Jonathan Pearson

BARBARA GRAZIOSI is the author of *Inventing Homer: The Early Reception of Epic* and *Homer: The Resonance of Epic,* among other works. A professor of classics at Durham University, Graziosi is a regular contributor to *Times Higher Education* and has been featured on several BBC television and radio programs on the arts.

ALSO BY BARBARA GRAZIOSI

Inventing Homer: The Early Reception of Epic

Homer: The Resonance of Epic (with Johannes Haubold)

Praise for

The Gods *of* Olympus

"Graziosi's writing is accessible and entertaining, her passion for her subject obvious. . . . A comprehensive and absorbing study."

—*Shelf Awareness*

"A delightfully entertaining study . . . In an impressive feat of research and synthesis, Barbara Graziosi has made the Greek gods vivid, accessible, and relevant for all of us. Graziosi's affection for her subject is exciting and infectious, and her beautifully seamless writing style, keen intelligence, and lovely sense of humor kept me eagerly reading. An excellent history."   —Rosemary Mahoney, author of *Down the Nile* and *For the Benefit of Those Who See*

"Humankind is at its most creative—and most revealing—in its desire for the divine, and its imagining of gods. Barbara Graziosi's absorbing history of the twelve Olympians follows their extraordinary journeys through the world and inside the human mind, where they have subtly coexisted with other gods, and continue to outlive us all."   —Patricia Storace, author of *Dinner with Persephone*

"Fun and well written . . . A great story, an unusual and fresh look at a pantheon that seems destined to live on long after we are gone."

—*San Francisco Book Review*

"An intelligent and entertaining examination of the Greek deities' timeless ability to 'express different, human truths' . . . Graziosi crosses the centuries elegantly, using the gods' constant presence to suggest that history is an ongoing continuum."

—*Publishers Weekly*

The Gods
of Olympus

=== A HISTORY ===

Barbara Graziosi

PICADOR   A METROPOLITAN BOOK   HENRY HOLT AND COMPANY   NEW YORK

www.picadorusa.com
www.twitter.com/picadorusa • www.facebook.com/picadorusa
picadorbookroom.tumblr.com

Picador® is a U.S. registered trademark and is used by Henry Holt and
Company under license from Pan Books Limited.

For book club information, please visit www.facebook.com/picadorbookclub
or e-mail marketing@picadorusa.com.

Designed by Kelly S. Too

The Library of Congress has cataloged the Henry Holt edition as follows:

Graziosi, Barbara.
    The gods of Olympus : a history / Barbara Graziosi.—1st ed.
        p. cm.
    Includes bibliographical notes and index.
    ISBN 978-0-8050-9157-1 (hardcover)
    ISBN 978-1-4299-4315-4 (e-book)
    1. Gods, Greek. 2. Goddesses, Greek. 3. Civilization—Greek influences. I. Title.
    BL783.G675 2014
    292.2'11—dc23

                                                                    2013025023

Picador Paperback ISBN 978-1-250-06234-5

Picador books may be purchased for educational, business, or promotional use.
For information on bulk purchases, please contact the Macmillan Corporate
and Premium Sales Department at 1-800-221-7945, extension 5442,
or write to specialmarkets@macmillan.com.

First published in the United States by Metropolitan Books,
an imprint of Henry Holt and Company, LLC

First Picador Edition: March 2015

10 9 8 7 6 5 4 3 2 1

To Johannes

CONTENTS

The Gods *of* Olympus

Simonides Was Wise

This book is a history of the Olympian gods—the most uncivilized ambassadors of classical civilization. Even in antiquity the gods were said to be cruel, oversexed, mad, or just plain silly. Yet they proved to be tough survivors: our earliest texts and images often depict them as travelers, and they managed to keep on the move for thousands of years. When the Greeks conquered Egypt, they started to resemble pharaohs; when the Romans conquered Greece, they merged with the local divinities of Rome; under Christianity and Islam, they lived on as demons, metaphors, allegories, and astrological principles; and in the Renaissance, they announced a new belief in humanity. Like many migrants, they adapted to new circumstances, while retaining a sense of their distant origins. This book traces the travels and transformations of the Olympian gods over more than two millennia, and over thousands of miles. It spans from antiquity to the Renaissance, because it is in this period that the Olympian gods made their most extraordinary journey—a journey that changed them from objects of religious cult to symbols of human creativity.

Some histories of classical civilization emphasize the similarities between antiquity and modernity; others insist on the differences.

This book attempts a different approach: rather than offer comparisons, it focuses on the processes of transformation. It tells a motley and miscellaneous tale, with many different characters, places, and encounters. The Olympian gods ranged widely; to follow in their tracks, one has to combine the insights of several academic disciplines, but it also helps to remain alive to the undisciplined vitality of the gods themselves. They were versatile and tenacious, managing to capture the world's imagination even after the death of their last worshippers.

When I look dispassionately at this project of writing about the gods, I realize that it must fail on at least two counts. Contemporary readers, even readers with a strong interest in classical civilization, do not seem to invest much in the Olympian deities. Conversely, people of earlier times invested so much thought and energy in them that it is impossible to do justice to their insights, visions, and experiences. Faced with the prospect of failing both my ancient interlocutors and my modern ones, I would instinctively like to carry on researching the gods of Olympus indefinitely, without actually writing a word about them.

There are, as it happens, good precedents for doing just that. The Roman orator Cicero, in his study *On the Nature of the Gods,* mentions the earlier Greek poet Simonides as his role model when dealing with the gods. This Simonides once found himself in a difficult situation: the tyrant of Syracuse asked him what a god was. Simonides pleaded to be granted a day to think about it. After one day, he asked for two, and then for four. When the amazed tyrant asked the poet what in the world he was doing, Simonides answered: "The more time I spend thinking about the issue, the more obscure it seems to me."[1] Simonides was wise, and I sympathize with his position. But I also sympathize with the idea that the gods thrive on conversation—that their characters, looks, and meanings are defined, and redefined, by people who talk about them and try to make sense of what others say. As Simonides implies, this is a conversation that lasts longer than a lifetime. It has already carried on for millennia and involved people from many different places. All I can do is join it, offer my perspective, and perhaps make one suggestion: that thinking about humanity must include at least some consideration of the Olympian gods.

A Family Portrait

The world of the ancient Greeks was full of deities: nymphs inhabited valleys and streams, Nereids lived in the depths of the sea, and satyrs roamed the woods. There were Titans, imprisoned deep in the bowels of the earth, and winged harpies, and sirens. . . . This unruly multitude of gods was hard to manage, or even count, but the Greeks trusted that they all answered to Zeus, the supreme god, and to his immediate relatives who lived with him on Olympus. The twelve Olympian gods were the most important deities of ancient Greece, and they could travel everywhere. Nymphs, Nereids, and satyrs remained confined within their native landscapes, but the gods of Olympus claimed the entire world as their own and demanded worship wherever they went: Homer, for example, described their travels all the way to Africa and northern Europe. It is partly because they were always conceived as universal powers that the gods of Olympus proved to be interesting to so many different people.

In ancient Greece, the personality of each god emerged from several sources. There were the local cults, with their specific rituals and unique atmospheres; the divine names of the gods, which had many possible explanations; the stories and poems that people shared; and the paintings and sculptures that represented the gods, particularly the cult statues housed in the temples. These elements combined and recombined in many ways across the Greek world. Similar cults attached to different gods; poems and myths traveled more swiftly than the adoption of new ritual practices; and images transcended even language barriers. All this makes it impossible to offer definitive and universal descriptions of the twelve gods of Olympus. It is always necessary to look in detail at the specific texts, objects, and places where the gods appeared and keep in mind that the relationships between them were constantly shifting.

As a group of twelve, the gods of Olympus came together primarily in poetry and art. Zeus was the most powerful of the twelve—but he was not all-powerful, because he needed and craved the company of his own family. For that reason, like all patriarchs, he had to settle for an uneasy compromise between power and comfort. Seated on Mount Olympus, he ruled over the entire world, but on the sacred mountain itself his family constantly undermined his authority. His wife, Hera, resented his affairs, challenged him, and sometimes even managed to trick him into doing what she wanted; his brother Poseidon demanded respect; his daughter Artemis charmed him in order to secure presents and promises; his son Apollo impressed and inhibited him; and little Hermes made him laugh, no matter how disobedient he was. Occasionally, Zeus threatened and thundered to remind his family that he alone was the ruler of the universe, but such outbursts were short and futile, for Zeus himself preferred the negotiations of family life to the loneliness of absolute power. After their mighty quarrels, the gods would make up over a big meal of nectar and ambrosia, tease one another, sing and laugh together—until Zeus and Hera, finally reconciled, would withdraw to their bedroom.[1]

One quick way to meet this lively family today is to visit them in London, where they still enjoy constant and devoted attention. Every day, hundreds of people walk down Great Russell Street, climb the steps of the British Museum, turn left past the souvenir shop, and walk straight to the main exhibit, in Room 18: the Elgin Marbles. There, visitors are confronted with the twelve gods of Olympus, seated on their thrones. The Parthenon frieze, whose design was overseen by Phidias in the fifth century BC, represents the gods surrounded by a grand procession of cavalry, chariots, elder citizens, musicians, women, magistrates, cattle, and sheep. This is a communal act of worship, which culminates in the ritual offering of a robe to the goddess Athena.[2] Today, these ancient worshippers are surrounded in turn by crowds of modern admirers, who also reverently file in front of the gods. The most alarming thing about the scene on the frieze is that the gods seem entirely uninterested in the human beings who are paying homage to them. We see them in profile, seated on their thrones and talking to one another, while in the midst of their gathering—or rather in front of it, according to the conventions of Phidias's art—the worshippers carry out their ceremony. The frieze tells a rather disheartening story about the relationship between gods and mortals, because Athena fails even to notice the offering and simply continues chatting to Hephaistos on her right. Yet precisely because the gods are so unconcerned with what happens on the human plane, we are given the thrilling opportunity to observe them at our leisure and discover how they interact with one another on Olympus.

To the left of the ritual offering, Zeus and Hera look each other straight in the eye. Hera holds up her bridal veil in a gesture that emphasizes her status as Zeus's wife, for it recalls the key moment in the ancient Athenian wedding ceremony when the bride lifts her veil and reveals her face to her husband. According to the Greeks, the entire balance of the universe rests, rather alarmingly, on the marriage between Zeus and Hera. Everybody knows that those two gods have a difficult relationship: Zeus is a serial adulterer, seducing or raping goddesses, women, and boys whenever the fancy takes him; and Hera's reactions are by turns resigned, resentful, enraged, and devious. There is something vicious and unstable about her

A line drawing of the twelve gods of Olympus on the Parthenon frieze. At the center of the composition, worshippers offer a robe to the goddess Athena. Moving from the ritual at the center to the left, we see Zeus (1), Hera with an attendant (2), Ares (3), Demeter (4), Dionysos (5), and Hermes (6). To the right of the ritual scene, we see Athena (7), Hephaistos (8), Poseidon (9), Apollo (10), Artemis (11), and Aphrodite with Eros between her knees (12).

mood swings, and Zeus realizes that he cannot trust her—yet she still sometimes manages to dupe him, particularly when she plays the part of the charming wife and enlists the support of the rest of the Olympian family. Their one and only son is, appropriately, the god Ares, a personification of war at its most senseless. Next to Hera stands a young female attendant, eyeing Ares with coquettish attention; the god, however, sits with his back to her, isolated and restless. With his hands clamped around his right knee and his feet lifted off the ground, he seems ready to get up and leave. Indeed, he has little business on Olympus—except, that is, for when he manages to sneak into bed with the goddess of love, Aphrodite. Zeus considers his own son Ares "the most hateful of all the gods of Olympus"[3] and cannot wait to see the back of him.

To the left of Ares, a lonely and mournful goddess sits with her hand on her chin in a pose of expectation. This is Demeter, goddess of agriculture. She resents her brother Zeus because he married off her lovely daughter Persephone to Hades, ruler of the underworld. Now she waits patiently for her daughter to visit her, which happens only once a year, in the spring. Demeter always ensures that the earth blooms to welcome her daughter when she finally emerges from the gloomy realm of Hades. Demeter's sorrow is the sorrow of many mothers: girls married young in classical Greece, at about fourteen or fifteen, and usually to men about twice their age. The story of the lovely Persephone and the ugly Hades must have sounded familiar to ancient people.[4] Anguish at the absence of her daughter drives a wedge between Demeter and Zeus. She visits the sacred mountain only rarely and always comes alone; Persephone and Hades are contaminated by their contact with the dead and have no place on Olympus. On the Parthenon frieze, Demeter holds in her hand the torch she used to look for Persephone when she first disappeared and which became a symbol of her secret rituals, the Eleusinian mysteries, where the Athenians learned from Demeter and Persephone how to negotiate the barriers of death, the gates of Hades.

A cheerful god holds up a cup of wine to Demeter's left. This is Dionysos, son of Zeus and Semele, a mortal woman who went up in flames on encountering Zeus and has continued burning ever since. Only half-divine, Dionysos struggles with recognition, especially since worshippers often take a while to acknowledge his powers. He is the god of orgiastic sex and drunkenness—experiences that make even mere mortals briefly feel divine, yet do not necessarily inspire respect. There is some uncertainty over Dionysos's Olympian status: not all Greeks agree that he belongs among the twelve main gods. Some suggest that Heracles has a better claim, because although he too is the son of Zeus and a mortal woman, he has at least completed twelve impossible labors, instead of encouraging drunken, sexy, and disorderly behavior.

On the frieze, Dionysos leans on his favorite brother: Hermes, son of Zeus and the minor goddess Maia. Hermes, the youngest god in the Olympian family, behaves like an unruly child: he steals, lies, plays tricks, and yet never gets punished. Indeed, he is the happy-go-lucky protector of tricksters and thieves—a stolen item is called a *hermaion* in ancient Greek, a "thing of Hermes." Hermes is equally dear to the gods of Olympus and those of the underworld, and he often acts as an intermediary between their different realms. He does not suffer like Demeter, or get trapped like Persephone, but crosses easily, with a light touch. He delivers messages to and from gods and mortals, relying on his ability to overcome all barriers.

Interpreters are under his special protection: successful communications with strangers and enemies, deities and dead people, are all the work of Hermes. (Today, the term *hermeneutics* still pays homage to his special powers of interpretation.) Everybody likes Hermes. On the Parthenon frieze, Dionysos leans on him with obvious ease, while Hermes himself sits at the end of the line of gods, looking at the Athenian procession. Placed between gods and mortals, he finds himself precisely where he likes to be.

On the other side of the offering, Athena turns her back on the robe that is meant to please her. Her powerful and relaxed attitude mirrors that of Zeus, and indeed Athena and Zeus tend to be of one mind—unsurprisingly, perhaps, since she was literally born out of his head. Rather than pay attention to her worshippers, Athena talks to Hephaistos, the god of forges and crafts. As a pair, the two balance out Zeus and Hera on the other side of the composition. The correspondence is not just visual, but also mythological: just as Zeus gave birth to Athena, so Hera conceived Hephaistos all by herself. Some accounts say that because Hera did not use male seed, her offspring turned out lame and ugly; others suggest that Zeus, enraged by the arrival of Hephaistos, hurled him off Mount Olympus, thus maiming him forever. Greek myth is flexible, embroidering different stories around the same basic intuition: that Hephaistos's lameness is somehow connected to his conception. Like her stepbrother, Athena presides over the arts and crafts: she is responsible for shipbuilding, chariot making, wool spinning, cloth weaving, and other activities that require technology and sophistication. Even in war, she favors tactics and discipline, having none of the mad, murderous rage of Ares. It is fitting that Athena and Hephaistos were the patron gods of Athens, a progressive and technological city. In fact, the Athenians had a special myth about these two deities. They said that Hephaistos once tried to rape Athena but ejaculated on her thigh, and his semen—wiped off and mixed with the earth where it fell—gave rise to the first Athenians. The myth expressed the close relationship between the Athenians and their patron gods: Athena was as nearly a mother to them as a virgin could be.

To the right of Athena and Hephaistos on the Parthenon frieze is a bearded, severe-looking god. This is Poseidon, another important deity in Athens. He tried to become patron of the city by offering Athenians the horse, but Athena trumped him with the bridle and chariot. He offered a sea-salt spring, and again she trumped him with the superior gift of the olive tree. While Athena offers the means to tame nature and bend it to human needs, Poseidon is violent and elemental, a powerful deity who needs to be treated with utmost respect. He is Zeus's own brother and has overall control of the sea. Prayers to Poseidon tend to express negative wishes: that he may not wreck a ship or cause an earthquake—or that he may inflict such things on the enemy. There is, in short, a huge amount to lose by getting on Poseidon's wrong side. Sitting next to him, his nephew Apollo seems to be aware of this: he has the respectful look of a young man being lectured by a forbidding uncle.

Apollo is Zeus's most beautiful and impressive son, but he is not a viable candidate for the supreme office because he is illegitimate, the offspring not of Hera but of the minor goddess Leto, who traveled all over the Aegean to find a safe place where she might give birth. Most localities were too afraid of Hera's jealous anger to welcome Apollo's future mother, but in the end the barren island of Delos offered her sanctuary. Apollo respects his father and knows he could never succeed him. What he does, instead, is act as Zeus's mouthpiece to people on earth: prophets and prophecies are under his protection. He loves beauty and measure, music and truth. His twin sister, sitting to his right, also loves music and dancing but is a more extreme character: Artemis adores wild creatures and hunting and shooting. And she hates the idea of being tamed by a man; indeed, her father, Zeus, has granted her permanent virginity. On the Parthenon frieze, she wears her hair gathered up, as suits a young girl, and pulls up her robe to cover her breasts in a gesture that is both sexy and coy. Aphrodite, sitting next to her, may have

Detail of the Parthenon frieze: Poseidon, Apollo, and Artemis.

eclipsed her beauty, but we can no longer tell that from Phidias's sculpture, because time has eroded her features. All we know is that she is pointing at someone in the procession and holding young Eros between her knees. Her body language reveals her aim: religious festivals were among the few situations in ancient Athens where unrelated men and women could meet and spend time together. The Greeks must have felt that Aphrodite regularly released Eros among the worshippers in real life, just as she seems poised to do on the Parthenon frieze.

The Parthenon frieze confronts viewers with a set of characters that are instantly recognizable: the husband and wife locked in a destructive marriage, the restless young man, the mother who misses her married daughter, the bearded uncle giving advice to his nephew, the young girl suddenly conscious of her budding breasts. At one level, the Greek gods are familiar to us because they are, quite simply, a family. But they are also familiar for a different reason: they have been a constant presence in human history, from antiquity to the present. When Rome conquered Greece, they acquired new names but kept their distinguishing features. And for all their subsequent disguises, they are still recognizable today.

Like the gods it portrays, the Parthenon itself changed identities several times in the course of its history. It was built in the 440s and 430s BC, at the height of Athenian self-confidence and power. Some four decades earlier, the Greeks had defeated the Persians, against all odds; the great battles of the Persian Wars—Marathon, Thermopylae, Salamis, Plataea—proved that the Greeks, though numerically inferior and politically divided, could resist the greatest empire of their time. Before withdrawing, though, the Persians had inflicted considerable damage. In 480 BC, they had seized and torched Athens, destroying its most important monument: the temple of Athena at the top of the acropolis. The Parthenon replaced that earlier temple and was conceived as the ultimate symbol of Athenian pride. Athena *Parthenos*, "the Virgin," was the patron goddess of the temple and the city, and she would not be defeated.

The procession on the frieze mirrored the actual procession that the Athenians performed in honor of their patron goddess at their most important city festival. Every July, they came together and filed in ritual order from the city gates, through the main square, and up to the acropolis, where they stopped by the Parthenon. There, at the head of the procession, a girl offered Athena an intricate robe woven by six women who had been specially appointed for the task. Afterward, the Athenians performed a sacrifice—the key ritual of ancient religion. They killed animals, offered their bones and fat to the gods, roasted their meat, and ate it in a massive communal feast. Given that it was difficult to preserve food in the ancient world, religious festivals were the ideal occasion for consuming a lot of meat while it was still fresh. (The comic playwright Aristophanes associated the festival of Athena above all with indigestion.) For many centuries, the procession of people and cattle carved on the Parthenon frieze matched the ritual performance carried out in front of it: the Athenians worshipped their patron goddess at their temple and recognized themselves in its sculptures. Then, in the fifth century AD, one thousand years after the Parthenon was built, it was converted into a church—a church dedicated to another *parthenos,* the Virgin Mary. Still, the Olympian gods survived intact and watched the new rituals with their immortal eyes. Another millennium passed, and they witnessed a further change: in the early 1460s, the Ottomans converted the church into a mosque, complete with minaret. Again, the gods on the frieze suffered no damage.

The real danger for them came in 1687, when the Venetians besieged Athens and bombarded the Parthenon mosque. The Ottomans had stored explosives there during the siege, so the building went up in flames. That the Venetians should have blown up the Parthenon in the wake of the Italian Renaissance exemplifies a simple fact: The priorities of soldiers and politicians are not the same as those of scholars and artists. Yet the ideals of the Renaissance did not die under Venetian artillery fire. The general Francesco Morosini himself admired—and looted—fragments of the sculptures he had just destroyed. Over a century later, in 1806, Lord Elgin followed suit: he removed all the Parthenon pieces he could find and sold them to the British Museum. And there they still are—though perhaps not forever. The Greek government urgently demands the return of the so-called Elgin Marbles to Athens, where a new museum is ready to house them. The current controversy over the return of the Parthenon sculptures is complex. It involves judgments about artistic integrity, national sovereignty, and—last but not least—tourist revenues, because visitors are sure to follow in the footsteps of the ancient gods. But above all, the controversy reveals a deeper truth: The Olympian gods by now are as at home in London as they are in Athens, and indeed in many other places as well.

PART I

Birth: Archaic Greece

How the gods first appeared, how they became specific characters, colonized Olympus, and formed into a family: Answers to these questions can be sought as far back as the first migrations to the Greek peninsula, the earliest traces of cult, and the great civilizations of the Bronze Age. And after that, they can be found in archaic Greece, where something happened between the eighth and the sixth centuries BC. It was then that the first temples were built, the first cult statues were housed in them, and Homer and Hesiod defined for the Greeks who the main gods were, how they were born, and how they behaved on Olympus.

Homer and Hesiod were considered great authorities on the gods—but they were never above question. In fact, as soon as their poems started circulating in the Greek world, people expressed doubts about their theological claims. Even with the gift of immortality, the gods of epic seemed too human, and too specifically Greek, to command respect as universal powers. The cult statues housed in temples were vulnerable to similar objections. Radical early critics questioned the anthropomorphic visions of poets and artists and thereby inaugurated a long tradition of debate—a debate that concerned not just the nature of the gods, but the interpretation of poetry and art.

1

At Home in Greece

Tall, broad, and covered in snow for much of the year, Mount Olympus stands alone, fully visible from every side. It dominates the landscape for miles; its dazzling peaks seem particularly incongruous when viewed from the hot, low plains around. From the sea, the mountain sometimes looks like a cloud.

In antiquity, Mount Olympus lay very much off the beaten track. People had little reason to go near it, and no incentive at all to climb it, but they could see it—and in turn they felt observed. The Greeks thought that the gods lived among the mountain's peaks and watched what happened down below. Poets elaborated on this notion. Homer described Mount Olympus precisely, mentioning its "many summits," "abundant snow," and "steepness" and giving an indication of just where it was. At the same time, he suggested that this mythical residence of the gods was not quite what it seemed: "Olympus is never shaken by winds, hit by rain, or covered in snow; cloudless ether spreads around it, and a bright aura encircles it."[1] So Olympus was both a particular landmark and a place of the mind. Greek communities could see the mountain, agree about its sacredness, and feel united by a shared sense of landscape; but

Mount Olympus.

they were also reminded that the gods did not live in our world and were never subjected to the indignities of bad weather.

It is unclear when the mountain first became associated with the gods. In the poems of Homer, the most important deities are explicitly called "the Olympians," but he was not necessarily the first to place them on the sacred mountain. The *Iliad* and the *Odyssey*, in the form in which we have them, date to the archaic period (roughly the eighth to the sixth century BC), and the Greek peninsula was settled long before that time. We can reconstruct, on linguistic grounds, that the Greeks were descended from speakers of a language also related to Sanskrit and Latin as well as to Germanic, Slavic, and other linguistic groups, and which is conventionally called "Indo-European." Migrating from central Asia, Indo-European speakers gradually settled in Europe and introduced broadly shared notions of the gods. So, for example, the Greek Zeus is related to the Sanskrit Dyáus Pitār: they are both versions of the same supreme god, ruler of the sky. It is unsurprising that in Greece, this Indo-European god settled on Mount Olympus, the tallest landmark in the area. It is more difficult to establish just when this happened.

Answering that question requires dating the Indo-European migrations and investigating the roots of Homeric epic—both of which are controversial subjects.

Impressive civilizations were already flourishing in Greece around 2000 BC, more than a thousand years before Homer's time. Monumental remains at Mycenae, Tiryns, and Pylos testify to this. In the twelfth century BC, however, these civilizations suddenly collapsed. A long period of decline followed, generally known as the Greek "Dark Ages." It was only in the eighth century BC that people living in Greece began to flourish again. The next two centuries were characterized by a sharp increase in the population, the rise of the city-state (*polis*), the construction of the first temples and cult statues of the gods, an upsurge in travel and trade, the foundation of new colonies, the reintroduction of writing (a technology that had been lost during the Dark Ages), and the phenomenal spread of epic poetry. Scholars used to think that the Dark Ages corresponded with the arrival of Indo-European tribes from Asia. The impressive archaeological remains at Mycenae and elsewhere were thought to predate that migration, and therefore have nothing to do with Zeus and the rest of the Indo-European pantheon. The many written tablets found at the Mycenaean sites were assumed to record a language unrelated to Greek, perhaps an early form of Etruscan. This theory crumbled spectacularly in the 1950s, when Michael Ventris and John Chadwick (who had worked as a code breaker during World War II) managed to decipher Linear B, the script of the Mycenaean tablets. To widespread amazement, they proved that the tablets actually recorded an early form of Greek.[2] This made it clear that Indo-European people had been living in Greece long before the Dark Ages and suggested that they worshipped essentially the same gods as later Greek communities, even though they did not have temples housing cult statues. Archaeologists had obviously misdated the Indo-European migration on the basis of the material record. This dramatic realization gave classicists hope of finding some snippets of Greek poetry among the

Linear B tablets, perhaps early versions of Homeric epic describing the Olympian pantheon. In fact, they discovered nothing of the kind: as far as we can tell, Linear B was used exclusively for matter-of-fact lists and inventories. Mount Olympus never featured, nor did any stories about divine doings. Still, by recording sacrifices and other offerings to particular gods, even the dry documents of Mycenaean bureaucracy did reveal some surprising facts.

Tablets from Pylos and Crete indicate, for instance, that Dionysos was already known in the second millennium BC. Homer barely mentioned him, and later Greek texts presented him as a newcomer to Greece, a recent import from the decadent East—but this was evidently not so. We now know that Dionysos was always considered a "new" and subversive god in need of recognition, no matter how long he had actually been worshipped in Greece.[3] His youth and exoticism are a matter of personality rather than historical age. Homer must have kept Dionysos out of Olympus not because he barely knew this god, as was once supposed, but because he was all too aware of his characteristics: Dionysos would have spoiled the party on Olympus with his drunken excesses. Linear B tablets produced other surprises, too. The god Apollo, for example, was apparently unknown to the Mycenaeans. This "most Greek of the gods," as a famous Hellenist called him, this paragon of beauty and measure, was in fact a rather late addition to the Greek pantheon, had no obvious Indo-European credentials, and was at least partly Semitic in influence, identified early on with the Canaanite god Resheph.[4]

There were, then, some differences between Mycenaean portrayals of the gods and their later appearance in archaic Greece—but there were also some definite connections and some suggestive echoes of old Mycenaean rituals in Homeric poetry. In the *Odyssey*, for instance, Poseidon receives special worship at Pylos in the Peloponnese, and that is precisely where most of the Linear B tablets concerning his cult have been found. Likewise, Hera is called "ox-eyed" in Homer, and Linear B tablets reveal that she had received rich cattle sacrifices from Mycenaean worshippers, richer even than those offered to Zeus. Perhaps early Greek speakers had looked right into the eyes of their sacrificial victims and seen in them a shadow of the goddess. Their impression was then passed on through the formulations of ritual and poetic language: *ox-eyed Hera* became a standard Homeric phrase. Beyond such poetic links, there was also an entirely solid aspect of continuity between the civilizations of the Bronze Age and archaic Greece: buildings. In the archaic period, people could still see the remnants of impressive fortifications at Mycenae, Pylos, and—most important—Troy, on the coast of Turkey, a city that had once been a Hittite protectorate. The Greeks wove stories around those ruins, imagining the great heroes who had once lived and died there. In the case of particularly impressive remains, such as the walls of Troy, it was even suggested that the gods themselves had built them.

One of the most remarkable features of archaic Greek poetry is how insistently, and precisely, it places its tales of gods and heroes in the Aegean landscape. It is as if, in the sudden explosion of travel and trade that characterized the archaic period, people wanted to exchange stories not only about their gods, but about landmarks, ruins, and sailing routes. Homer described the whole eastern Aegean, mentioning hundreds of place-names, in a massive Catalogue of Ships in the second book of the *Iliad*. Hesiod, in his *Theogony,* revealed how the gods were born and simultaneously placed them on a map. Zeus grew up in Crete, he said; Aphrodite came out of the waves near Cyprus. As well as listening to poems about divine travel, the Greeks were increasingly prepared to travel themselves in order to worship the gods. According to our ancient sources, the first Olympics took place in 776 BC. Athletes, dancers, poets, and musicians from many different Greek city-states gathered to compete against one another at the small village of Olympia, probably so named after the residence of Zeus. The games were put on precisely as a spectacle for Zeus, but they also attracted enthusiastic human crowds. At roughly the same time, the Delphic oracle opened for business, delivering Apollo's prophecies to all who made the journey to it. Soon, Delphi also started to host competitions in athletics and poetry, in order to make sure that Apollo did not miss out on the celebrations his father enjoyed elsewhere. Crisscrossing the Aegean in poetry and sailing ships alike, the Greeks took possession of the landscape and placed their gods in it.

The *Homeric Hymn to Apollo,* a beautiful archaic poem telling the story of Leto's search for a place to give birth, illustrates the process. After nine days of travel and labor, Leto finally delivers Artemis and Apollo on the barren island of Delos, holding on to a palm tree. A sanctuary is built near the sacred palm, and worshippers begin to visit the island, bringing their offerings and gifts. Rewarded for its kindness to the pregnant goddess, Delos becomes rich, despite its rocky soil. The island also sets a pattern for the cult of Apollo: when the god grows up, the *Hymn* continues, he travels to another daunting place, "a cliff hanging below Mount Parnassos, and a rugged glade below." There, at Delphi, Apollo defeats a snake-like monster called Python and decides to build a second temple for himself, where he will deliver oracles to inquiring mortals.

The poem tells us that Apollo needs priests for his inhospitable sanctuary at Delphi and, while considering the problem, "becomes aware of a swift ship on the wine-dark sea," sailing hundreds of miles away between Knossos and Pylos. Deciding to turn the Cretan crew into his priests, he transforms himself into a dolphin and leaps into the ship, rocking it fearfully as the Cretan sailors struggle in vain to catch him and throw him overboard. Terrified, they sail past Pylos, their destination, and farther north until the wind bends their course eastward, into the Gulf of Corinth, and they are finally stranded at Krisa, near modern Itea. There Apollo suddenly reveals himself in a shower of sparks. He tells the Cretan sailors that they must abandon their trade, climb the mountain looming above the coast, and tend to his newly founded sanctuary. They will make a good living, he adds, despite their unlikely location, because pilgrims will provide a constant supply of gifts.

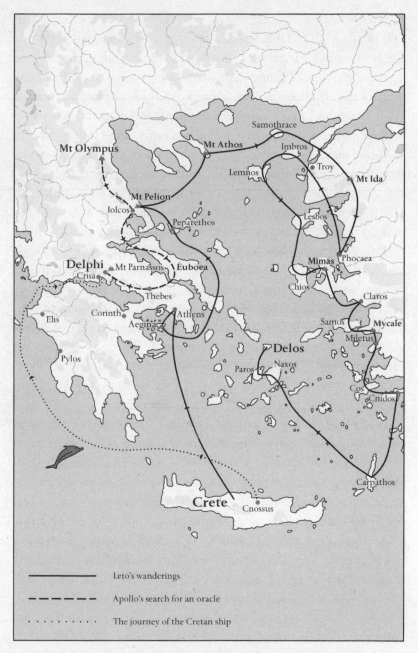

Leto's wanderings

Apollo's search for an oracle

The journey of the Cretan ship

The journeys described in *The Homeric Hymn to Apollo*.

It seems that the actual priests who worked at the sanctuary in Delphi really did claim Cretan descent and explained their life hundreds of miles from their ancestral home by telling the story of Apollo the dolphin. Strange as their tale may seem, it captured the spirit of the age. Everybody was on the move in the archaic period. Trade flourished, new cities were founded, and communal worship became part of a quickly expanding economy. The *Homeric Hymn to Apollo* mentions scores of place-names when describing the journeys of the Cretan sailors, Apollo, and his mother, Leto, thus offering a virtual tour of the ancient Greek world (see map on p. 23). Modern readers struggle to locate all the ancient toponyms and can easily get bored; but archaic Greek audiences must have been thrilled, for they recognized their own hometowns and landscapes and realized that they all played a role in the biography of the god. It was through such stories that Greek speakers began to realize that they belonged together and inhabited the same world. In the fifth century BC, Herodotus claimed that Greekness was a matter of "common blood and language, shared temples of the gods, rituals, and common habits."[5] Panhellenic centers of cult like Delphi and Olympia were of cardinal importance precisely because they helped to establish the "common habits" of the Greeks.

For modern tourists, visiting Delphi remains one of the most effective ways of experiencing that ancient sense of Greekness, that early connection between place, poetry, and religion. It is best to approach the sanctuary from the sea—as Apollo and his priests did, according to the *Hymn,* and as ancient worshippers arrived in real life. From the coast near Itea, the ancient sanctuary looks like a tiny white speck of marble against the dark cliffs of Mount Parnassos. The ascent is sharp and difficult, but those who follow the country road as it snakes up the mountain are amply rewarded. Up in Delphi, the view is spectacular and the air bracing, crystal-clear; just to be there is a spiritual experience, even today. To the south there are open views of blue mountains and a wide-open valley filled with a sea of silvery olive trees. Beyond them, the actual sea glitters, bright blue, in the distance. When one turns north, the outlook changes sharply: up close a sheer rock face looms over visitors, and beyond it rise the twin peaks of Mount Parnassos. The cliffs and crags seem impenetrable, but right there is where the *Hiera Hodos* starts, the

Remains of the temple of Apollo at Delphi. Pilgrims undertook a difficult journey in order to reach this sanctuary and interrogate Apollo on the issues that most mattered to them, from questions of paternity to the likely outcome of wars. His oracles always turned out to be true, though they were hard to interpret.

ancient Sacred Way that leads through the sanctuary of Apollo up to the temple where his oracles were delivered.

The sanctuary complex is built on narrow terraces cut into the steep mountainside, exploiting the small space to the full. Inside the sanctuary, the Sacred Way climbs upward, making two hairpin bends. The remains of elaborate buildings crowd it on both sides, so that visitors are constantly confronted with unexpected sights. This must have been even more true in ancient times, when intact structures would have impeded an overview of the sanctuary. Clustered around the entrance were once many life-size statues raised on pedestals, commemorating assorted wars between Greek city-states— Tegea's victory over Sparta, for example, and Sparta's victory over Athens. A few statues also celebrated peaceful activities: the people of Corfu, for instance, set up a large bronze bull in thanksgiving for an extraordinary catch of tuna. After the statues, a little higher up, the Sacred Way was flanked by small, room-size shrines, or "treasuries," built by individual city-states to house their votive offerings to Apollo. There were once thirty or more treasuries, and judging from those best preserved, they were exquisite. The Athenians built theirs on one of the best plots, a small triangular terrace just after the first sharp turn. It stood at an angle from the road, showing off both side and front to everyone as they went up and presenting a dramatic sight to those descending as well. The treasury was built entirely of Parian marble and had a beautiful frieze running all around it. The Athenians were probably trying to outdo the intricate treasury built just down the road by the people of Siphnos, but it is not clear that they succeeded. The Siphnian shrine, with its two beautiful sculpted women holding up the roof as if they were columns, is hard to surpass. The treasuries exemplified the competitive stance of ancient Greek city-states but also revealed a sense of common purpose, showing that all cities and communities paid homage to Apollo. It made sense for the Greek city-states to lavish on their treasuries at Delphi the best craftsmanship and materials they could afford, since the buildings advertised their piety, wealth, and achievements to the many pilgrims and diplomats who traveled to Apollo's oracle from all over the Greek world—and indeed from even farther afield.[6] As visitors climbed the Sacred Way toward the temple of Apollo, they essentially walked past a small-scale version of Greece, city-state by city-state. The experience of modern tourists is, in that respect at least, not so different: a visit to Delphi, with its treasuries huddled together in one place, still offers a privileged overview of the ancient Greek world.

After the second sharp bend, the Sacred Way leads to the main temple, on the facade of which was carved a scene of Apollo's first arrival at Delphi. The image recalled the story told in the *Homeric Hymn to Apollo* and mirrored the pilgrims' own travel to the sanctuary: Apollo's journey was the same as those of his priests and worshippers. It was at the temple, at this point of convergence and arrival, that momentous conversations took place. Apollo, through the utterings of the Pythia, his venerable priestess, answered questions put to him by his visitors. Pilgrims made inquiries about the things that most mattered to them, from issues of paternity and infertility (which seem to have been especially frequent) to the outcome of wars and the possibility of settling new lands. The Pythia offered authoritative but rather obscure answers, and several other priests were then at hand to interpret her utterings for a fee. Pilgrims often continued to ponder Apollo's responses, and consult further experts, back home. After that long process of consultation and interpretation, Apollo's revelations usually crystallized into lines of hexameter poetry and were always found to be true—even if the correct interpretation sometimes emerged only after the relevant events had come to pass.

The proceedings at Delphi might seem baffling from a modern perspective: it is hard to see why the Greeks took such pains to travel across the sea and up a mountain in order to get some sort of mystifying, unclear response. But I suspect that visiting Delphi may really have offered concrete help, in at least two ways. First of all, because the oracle was open for consultation only for a brief period in summer (Apollo was thought to spend the rest of the year in the far north of Europe), those who wanted to interrogate the god generally had to wait. Crucially, the process slowed things down and gave people time to consider their decisions. Taking time over important questions must have helped, no matter what the Pythia actually said. A visit to Delphi also encouraged people to put their own troubles into perspective. As they walked up the Sacred Way, past all the votive offerings and treasuries, they must have realized that many other people, from many different parts of the world, had also asked Apollo for help in the same way. When visitors reached the temple, an inscription advised them: "Know Yourself." They were invited to reflect on the difference between themselves and the god Apollo but were also forced to consider how they were similar to all other ordinary mortals who had been confronted with that injunction. A consultation at Delphi offered the advantages of time and perspective and suggested to all Greeks that they belonged together.

It was at Panhellenic centers of cult like Delphi that the personalities of the gods became embedded in the collective memory of the Greeks. Visitors were told the same stories, heard the same poems, saw the same sculptures, and underwent the same experiences at Delphi; so they began to feel the same way about Apollo. Likewise, at Olympia, visitors from many different city-states saw the same games in honor of Zeus and felt the god observing them as they gathered and competed in that particular place of worship. In the archaic period, Greek mythology developed as a form of entertainment, for both gods and mortals, at religious gatherings. It was highly imaginative, but it was also rooted in a very real landscape—a landscape dominated by Mount Olympus and its gods.

2

Epic Visions

Homer and Hesiod were thought to have a special ability to see and describe the gods. According to Herodotus, it was those two poets "who first revealed to the Greeks how the gods were born, what they were called, which honors and powers they enjoyed, and how they looked."[1] This task, however, was far from straightforward. For example, when Hesiod set out to compose his great poem about the origins of the gods, the *Theogony,* he had a lot of trouble deciding where to start. He knew that as an epic poet, he must begin with the Muses and ask them for information—but the Muses, daughters of Zeus and Memory, were rather recent goddesses, and he wanted to tell about a time before their time, a time even before Zeus's time, a time before the beginning of everything. Eventually, he decided to compromise by offering several false beginnings. The *Theogony* starts with a proper invocation to the Muses, and immediately Hesiod adds that these goddesses can sing not only about Zeus, Hera, Athena, Apollo, Artemis, and the other Olympian gods, but also about earlier deities: "Kronos the crafty counselor, Dawn, the Sun, the bright Moon, and Earth, great Oceanus, and dark Night."[2] Having established the Muses' ability to trace the genealogies of the gods back in time, Hesiod begins again, telling how he himself first met the goddesses of poetry. The Muses approached him while he was tending sheep on Mount Helicon, he says, and were quite rude about his work. They called all shepherds "wretched, shameless creatures, mere bellies!"[3] They then suggested a new profession for Hesiod, teasing him a little longer: They could turn him into a poet, they claimed, because they knew how to sing the truth. But then again, they could also fool him, because they knew how to sing lies that sounded like the truth. In the end, they decided to tell Hesiod "true things" about the gods—so he rewarded them by starting his poem again, for a third time, with a hymn in their honor. He now sang about the birth of the Muses in a remote land "in the glens of Eleutheros" and revealed how they had first climbed Mount Olympus, greatly pleasing their father with their singing and dancing. And this was the content of their first song: how Earth first had sex with Heaven, beginning the genealogy of the gods, and how Zeus himself was born and became ruler, after defeating his father, Kronos, son of Earth and Heaven. The opening sequence in the *Theogony,* with its elaborate songs within a song, established the basis for Hesiod's authority. The Muses could recount the origins of the gods from the beginning, and so could Hesiod, because he was a friend of theirs; he had met them on Mount Helicon. The Muses pleased Zeus with their song, and Hesiod's poem would also please the supreme god—because he was voicing their song.

After all these preambles, the *Theogony* now begins in earnest, at the beginning of everything, *ex archēs.*[4] And in the beginning Earth emerges from *chaos,* a word that probably means "gaping void" in Hesiod's poem. Then Earth gives birth to time, in the form of the twins Night and Day, and to space: Heaven, Ocean, Mountains, Valleys, Seas, and Islands all come from her. Soon Heaven becomes Earth's lover, and that proves to be his undoing. Heaven is a jealous partner—he resents Earth's ability to generate on her own—and a hateful father, afraid that his own children will grow up to be stronger than him. He therefore tries to keep his offspring pressed inside Earth's body, obstructing the process of birth. At that,

Earth plans her revenge: she arms her son Kronos with a sickle while he is still inside her, and when Heaven approaches Earth, "spreading himself all over her, demanding sex," Kronos comes out of his mother's body and castrates his father.[5] Heaven's genitals fall into the sea and float to the island of Cyprus, and from them Aphrodite is born.

Kronos then replaces his father as ruler of the universe and in turn immediately starts plotting against his own children. He decides to prevent them from growing up by eating them as soon as they are born. The *Theogony* sounds rather Freudian here (and in fact Freud was interested in it): Kronos's decision to keep his children inside his own belly can be interpreted as a remarkable case of uterus envy. Understandably, Kronos's wife, Rhea, resents his behavior and eventually devises a trick to save her offspring. After delivering her youngest son, Zeus, she hides him in Crete and serves Kronos a swaddled stone instead. Kronos throws up that stone, and it lands at the precise spot in Delphi where Apollo will one day set up his oracle. The stone—which in a sense prophesies where Apollo's place of prophecy will be—becomes a prize exhibit at Delphi. Known as the *omphalos,* "the belly button," it is said to mark the navel of the earth.

The stone—in the *Theogony* as in Delphi—symbolizes the end of Kronos's supremacy and the beginning of the rule of Zeus. And now the problem of succession arises again. To prevent his own children from replacing him, Zeus combines the strategies of his father and grandfather, swallowing his pregnant wife, Metis, before she can give birth. This procedure finally works: he lets out of his head only his daughter Athena, while her twin brother, who was going to succeed his father, never sees the light of day. By swallowing his wife, Zeus acquires the resources of female intelligence, the very resources that had defeated his father and grandfather in previous generations (*metis,* in Greek, means "clever thinking"). Athena becomes the ultimate symbol of androgynous wisdom: she has the resources of her father and mother combined—power and brains.

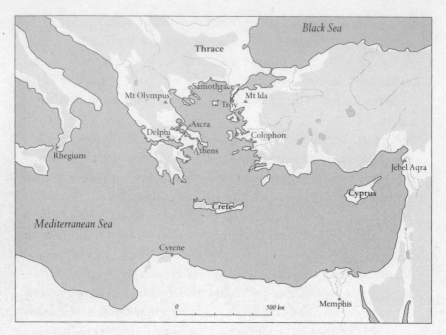

The eastern Mediterranean.

But she is sterile, a virgin forever, and therefore no threat to the rule of her father. Zeus now colonizes Olympus, installing his own freed siblings there along with his most powerful children. The secret of his success is that he has no viable successors. He never lets his son by Metis come out of his head, and Ares—his only son by his sister and second wife, Hera—is too violent and stupid to command consensus. Apollo is Zeus's most impressive son, but he is illegitimate and sees his role as supporting the rule of his father rather than challenging it. As for Zeus's daughters, they are mostly virgins and therefore unable to threaten him by giving birth to a powerful grandson. Zeus has the sense to marry Aphrodite off to the disabled, lame Hephaistos, and that neutralizes her. And so it is that after a period of generational strife and cosmic upheaval, the Olympian family settles down into a stable order. It becomes frozen in time: children remain children, and Zeus remains "the father of gods and men," in the standard epic formula, for all eternity. Succession—and the kind of powerful alliances between mothers and sons that toppled the ruling god in the first two generations—remains a problem only for mortal men on earth.

Hesiod's myth of origins makes for a strange and disturbing story, and for readers today one of its most puzzling aspects is the constant fluctuation between divine narrative and family dysfunction. Heaven (or Ouranos in Greek) is simultaneously the sky and a recognizable personality type, the violent husband. Hesiod's Earth is clearly the actual earth—with mountains, rivers, caves, and valleys—but she is also the Earth Mother, the goddess Gaia, an anthropomorphic deity ready to castrate her partner in order to nurture her children. Modern editors have great trouble deciding when to capitalize Earth's name and when to leave it lowercase, treating the term as referring simply to matter. The ancient Greeks did not have that problem, because they had only one letter size, but the real issue is not typographical but conceptual: Hesiod does not distinguish among cosmic principles, anthropomorphic deities, and material realities. The power of his gods resides precisely in a mixture of different apprehensions. Earth is the physical earth, but also a "broad-breasted" goddess. A cave is a cave, and it is also her womb: monsters and gods are nurtured there. Athena, for her part, is both an anthropomorphic goddess and rational thought.[6]

There is no single, orthodox way of understanding the gods, and the Greeks clearly thought they could always discover new things about them, not least by considering the views of faraway people. Very similar narratives to Hesiod's *Theogony* circulated around the Jebel Aqra, an imposing mountain on the coast of Syria (see map on p. 32). The Hittites on the north slope of this massive peak told stories about their thunder-god, Tarhunta—how his father had tried to eat him but had broken his teeth on a stone instead and how Tarhunta had replaced his toothless father. The stone that enabled Tarhunta's ascent to power had become a local object of cult. Meanwhile, the Canaanites, on the south slope of the Jebel Aqra,

Kronos was tricked into swallowing a stone rather than his own son Zeus. He eventually threw up that stone and it landed in Delphi, where it was thought to mark "the navel of the earth." This *omphalos,* or "navel," dates to the Hellenistic period and is decorated with umbilical cords. It is now kept at the Archaeological Museum in Delphi, while an ordinary conic stone marks its place in the sanctuary itself.

celebrated Baal, lord of the thunderbolt, as their own supreme god. Greek travelers would have found it easy to identify their own Zeus with the Hittite Tarhunta and the Semitic Baal. There were sailing routes that linked Delphi to Crete, as the *Homeric Hymn to Apollo* shows, and archaeological finds suggest that Crete was also linked to Cyprus and ultimately the Syrian coast. It should not surprise us that myths traveled swiftly along those watery paths and that the *Theogony* echoed the stories that swirled around the Jebel Aqra. Hesiod was not trying to create a parochial little myth for his own home village of Ascra, "bad in winter, awful in summer, and good at no time," as he described it.[7] His gods were universal powers, and insights about them could be gathered far and wide.

Indeed, both Hesiod and Homer carefully avoided references to local cults, legends, or traditions. What they offered instead was a vision of the Olympian gods calculated to appeal to everyone, or at least to everyone who understood their language (which was an artificial mixture of several different Greek dialects). The winning trick of their poetry was simple: instead of describing the relationship between the gods and their assorted local cults, they revealed to all Greek speakers how the gods related to one another on Olympus. Those were topics of general interest, no matter how particular communities chose to worship. When the Greeks listened to Homer and Hesiod, they were eavesdropping and spying on the gods; they were discovering even what the gods themselves had tried to keep secret—their schemes, love affairs, and quarrels. These visions had immense power because they revealed the individual characters of the gods, how they thought and behaved, to all the Greeks.

The most scandalous affair on Mount Olympus is the adulterous relationship between Ares and Aphrodite, wife of Hephaistos. In the *Odyssey*, that story is the subject of a cameo performance delivered by a blind bard called Demodocus. In book 8, when Odysseus finally reaches the hospitable land of the Phaeacians after much suffering by land and sea, he is treated to a great banquet and proper entertainment. The highlight of the evening is Demodocus's story of how the ugly Hephaistos caught Aphrodite in bed with Ares. He used his craft as the god of smiths to make some very fine chains—so thin that they were invisible to the naked eye. With them, he turned his own bed into a trap and snared Ares and Aphrodite together. Helios, the sun-god, shone down on the naked couple and all the gods had a good look at the captured lovers. After much divine hilarity and humiliation, the pair was finally set free; Ares went to visit the warlike Thracians, whereas Aphrodite left for her native island of Cyprus, where the Graces gave her a restorative bath.[8] The most amazing thing about the story in this Odyssean telling is that the blind bard Demodocus can evidently see and report on the gods' private lives, from Hephaistos's scheming with his fine chains to the spectacle of the naked Ares and Aphrodite. Homer explicitly says that Demodocus's poetic power is a compensation for his disability: "The Muse loved him exceedingly, and gave him a good gift

Aphrodite emerges from the sea, on a relief dated to about 460 BC and known as the Ludovisi Throne. The restorative bath that the Graces gave to Aphrodite after the humiliating episode with Ares was, in effect, a reenactment of her birth.

and a bad one. She deprived him of his eyes, but gave him sweet song."[9] In this account, poetry is a form of vision, and Odysseus later compliments Demodocus because he can sing about the exploits of gods and heroes "as if he had been there himself" and seen them with his own eyes.[10] Like Demodocus, Homer was thought to be blind. The Greeks believed that the divine power of his poetry was similarly a mirror image of this terrible disability in life.

Homer's supernatural vision allowed him to track down the gods no matter where they were or what they were up to. The beginning of the *Iliad* makes this abundantly clear. As the story opens, the gods have left Olympus to have a banquet with the Ethiopians, and Achilles has to wait for twelve days before they finish their celebrations, come back to their sacred mountain, and finally pay some attention to his grievances. But while Achilles is kept waiting, Homer can see and relate just what the gods are doing. He can also tell us what happens when Zeus finally returns from the African banquet: the minor goddess Thetis, Achilles's mother, tells Zeus that the Greek commander in chief, Agamemnon, has taken possession of Achilles's concubine and slave and that her enraged son has withdrawn from the fighting in order to teach the overbearing commander a lesson.

Zeus agrees to support the Trojans for as long as Achilles refuses to fight. The Greeks will suffer heavy losses, and that will force Agamemnon to recognize his error and make amends.

In the subsequent narrative, too, the poet is aware at all times of the gods' thoughts and actions; he can even tell us when Zeus gets distracted and thereby falls short of his promise to Achilles's mother. In book 13, he describes how Zeus—who is enjoying a quiet moment by himself on top of Mount Ida—turns his gaze away from the war raging below him on the Trojan plain and glances farther afield, to the Thracians and other people of the distant north. Poseidon, meanwhile, is keeping watch from another mountaintop, on the island of Samothrace, and notices Zeus's distraction. He immediately decides to take advantage of it and help his beloved Greeks in their assault on Troy. In three huge steps (the earth shakes at his progress), he leaps down from his perch and plunges into the sea, arms himself in his underwater palace, and emerges with an entourage of sea monsters darting about in his wake. The god then joins the Greeks on the Trojan plain, helping them while Zeus is still looking to the distant north. Hera, from her own vantage point on top of Mount Olympus, realizes what is going on and—because she too wants to help the Greeks, against Zeus's wishes—decides to visit her husband on Mount Ida, seduce him, and buy Poseidon some more time.

Through Homer's eyes, we are supernaturally in a position to see Zeus and Poseidon perched on opposite mountaintops, staring down at the Trojan plain between them, while Hera keeps watch from Mount Olympus. We can pinpoint the gods in a vast landscape and plot their lines of vision across hundreds of miles. As soon as Zeus turns his gaze away from the Trojan plain, we hear how the other gods spring into action. It is no wonder that the Greeks regarded Homer's ability to describe the gods as divine. Not only could he view the entire panorama of the eastern Mediterranean at a glance and place the gods in it; he could even offer a detailed account of events that had happened long before his time, since the Trojan War was in the distant past. There was something extraordinarily vivid and true about his poetry—and its authority was enhanced by the fact that it agreed, in broad outline, with Hesiod's accounts. These two poets shared the same epic language and the same overall understanding of the gods. Most of the discrepancies between their poems were merely a matter of tone, a product of their different settings. The *Theogony* described the early cosmic struggles that led to the rule of Zeus, and its atmosphere was accordingly raw and threatening. The *Iliad* and the *Odyssey* were set at the time when Zeus was already firmly in control, so disagreements among the gods now seemed lighthearted and at times even farcical. For example, when the gods themselves enter battle in *Iliad* 21 and line up against one another, their conflict is presented as a piece of entertainment for Zeus, who settles down to watch it ensconced in a comfortable "glade on Mt. Olympus."[11] He is in charge, and if the gods want to fight, siding with either Greeks or Trojans, that is no great worry to him; in fact, he looks forward to the spectacle, in much the same way he watches the war between mortals, or indeed sporting events at Olympia.

The only really serious theological disagreement between Homer and Hesiod concerns one single issue: the genealogy of Aphrodite. According to Hesiod, Aphrodite was born out of the castrated genitals of Heaven, a story that spoke of primordial powers of destruction and generation. In Homer, by contrast, Aphrodite was a petulant young goddess, a daughter of Zeus and Dione. No longer a generation older than the supreme god, as she was in Hesiod, Homer's Aphrodite easily slotted into Zeus's permanent patriarchal order. That Homer and Hesiod disagreed about the genealogy of Aphrodite troubled some Greeks. Plato famously claimed that there were two different goddesses called Aphrodite, corresponding to two different kinds of love: "Heavenly Aphrodite," daughter of Heaven, patron of the superior love between men, and "Pandemic Aphrodite," in charge of the common type of love, that between man and woman. But even before Plato's influential theory, epic performers noticed the difficulty with Aphrodite's ancestry and tried to patch over the differences between Homer and Hesiod. They felt the need to create a semblance of coherence, in order to uphold both poets as authorities on the gods.

One poem in particular, a short hymn to Aphrodite designed to be performed at a poetry contest in her honor, started with a polite retelling of Hesiod's myth:

> The strong wind's moist breath conveyed her,
> through crashing waves, all foaming, to shore.
> The Seasons who wear golden ribbons gave her a welcome of joy,
> and wrapped her in deathless clothes. Upon her immortal head
> they placed a beautiful crown of intricate gold;
> they pierced the lobes of her ears with flowers of mountain's
>   copper
> and costly gold, and about her soft neck and gleaming breasts
> they adorned her with chains of gold . . .

This was a cunning opening. Men no doubt often undressed Aphrodite in their minds, summoning the goddess to their bedrooms when confronted with lesser females. The poem, more respectfully, dressed her instead but still looked her up and down in the process. After that Hesiodic beginning, the narrative suddenly swerved in the direction of Homer, suggesting that the other gods were already born and assembled on Olympus when Aphrodite emerged from the waves. Just how that could have happened, the poem did not say. Perhaps Heaven's genitals had floated around for a while before reaching Cyprus, and meanwhile Zeus was born, had his own children, and settled on Olympus. At any rate, when Aphrodite emerged from the foam, the other gods were ready for her:

> . . . her adornment complete,
> the Seasons led Aphrodite to the other gods, and they were amazed
>   at the sight.

They gave her their right hands in greeting, and each god prayed
    that she be
his own wedded wife to bring home, so amazed were they at her
    beauty.
Farewell to you, dark-eyed goddess whose spirit is sweet and kind;
in the poetry contest permit this singer to win, and make ready my
    song.[12]

The poem did not explicitly talk of Heaven's severed genitals
and also remained tactfully silent about Zeus's decision to marry
Aphrodite off to the ugliest Olympian, the lame future cuckold
Hephaistos. All that trouble, that ugliness, that complication, lingered just outside the confines of the hymn, a dark frame around
the luminous goddess.

Modern readers tend to treat the gods of early Greek poetry as
silly fictions, or "sublime frivolities," as they have often been called.[13]
They suppose that epic poetry is essentially free to invent whatever
it wants, and that contradictions between poems do not matter
much. Our *Hymn,* however, shows that in some circumstances contradictions did matter, and tact was required. Composed as an
offering for Aphrodite, the poem needed to steer a respectful course
between different views of the goddess. In general, epic poets were
mindful of the gods, though they never suggested that the gods were
morally perfect—indeed, that notion would have seemed absurd to
them, given that the deities evidently inflicted horrible things on
innocent mortals. The task of the poets was not to defend the Olympians, who needed no human defense in any case. What they aimed
to do, rather, was offer a clear vision of the gods and their actions,
so that mortals might begin to understand them.

That epic poetry influenced how the Greeks related to the gods
is beyond doubt. For example, the travels of the gods described in
poetry affected the operation of their sanctuaries in real life. Delphi,
as we have seen, was open only in summer, because that was when
Apollo was said by poets to visit the place. Unlike the omnipresent

God of Christian theology, the Greek gods were either present or absent, and when they were away, oracles did not work and prayers remained unanswered. The word *atheos* did not usually mean "atheist" in ancient Greek. Instead, it often described someone whom the gods had abandoned.

An inscription discovered at the healing sanctuary of the god Asclepius, son of Apollo, in Epidauros, confirms this, showing how divine travel could shape actual religious practices.[14] The inscription reports the experiences of one Sostrata, who went to the temple hoping to be healed from a "false pregnancy." She followed the ritual practice of incubation—that is, she slept in the sanctuary overnight, hoped that Asclepius would visit her in a dream, and expected that his visitation would cure her. Unfortunately, when she woke up after her incubation, she felt even weaker than she had the day before. The god had failed to cure her, and her relatives had to carry her away on a stretcher. The inscription tells us that as the distraught party made their way home, they met a handsome young man, who asked to examine Sostrata there and then. He made an incision in her abdomen, removed two basins of something (the inscription is hard to read at this point), sewed up the incision, and thereby managed to cure her. What this stranger did may strike us as effective medical practice—and indeed we know from Hippocratic writings that such empirical approaches to medicine were developing around the fourth century BC, the time of this incident— but Sostrata concluded that she had met with the god Asclepius himself, disguised in human form. She surmised that he was traveling back to his temple, after a period abroad. The inscription at Epidauros recorded her gratitude to Asclepius and advertised his healing powers to other ailing pilgrims. Clearly, Sostrata's testimony was useful for its account of initial failure as well as eventual success. If the god was not always present at his sanctuary in Epidauros, not all pilgrims could expect to be healed at all times. Local priests could have used Sostrata's story to explain failed incubations, to encourage pilgrims to return—and perhaps to suggest that successful instances of hands-on healing were ultimately also the work of their patron god.

Stories about the gods—especially the epics of Hesiod and Homer—offer the most amazing descriptions of how the deities walked in and out of people's lives, how their changeable moods and movements shaped everyone's experiences. One reason these accounts remain impressive, even today, is that they do not try to *explain* what the gods are or how they operate. Mixing metaphor and reality, they suggest that ordinary mortals can never quite grasp the divine power of the gods. At times the gods of epic seem entirely anthropomorphic, but they can suddenly become more abstract and mysterious. When Hera travels to Mount Ida to seduce her husband, for example, she takes her time, making her journey as any real-life sailor would do: up the east coast of Greece, across to Turkey, and down the Asian coast, avoiding the open sea. But when Zeus wakes up and sends her packing to Olympus, she moves quite differently:

> . . . like an idea that flashes in the mind of a man
> who has travelled far and wide, and thinks in his mind's awareness,
> "I wish I were in that place, or this," and imagines many things;
> so swiftly travelled Hera in her haste, a goddess.[15]

The Olympian gods are, and are not, like human beings. They travel like sailors, but also at the speed of thought. They belong to our world and transcend it. The early epic poets were on intimate terms with the gods; they could see them and even talk to them directly. But their ultimate accomplishment was to describe to us the gods of Olympus in words, experiences, and images that are fully our own.

===================== 3 =====================

Critical Views

It is through their vivid accounts of the gods that Greek epics capti-
vated their audiences and continue to speak to us many centuries
later. When we read the *Iliad,* for example, we can almost feel Poseidon's heavy steps in our bones as he strides down Samothrace, and
"the high peaks and the timber / shake under his immortal feet."[1]
Here Homer takes inspiration from a cult title of Poseidon, "the
earth-shaker," and turns it into powerful poetry. Sappho, the most
celebrated woman poet of antiquity, offers equally memorable portraits of the gods—describing, for example, the pain of falling in
love with a girl and the fulfillment that Aphrodite can bring. The
goddess comes to Sappho's rescue from Olympus, "in a chariot
drawn by fluttering sparrows, flapping fast their wings over / the
dark earth."[2] To this day, we can still recognize Aphrodite in a host
of sparrows flying across the sky, even if we cannot quite make out
her chariot. Poetry works through detail, and it is in the detail of
their poetic appearances that the Olympian gods still enchant us.
But this level of specificity can also become a problem: the Olympian gods seem so very Greek, in their chariots and sandals, that
their universal credentials can easily be questioned. Anthropomorphic art makes the problem all the more obvious. Do the gods

really look like mortals? And if so, which mortals? Why should the gods look especially Greek, if they are supposed to rule over the entire universe? Could they not have black skin, for example, or blue eyes?

These questions sound modern, but they actually belong to the sixth century BC. Xenophanes of Colophon, the earliest known critic of Homer, made the following observation about the gods:

> The Thracians think that the gods are red-haired and blue-eyed;
> the Ethiopians that they are snub-nosed and black.

In a polemical flourish he added:

> If cattle and horses and lions had hands, and could paint
> with their hands and accomplish works like men,
> horses would paint the gods in the image of horses, cattle of cattle,
> and they would each shape the bodies of gods in the shape of their
>   own.

Xenophanes was not interested in the actual views of Thracians or Ethiopians. He mentioned them because they featured in Homer. At the beginning of the *Iliad*, as we have seen, the Olympian gods were said to be visiting the Ethiopians, and later on in the poem Zeus observed the Thracians from Mount Ida. So it made sense to ask what these distant people made of Zeus and whether he resembled them. Xenophanes also had other objections against the gods of epic:

> Homer and Hesiod ascribed to the gods every action
> that causes shame and reproach among human beings:
> theft, adultery, and cheating each other.

True divinity had to be quite different, in Xenophanes's view. He argued that there must be "one god, the greatest among gods and men, not at all like mortals in appearance or thought." This supreme being would not travel hither and thither like the gods of Olympus, but keep completely still:

> Always he remains in the same place, moving not at all;
> for it is not fitting for him to travel here and there,
> but without effort he shakes everything by the thought of his mind.

Xenophanes proposed not only a different theological order, but a new basis for human knowledge. He dismissed divine inspiration, and all Muse-given truths, claiming that "in time, by searching, human beings find out better."[3]

He was not alone in this enterprise. Not far from his native city of Colophon, in Miletus, other Greek thinkers—Thales, Anaximenes, and Anaximander—also set out to reexamine the fundamentals of human knowledge without relying on inherited Greek views about the gods. They left aside the complicated atmospheres of poetry, myth, and cult and tried to establish what was actually the case through direct observation and logical thinking. The focus of their inquiries was nature (*physis*); they were interested in first principles, celestial bodies, and the "order" of things (*kosmos*, in Greek). Thales, Anaximenes, and Anaximander wanted to describe the material principles of the universe, and we know that Anaximander saw the divine not as a family of gods, but as an organizing mind that made order out of matter. Heraclitus, in the nearby city of Ephesus, also dismissed common Greek notions of the gods. People who prayed to statues were wasting their time, in his opinion: the practice was like "holding conversations with houses."[4] For him, the true divine was something different, a single unified principle steering all things. That principle was "both unwilling and willing to be called by the name of Zeus."[5]

Thales, Anaximenes, Anaximander, Heraclitus, and Xeno-phanes are now hailed as the founding fathers of Greek philosophy, but they came from an environment that was by no means exclusively Greek, and their views might well have been shaped by their place of origin. Xenophanes's Colophon, on the coast of western

Turkey, was a city where Greeks, Lydians, Carians, and Persians came into close—and often hostile—contact. Xenophanes must have realized that the poetry of Homer and Hesiod meant nothing to those who could not understand its language and conventions. Accordingly, he strove for a divine that was truly universal, equally relevant to all human beings on earth. Thales, Anaximenes, Anaximander, and Heraclitus, living in similarly mixed environments, likewise sought to offer arguments that would appeal to anyone who considered matters dispassionately.

Except for Xenophanes, all of these thinkers wrote prose, which was in itself a bold and innovative choice that distanced them from poetic Greek ways of singing about the gods. Xenophanes, in a sense, was the most traditional: he criticized poetry from within, by composing verse. Exactly what theological views he held is hard to establish. We have very few fragments of his work, and only in the form of quotations and paraphrases in later (often Christian) authors. Because the remnants of Xenophanes's work have been specifically selected for us by advocates of monotheism, it is difficult to figure out how large a role the supreme god played in his thought. His longest-surviving poem shows that he did endorse some traditional aspects of Greek religion, such as proper ritual behavior before a feast: he insisted that hands should be washed, garlands worn, and wine poured out into a special vessel—or onto the ground—as a libation to the gods.

Xenophanes's very obsession with Homer and Hesiod indicates that he took them seriously as authorities on the gods of Olympus. They provided the materials against which he sharpened his own thinking; they shaped his views about what was important and what needed correction. Ethiopians and Thracians featured in Homer—and Xenophanes wrote about them, rather than any real-life Lydians or Carians he may have encountered in Colophon. Divine adultery, theft, and cheating were key themes in both Homer and Hesiod—and they were the divine faults that most exercised Xenophanes. But he was also more generally concerned with anthropomorphism and its expression in painting and sculpture. His thought experiment about horses, cattle, and lions focused, after all, on image making rather than storytelling.

By criticizing Homer, Hesiod, and anthropomorphic art, Xenophanes hit right at the heart of Greek religious culture. His objections were muscular but—like all polemical statements—trivialized the opponent. Greek visions of the gods were, in fact, more accommodating of the foreign and the unknown than his arguments suggested. Homer's Hera, who might travel like a Greek sailor but also move at the speed of thought, shows that the gods were not always just like mortals.[6] In art, too, there was greater variety and flexibility than Xenophanes implied: anthropomorphic images were not the only way in which the Greeks represented their gods. They also worshipped stranger, older cultic objects, some of which were no more elaborate than plain wooden planks. On the island of Ikaros, for example, a basic piece of wood was revered as Artemis. Even in Athens, and even after the most famous Greek artist, Phidias, sculpted a marvelous gold-and-ivory statue of Athena for the Parthenon, people continued to venerate an older image of the goddess in a nearby temple, the Erechtheion. This older Athena seems to have been a rather featureless piece of olive wood—yet at the great city festival in honor of the goddess, it was this ancient piece of wood that received the ceremonial offering of a robe, not Phidias's sculpture. Women tended the olive wood, washed it, adorned it with jewelry, and wrapped it up in the ritual garment. Despite the jewelry and the clothing, the piece of wood was hardly an anthropomorphic statue, nor was it even regarded as a work of art. At least according to later Christian sources, the olive wood had not been modeled by human hands at all, but had fallen directly from the sky.[7]

The Greeks assumed that the gods had originally been worshipped in the form of unshaped pieces of wood or stone and realized that cult statues were a relatively recent development, a human improvement on those earlier cultic objects.[8] Indeed, they saw anthropomorphism as a specifically Greek mode of representing the gods—and had their doubts about it for precisely that reason. In the fifth century BC, Herodotus claimed that Homeric and Hesiodic visions of the gods were only rather recent and that the Egyptians had much more ancient and authoritative traditions of divine knowledge. He also made the following comments about the religion of the Persians:

> Now, the Persians, to my certain knowledge, have the following practices. It is not one of their habits to construct statues, temples, and altars; in fact, they count those who do so as fools, because (I suppose) they do not anthropomorphize the gods as the Greeks do. Their worship of Zeus consists in going up to the highest mountain peaks and performing sacrifices; they call the whole vault of heaven Zeus. They also sacrifice to the sun and the moon, and to earth, fire, water, and the winds. Originally, these were the only deities to whom they offered sacrifices, but since then they have also learnt from the Assyrians and Arabs to sacrifice to the Heavenly Aphrodite. Aphrodite is called Mylitta by the Assyrians, Alilat by the Arabs, and Mitra by the Persians.[9]

This bewildering (and quite inaccurate) ethnography of the Near East was typical of Herodotus. It suggested that the gods roamed freely, taking different names and guises; but it also made a more specific point. Worshipping statues, and imagining that the gods behaved like mortals, could seem rather foolish, Herodotus admitted. He was echoing here not just the views of potential foreign interlocutors, but a long Greek tradition skeptical of anthropomorphism, which had been clearly articulated by Xenophanes and picked up by a significant number of others.

The power of Xenophanes's skepticism was such that already during his lifetime, in the sixth century BC, Theagenes of Rhegium issued a defense of the Homeric gods aimed precisely at protecting them from charges of anthropomorphism and immorality. At first sight, it may seem unlikely that Theagenes was responding to Xenophanes's critique of the epic gods, since the two men lived more than six hundred miles apart as the crow flies (see map on p. 32). Yet they were both thoroughly familiar with Homeric epic, and their own work may well have traveled along epic routes. We can imagine traveling rhapsodes, public performances, and ensuing discussions about the nature of the gods. Whatever the exact relationship between Xenophanes and Theagenes, it is clear that ideas spread fast across the ancient Mediterranean and that the nature of the epic gods was a major concern indeed in the archaic period.

About Theagenes's writings we know even less than about Xenophanes's poems; what remains of his thought has come down to us largely through marginal notes, called scholia, found in some manuscripts of the *Iliad* from the Middle Ages. The longest note we have concerns the battle of the gods in books 20 and 21 of the epic. It starts by admitting that some readers find it "unseemly" that the gods should fight one another but points out that according to others, the Olympians should be interpreted allegorically, "on the basis of the form of expression used" (whatever that means, exactly).[10] The note goes on to describe the gods as physical properties, which would allow the battle to be interpreted as an opposition between different elements: for example, Poseidon (water) fights against Apollo (fire). Alternatively, it says, the Olympians can be taken to represent psychological qualities: Athena (wisdom) opposes Ares (folly); Hermes (intelligence) fights Leto (oblivion). All this sounds rather medieval on first hearing, but the note ends with a surprising flourish: "This form of defense is very old, and goes back to Theagenes of Rhegium, the first man who wrote about Homer."

It is hard to know just how much to make of this claim: for the author of the note, Theagenes is clearly little more than a name, a convenient "first inventor" of a kind of interpretation that developed over centuries and proved useful for moralizing lovers of epic. Whether Theagenes actually interpreted the battle of the gods precisely along the lines suggested is doubtful; the identification of Apollo with fire, for one thing, is probably later than the sixth century BC. On the other hand, for Theagenes to have advanced that general form of thinking about the gods is plausible, given his place on the continuum of Greek thought. We know that interpreters of Homer who worked about a century after Theagenes offered full-blown allegorical interpretations of the Olympian deities. They did not call them "allegories" yet (their technical term was *hyponoiai*, "underthoughts"), but clearly allegories is what they were. Metrodorus of Lampsacus, for example, argued in his treatise *About Homer* that "neither Hera nor Athena nor Zeus are that which people think they are when they establish their sacred sanctuaries, but are the substances of nature and arrangements of the elements."[11] And punning interpretations of divine names, linking gods to physical phenomena, already feature in the Homeric poems themselves. In the *Iliad*, for example, we read that Hera spread a thick mist, *ēera,* to protect her beloved Greeks.[12] Theagenes may have teased out some of the implications of these Homeric word games in order to suggest that the Olympian gods were not what they seemed to be—and that, as a result, charges of immorality did not apply to them. A thick mist, after all, could hardly be faulted for deceptive behavior.

The long-distance conversation between Xenophanes and Theagenes seems to have inaugurated a long tradition of debate. In the first century AD, for example, a treatise entitled *Homeric Problems* starts with this crystal-clear alternative: "Everything is impiety if nothing is allegory."[13] Here is the lasting mark left by our two early critics: either the Homeric gods are anthropomorphic and therefore morally reproachable, as Xenophanes maintained, or they are not what they seem to be, as Theagenes apparently argued. Either the epic gods are "fictions," "creations" of the poets, in Xenophanes's words,[14] or there is some deeper truth to them that we readers must decipher—perhaps along the lines suggested by Theagenes. This disagreement has had two main legacies. The first is an open-mindedness about the gods of Olympus, a willingness to debate their nature, which characterizes their entire history. The second—no less important—is an abiding interest in human creativity, in how poets and artists choose to represent the gods, and how we in turn must interpret their work.

PART II

Dialogue: Classical Athens

In the first decades of the fifth century BC, Athens became a democracy, thus inaugurating a system of government that was soon adopted by many other Greek city-states. A new confidence in the abilities of ordinary men to govern themselves fueled broad-ranging discussions about the Olympian gods. If citizens could take care of their own affairs without the help of aristocratic rulers, it was no longer so attractive to picture the gods as members of a grand and immortal family who held sway over all the people on earth. Perhaps the gods were only fictions, after all—embodiments of human fears and hopes. Perhaps Aphrodite was just another name for lust, and Zeus's thunderbolts were actually produced by rubbing atoms.

The Athenians found such thoughts intriguing, but also deeply alarming. Toward the end of the fifth century BC, they rebelled against such notions and became hostile to philosophers who promoted them. Most famously, they sentenced Socrates to death for "not believing in the gods in whom the city believes, introducing new gods, and corrupting the young." In the stunned bewilderment that followed his execution, the Athenians agonized anew about their political and religious commitments. What was wrong with Socrates's views? And how could the truth about the gods be established, if not precisely through the kind of free and open dialogue he had advocated in life?

4

An Education for Greece

The gods of Olympus were deeply involved in the developments of the classical period (the fifth and most of the fourth century BC), starting with their key role in getting Greek communities to unite against the Persians. At the beginning of the fifth century BC, some Greek cities in Ionia (the western coast of what is now Turkey) rebelled against Persian control, and other Greek city-states, including Athens, offered them military support. The Persians reacted immediately: Darius I, King of Kings, attacked and defeated the rebel Ionian cities, then launched an offensive against other city-states in the Aegean islands, and finally disembarked his troops on mainland Greece, determined to teach the Athenians a lesson. Against all odds, however, the Athenians defeated his army at Marathon. Darius's son Xerxes launched an even larger attack a few years later, but he too was defeated by the Athenians—beaten back in the naval Battle of Salamis after the Spartan general Leonidas, at the head of three hundred soldiers, had heroically managed to delay the Persian army at the narrow pass known as Thermopylae. In 479 BC, the allied Greeks at last routed the Persians decisively at the Battle of Plataea. To be prepared against possible future attacks, Athens then formed an alliance of Greek city-states under the protection of Apollo. Its meetings were held on the rocky island of Delos, and the shared funds were kept there as well. Greeks from many different city-states already knew the island as the place where Leto had given birth to Apollo and Artemis, and now they saw it as the hub of their alliance. A shared place of cult turned into a symbol of Greek resistance against the invaders.

Soon, however, complications arose—and Apollo found himself embroiled in an extended intra-Greek struggle for power. The Delian League, which had started out as a defensive pact, quickly began to turn into an instrument for the Athenians to establish their control over other Greeks. Contributions from "allies" were used for various Athenian projects, including the construction of the Parthenon, and defections were not tolerated. A city that tried to leave the alliance could find itself under military occupation, its walls destroyed, and its secessionist leaders on trial in Athenian courts. The true nature of the league became especially obvious when Pericles transferred its common funds from Delos to Athens, where allies were forced to parade their contributions in the theater of Dionysos at the annual festival in honor of this god. Apollo and Dionysos had often been rivals in myth and cult; now the move from Delos to Athens, from the realm of Apollo to the Dionysian festival, marked a fundamental shift of power in the Greek political world.[1] A defensive alliance against the Persians had become the basis for an Athenian empire. Not all city-states were happy with Athens's supremacy, nor indeed with the role of Dionysos in establishing it. Phidias did what he could for this god by including him among the twelve on the Parthenon frieze, but his Olympian status was never universally accepted. Apollo, for his part, had to suffer rather unsympathetic treatment in plays performed in the Athenian theater of Dionysos—all the more so because Delphi, Apollo's main Panhellenic center of cult, had been hostile to the Athenian cause.

The shifting fortunes of the various gods reflected the unstable politics of the classical period. But the controversies of this time were not limited to the relative standing of the gods vis-à-vis one another; they also involved a fundamental reassessment of divine power in relation to human self-determination and autonomy. The democratic system of government, which the Athenians first developed in the early fifth century BC, proved to be attractive: by the end of the century, hundreds of Greek city-states had founded their own democracies (partly under Athenian coercion, to be sure, but partly also through the impetus of local people rebelling against their own rulers). For Athens, democracy and empire easily went together, though for other Greek city-states it was harder to establish what self-determination should entail. Some cities (most notably Sparta) resisted Athenian control; others sided with Athens and, in many cases, turned against their own ruling elites. Predictably, constant warring was the result. Yet even amid all the violence, a new confidence in humankind, in people's ability to determine how they should live and die, became palpable. "Man is the measure of all things," intoned Protagoras, capturing the spirit of the age.[2] It was this attitude that had the most radical effect on the gods. Ordinary mortals felt that they were now in a position to question all forms of power. Of course, Xenophanes and other thinkers had already asked probing questions about the gods in the sixth century BC, but now wondering about the true extent of the divine might became a mass phenomenon. An audience of some fifteen thousand people seated in the theater of Dionysos heard, for example, that "habit" was stronger than the gods, because it was through habit that people believed in them in the first place.[3] Thus, while the rituals of religion remained largely stable (for, after all, men and women still needed the comfort of habit), doubts about the gods spread fast.

Metrodorus of Lampsacus, as we have already seen, claimed that the gods of epic were not what ordinary worshippers imagined: they were allegories, in fact, and had nothing to do with what happened in sanctuaries. Protagoras, who thought that man was the measure of all things, claimed to have no views about the gods: "I cannot say either that they exist or that they do not, nor how they are constituted in form; for there is much which prevents knowledge—the obscurity of the subject, and the shortness of human life."[4] It would be interesting to know how his treatise *On the Gods* continued after this devastating opening statement, but it has not survived. Melissus, on the island of Samos, echoed Protagoras's feelings, claiming that there was no way of establishing whether the gods existed.[5] And it was also at this time that the poet Simonides, in Sicily, told the local tyrant that he needed just one more day, and two more, and then four, to figure out what a god might be.[6]

Meanwhile, Prodicus, a philosopher from the island of Keos, offered new theories about the names and the nature of the gods. In his view, back in the early history of the world, primitive human beings called "god" whatever they found useful, such as the sun, the moon, moisture (which they called "Poseidon"), and fire (which they called "Hephaistos"). Eventually, he said, some men and women started to travel and teach new skills, such as the cultivation of plants, and the results of what they taught also seemed divine to their pupils: "Demeter" was in fact a name for corn, and "Dionysos" signified wine.[7] Many miles away, in the northern city of Abdera, Democritus developed similar views about the origins of the gods but claimed that they emerged out of human fears, rather than any sense of gratitude. Thunderbolts terrified people, for example, so they imagined an angry Zeus.[8] Democritus dismissed the notion that lightning was really produced by a god, arguing that it was instead a physical phenomenon caused by the rubbing of atoms—minuscule, indivisible particles of matter that constantly combined and recombined, creating all that exists. And Anaxagoras of Clazomenae, who got interested in a fallen meteorite, concluded that Helios, the sungod, was in fact a blazing lump of stone, "larger than the Peloponnese."[9]

New ideas about the gods crisscrossed the Mediterranean in the course of the fifth century BC and gathered strength as people talked to one another. Some thinkers emphasized a single divine principle (much to the delight of later Christian readers), some were truly agnostic, and we know that at least one man—Diagoras of

Melos—developed a reputation for genuine atheism. According to one anecdote, on seeing votive gifts made by shipwreck survivors, Diagoras pointed out that there would have been more gifts if the many drowned at sea had also been in a position to leave offerings for the gods.[10] (Because of his reputation for atheism, Diagoras's religious hymns became something of a joke in antiquity.) Beyond the different aims and views of individual thinkers, however, there was a common thread to their endeavors: they all questioned traditional assumptions about the Olympian gods and cared little for religious ritual.

Artists, by comparison, seemed more wedded to tradition—not just because their commissions were often linked to temples and religious festivals, but also because anthropomorphic gods offered such wonderful opportunities for exploring the human form. Still, even while working within the constraints of their commissions and conventions, they began experimenting. In the course of the early fifth century BC, the rigid schemes of archaic sculpture gave way to more naturalistic, free, and fluid representations of the human body, suggesting living, breathing people. As a result, it became much easier to recognize individual gods: they now looked like specific types of human characters. Artemis was established as a young girl at the brink of sexual maturity, Apollo as a beautiful youth, Demeter as a mournful mother holding a torch, and Dionysos as a jolly god with a cup in his hand. Before this, archaic statues had been so inscrutable that they could be deciphered only by context. A male figure in a temple of Apollo could be assumed to be a representation of the god, for example, even if its actual appearance gave nothing away. The gods that Phidias carved on the Parthenon frieze did away with such stiff formalism: they had individual bodies and characters and conveyed a lively sense of movement. They could easily be seen as studies of the human form, in fact, rather than theological statements. Only Phidias's cult statues attempted to capture the awe-inspiring feeling of an epiphany, an actual encounter with a god. His statue of Athena inside the Parthenon, for instance, was fully twelve meters high and was entirely covered in gold and ivory. A shallow pool of water in front of it reflected light from the outside and projected it onto the statue, adding to the dazzling effect. Phidias's Athena immediately set a new trend. A few years after the Parthenon was built, the authorities at Olympia invited him to sculpt a monumental gold-and-ivory statue of Zeus for their own temple. He made a massive Zeus seated on a throne, a figure so realistic

A Roman copy of Praxiteles's *Apollo Sauroktonos*, ca. 350 BC. The god originally held an arrow in his hand and idly used it to torment the lizard on the tree trunk, biding his time until killing the animal would give him the greatest pleasure. If the harmless creature symbolized the fearful monster Python, whom Apollo had famously killed at Delphi, then what did the languid, beautiful body of Apollo represent? Praxiteles's art posed interesting theological questions.

that ancient visitors speculated that this sculpted god could stand up and take the roof off the temple.[11]

Exceptional size and luminosity served, in these cases, to distinguish the statues of the gods from those of ordinary mortals, but classical art focused above all on conveying a naturalistic impression of the human body. From a religious perspective, this posed some problems. If the gods looked like beautiful, living, breathing mortals, then what exactly was divine about them? Whereas earlier artists had taken anthropomorphism for granted, without asking too many questions about it, in the classical period artists began to reflect explicitly on the issue of anthropomorphic representation, partly no doubt because everybody was beginning to question it. Praxiteles, for example, made a statue of Apollo in the act of killing a lizard. His sculpture recalled the myth of Apollo's arrival at Delphi, when he had killed the horrific monster Python, but the scene was now far from ominous. The terrible monster had become a little animal, and Apollo himself was a languid youth idly tormenting the creature with an arrow. What was the connection between human representation and divine reality? Where was the mythic monster, and what were we to make of the god? It was the unthreatening animal, even more than the human-looking god, that pointed to a newly formulated problem: If a tiny lizard could stand for a frightful monster, then what did the youthful, aimless Apollo stand for? Praxiteles's work was naturalistic but also posed transcendental questions. The effect was sophisticated, witty, and deeply puzzling.

Even before Praxiteles sculpted his *Apollo Sauroktonos*, "the Lizard-Slayer," artists had begun to reflect explicitly on the nature of the gods. From about the middle of the fifth century BC, a new subject began to feature on Greek vases: scenes showing the cult statue of a god and, next to it, the god himself. The statue was usually archaic in style—a rigid pose, often with one foot forward, a stiff neck, symmetrical drapes, and muscles—while the god was depicted in the new, flowing, classical style. The vases told a story about progress in art. Classical painting represented the "actual" god,

An archaic cult statue of Apollo, inside a temple, next to the actual god, depicted in the more flowing classical style. This fragment of a south Italian vase, dated to the early fourth century BC, suggests a story of artistic progress yet also invites us to reflect on the limits of art.

while archaic statues began to look, by comparison, stilted and conventional. At the same time, the vases also drew attention to their own imperfection. It was always possible to imagine the real god picking up the vase, making even the classical painting of himself look unrealistic by comparison. This game of Chinese boxes—the god inside the statue, inside the vase, inside our ability to visualize the gods—was an invitation to reflect on the limits of art. The divine, whoever or whatever it may be, was elsewhere, in a different realm, always beyond human attempts to represent it.

Such philosophical vases depicting the gods next to their archaic statues originated from many different places, and so did radical theories about the gods. New ideas sprang up everywhere and spread fast through the entire Greek world, from southern Italy to the Ionian coast. But it was in Athens that they took root with the most vigor. There was something special about this city, something ruthless and open, that made it particularly susceptible to questioning the gods. People there believed that difficult problems were best

resolved by engaging in open and frank debate. They also maintained that ordinary citizens were perfectly able to make up their
own minds about everything, including the nature of the divine.
Many of the radical thinkers I have already mentioned—including
Metrodorus, Protagoras, Prodicus, Anaxagoras, and Diagoras—
settled in Athens in the course of the fifth century BC because they
thought their ideas would be well received there. And they were
right about that, at least initially.

Pericles's celebrated speech in honor of the war dead, as recorded
for us in Thucydides's *History of the Peloponnesian War,* offers the
clearest statement of how Athenians liked to think about themselves, of how confident and unconventional they were:

> Our constitution is called a democracy because power is in the hands
> of the whole people, rather than a minority. When it is a question of
> settling private disputes, everyone is equal before the law; when it is
> a question of putting one person before another in positions of pub-
> lic responsibility, what counts is not belonging to a particular class,
> but the actual ability which the individual possesses. No one, so
> long as he has it in him to be of service to the state, is kept in politi-
> cal obscurity because of poverty. And, just as our political life is free
> and open, so is our day-to-day life in our relations with each other.
> We do not mind our next-door neighbor if he enjoys himself in his
> own way, nor do we give him the kind of black looks which, though
> they do no real harm, still do hurt our feelings. We are free and tol-
> erant in our private lives; but in public affairs we keep the law. . . .
> Our love of what is beautiful does not lead to extravagance; our
> love of the things of the mind does not make us soft. We think that
> wealth is something to be properly used, rather than something to
> boast about. . . . Taking everything together, then, I declare that our
> city is an education for Greece.[12]

Pericles offered an idealized picture, of course. Athens may have
been "an education for Greece," but it is equally true that intellectuals

from all over the Greek world flocked to Athens in order to educate
its citizens. Pericles's statement that "the whole people" held power
was equally misleading. What he actually meant was that adult Athenian men did. Out of a total population of about 350,000—including perhaps as many as 100,000 slaves—only about 50,000 to
60,000 were regarded as citizens and eligible to take part in the
political process. Still, those men were genuinely included, and their
participation was radically direct. Whereas we elect politicians who
govern for us, in Pericles's time most Athenian officials (and all jury-
men) were selected by lot from the entirety of the citizen body,
because elections were thought to favor rich candidates. Major decisions, such as whether to go to war or raise taxes, were taken by vote
in a public assembly open to all citizens. Officials—whether appointed
by lot or elected—were held to the closest scrutiny in the council
and the assembly, and sometimes in the courts, too, where juries of
thousands made instantaneous decisions about the cases that were
presented to them. In the fourth century BC, the Athenians even
devised a system of public compensation so that poorer citizens
could attend the assembly, be selected for office, and serve as jurors
without loss of earnings. In short, Athenian citizens were utterly
committed to their own ability to make decisions and govern their
state. Some even went as far as suggesting that women and slaves
would also be able to govern—if given the appropriate opportunities and education.

All this confidence in human self-government had the effect of
marginalizing the gods, at least in some public contexts. Pericles
himself never once mentioned the Olympians in his funeral oration.
The fallen Athenians had died on the battlefield not in order to obey
the will of the gods, but because they wanted to impose their own
will on other Greeks. Likewise, political and legal speeches rarely
appealed to the gods. Speakers addressed themselves instead to the
"men of Athens" and trusted their fellow citizens to judge what
was right and wrong. Thucydides, who recorded Pericles's speech,
was deeply influenced by the culture of the assembly and the courts.

His *History of the Peloponnesian War* barely mentioned the gods and never once suggested that they influenced human affairs. In fact, Thucydides implied that relying on the gods and on divine justice was politically naïve. He made that point most clearly when discussing the hostilities between Athens and the island of Melos, in the southern Aegean. The Melians insisted on remaining neutral in the first stages of the Peloponnesian War between Athens and Sparta, but Athens confronted them with a stark choice: Either join the Delian League or be destroyed. The Melians objected that they had done nothing wrong and that the gods would therefore protect them. The Athenians replied that "the strong do as they like, and the weak suffer what they must."[13] They then conquered the island of Melos, killed all adult males, and enslaved everybody else. Thucydides never again mentioned the gods in his account of the Melian affair. They featured only in the Melians' own empty hopes for divine justice.

Without trust in a divinely appointed order, it was easy to reach the conclusion that might was right. And that is precisely the conclusion the Athenians reached—at least as far as their foreign policy was concerned. Within their own city, the picture was more complicated. Pericles described Athens as a free and open society, where people never gave one another "black looks" for what they did in private and justice was supposedly guaranteed by the principles of equality before the law. But, again, his description was idealistic, even actively misleading. Archaeologists have discovered hundreds of curse tablets in the soil of ancient Athens. People scratched the most extreme and detailed maledictions on cheap pieces of lead, hoping that the gods would be induced to harm their neighbors, relatives, business associates, love interests, sporting rivals, and friends. Sometimes the tablets were even accompanied by ancient Greek equivalents of voodoo dolls. Judging from the sheer number of these curses, it seems that people were constantly trying to harm one another in classical Athens. Notably, many of the tablets referred to court cases: litigants evidently felt that bringing their complaints before the law was not enough and asked the gods to crush their adversaries, render them incoherent in court, or, better still, make them have a fit and die on the spot before the jury. Requests of this kind were generally addressed to the most sinister deities—Hades, ruler of the underworld, featured particularly often. But some Olympians also made an appearance on curse tablets, together with epithets that specified their more sinister powers: Hermes *Chthonios,* "of the Underground," and Demeter *Chthonia* were apparently powerful gods for cursing. Although the gods were hardly mentioned in official legal proceedings, people seem to have thought that they could affect what happened in court. The principle of equality before the law did not fully reassure the Athenians after all, and a human jury was not entirely trusted to deliver what was needed.

Free, rational, and egalitarian on the surface, Athens hid a meddlesome and malignant core. The Athenians insisted on their own human ability to govern themselves, but at the same time they enlisted the occult power of the gods in order to harm one another. It was not easy to live up to fully democratic principles, to believe that people could rule themselves and properly judge one another. The gods were needed precisely because they could be partial and unfair. Pericles claimed that Athens was "an education for Greece," yet the city offered no easy lessons—not about how to live with one another and not about the gods.

5

Exile and Death

When Gorgias of Leontini arrived in Athens in 427 BC, people took notice. He was physically imposing, but, more important, there was something amazing about the way he spoke: there was a rhythm, a symmetry, a rhyme, to what he said. Words seemed to reveal their deeper meaning simply by the way in which he arranged and articulated them. He had no trouble at all convincing the Athenians that they should offer military support to his native city of Leontini, in eastern Sicily—in fact, they listened to him as if spellbound. And Athens cast a spell on Gorgias, too. He returned home a hero, but he no longer cared about Leontini's affairs. At the first opportunity he returned to Athens and began to teach rhetoric there. He knew he could charge whatever fees he liked: the Athenians were desperate to sound like him. Even today we can still hear his voice and his turns of phrase—they're there in the scripts of Athenian drama, in Thucydides's *History of the Peloponnesian War,* in Athenian political speeches and philosophical dialogues. That is how deeply his teaching took root. Never one for understatement, Gorgias eventually became so rich that he commissioned a statue of himself entirely covered in gold and exhibited it at Delphi.

Gorgias was one of several foreign intellectuals who contributed to a mounting feeling of moral and religious anxiety in Athens in the last decades of the fifth century BC. He did this by mixing up different ways of thinking about gods and men and causing a lot of confusion. To train his pupils in public speaking, Gorgias did not use the specifics of Athenian law (which he probably did not even know), but rather relied on the poems and myths that belonged to all the Greeks. The result was that traditional views about the gods were subjected to a new kind of quasi-legal scrutiny. In one rhetorical stunt, for example, he set out to defend the most reviled woman on earth: Helen of Troy. It was true, he admitted, that she had left her husband, sailed off with Paris, and caused the Trojan War—but, after all, she was acting under the influence of Aphrodite and, as Gorgias pointed out in his typically assonant style, it was impossible "to hinder a god's predetermination by human preconsideration."[1] Gorgias added many more reasons why Helen should attract pity rather than blame. For example, he suggested that Paris had seduced her through irresistible language: "Speech is a great power, which has the most minute and invisible body, but accomplishes the most divine works; for it can stop fear and soothe sorrows, create joy and increase pity."[2] With this argument, Gorgias cast his lot with Helen's. If his speech—his own invisible yet mighty creation—managed to persuade, then Helen had to be judged innocent.

There was something thrilling and immoral about Gorgias's arguments. Nobody in the ancient world thought that it was all right for a real-life woman to behave like Helen, and Gorgias reveled in the very outrageousness of his suggestion. He concluded his performance by saying that he had offered "a speech in praise of Helen, and an amusement for himself."[3] So Gorgias and Helen were not in the same boat after all. She remained a shameless woman, whereas he was simply amusing himself—or so he claimed. What exactly Gorgias thought, and what exactly he was teaching, remained uncertain. He famously wrote a treatise called *On Not Being or On Nature,* where he argued that nothing exists; that even if something existed, we could not know it; and that even if we did know it, we could not communicate it to others. Was that too just a piece of fun, or was it a serious argument aimed at emancipating words from reality? To this day, some people take Gorgias seriously as a philosopher, while others dismiss him as merely an impressive clown. In Athens, Gorgias's claims were exploited to both serious and comic effect, but above all they were regarded as genuinely useful. A whole industry of rhetorical training soon sprang up to teach people how to speak for or against anything at all. Certain moral propositions could be true or could be false—it all depended on what sounded persuasive in a specific context.

A collection of *Double Speeches* in this tradition has survived from classical Athens, formally setting out both sides of specific arguments. *On What Is Fine and What Is Shameful,* for example, starts with a straightforward position ("Adultery is always shameful") and then shifts to cultural relativism: Spartans, Athenians, Thracians, and Egyptians have different views about adultery, so we must conclude that adultery is perfectly fine in certain circumstances. This treatise ends with an attack on poetry: the authority of the poets cannot be adduced when it comes to moral judgments, it insists, because "the poets compose to give pleasure, rather than offer the truth."[4]

In this climate, Homeric epic became suspect. When Gorgias argued that Helen was innocent because Aphrodite forced her to commit adultery, he was taking his cue from a passage in *Iliad* 3 where the goddess, disguised as an old woman, went to fetch Helen from the city walls and told her to return immediately to her bedroom.[5] On that occasion, Helen had lashed out against the goddess: she had refused to join Paris in bed and tried to stand her ground but had been crushed by Aphrodite's superior power. The Homeric exchange between Helen and Aphrodite seemed puzzling even in antiquity. Was Helen talking to her own sexual desire? Or did she really have no physical control over her actions? Homer claimed that Aphrodite had actually, bodily, removed Helen from the city walls and dumped her in Paris's bedroom against her will. But was this Homeric account plausible? In Gorgias's prosaic retelling, it began to sound highly unlikely: a piece of immoral sophistry, rather than a poetic exploration of divine power.

The playwright Euripides echoed Gorgias by staging a court case against Helen in one of his tragedies, *The Trojan Women*. The play is set in the bleak aftermath of the Trojan War. The city of Troy is a pile of ashes in the background, and the enslaved Trojan women are waiting to be allocated to their new Greek masters. In the midst of all the devastation, Helen appears onstage dressed to the nines, ready to leave the Trojan women to their terrible fate and resume her former life with her first husband, Menelaos, after her ten-year escapade. Because she realizes that both Greeks and Trojans have reason to resent her, she delivers an articulate speech in self-defense. The Trojan War was not her fault, she says: it was a plan hatched by the gods. Menelaos is prepared to go along with this—but then he would, since Helen's beauty offers all the persuasion he needs. Indeed, his only concern is whether she has gained any weight since he last saw her. The Trojan women are a tougher audience for Helen: "Aphrodite is just another name for folly," barks Hecuba, former queen of Troy.[6] Hecuba is right, of course. But she is also badly wrong. Aphrodite was not just Helen's personal lust, and the Trojan War was not simply the fault of one beautiful woman. There was, in fact, no plausible explanation for that war. And the gods of Olympus tended to appear precisely when history became implausible, when people behaved in ways that seemed unaccountable.

Gorgias and Euripides forced the Athenians to think hard about the gods and their relationship to human action and responsibility. In Homer, both gods and mortals brought about what happened, acting together; but now there were courtroom choices to be made. Either Helen was guilty of choosing to behave badly or she was not. And if she was guilty—if she hadn't been dragged into Paris's bedroom against her will—then Aphrodite's power was called into question. This was new. People were used to applying different standards of reasoning to claims of divine power depending on context.

In a real courtroom case, declaring that "the gods made me do it" had no place at all, while in poetry the power of the gods seemed real—it explained, for example, why people behaved in ways they knew were wrong. Now these different perspectives on the gods were forcefully driven against each other and made to clash.

It was above all on the Athenian stage that the collision happened—partly, no doubt, because the theater was both a religious and a political institution. Athenian tragedies and comedies were staged in honor of the god Dionysos at his yearly festivals, but they were also important civic occasions. At some point, as with political and jury service, the Athenians even introduced state subsidies for poorer citizens who wanted to attend Dionysos's festivals but could not afford to take time off from work. Clearly, going to the theater was deemed as important as serving on a jury or participating in the assembly. The plays imparted no straightforward political agenda, however, nor did they even affirm a clear religious creed. Instead, they offered something interesting, magnetic, and hard to interpret. Perhaps their political value lay precisely in the fact that they made people think and thus trained them in deliberation.

The plays of Euripides confronted the Athenians with intractable questions about the gods—and not just in his *Trojan Women*. His tragedies often began with a traditional myth, only to subvert and ultimately destroy it. *Heracles,* for example, was based on a well-known story: Hera, jealous of Zeus's liaison with the mortal woman Alcmene, inflicted madness on Heracles, the son born of that union, and induced him to kill his own wife and children. Then the play took an unexpected turn. Once the madness subsided, Euripides's Heracles asked himself how Hera could possibly be so cruel as to make him kill his own family, and who would ever want to worship a goddess like her. Indeed, he continued, the whole notion that the gods had sexual partners, suffered jealousy, and took out their frustrations on mortals made no sense at all: "The god, if he truly is god, needs nothing; everything else is just the wretched words of poets."[7] The paradox of the play, of course, is that by expressing such thoughts, Heracles was calling his own existence into question. As a character in a play, he was himself the product of "the wretched words of poets." More specifically, because he was the son of Zeus and a mortal woman, it was ironic that he—of all characters—should doubt the notion that the gods experienced sexual desire. Euripides did not resolve the paradox within the play itself. One way of interpreting *Heracles* is that when Heracles doubts Hera's cruelty and his own ancestry, he is in fact still mad. But if he is not mad, and right to claim that true divinity needs nothing, then it suddenly becomes unclear why the Athenians should gather in the theater of Dionysos and celebrate a festival in his honor.

Such ideas shocked the city of Athens. One comedian claimed that sellers of wreaths and other religious paraphernalia all went out of business because "Euripides persuaded people that the gods do not exist."[8] There is no reason to take this quip at face value. In reality, people continued to worship. Festivals and sacrifices continued to follow the traditional Athenian calendar; priests were still appointed, offerings made, and wreaths, no doubt, woven and sold. Euripides himself continued to write plays for the festival of Dionysos, no matter what outrageous things he made his characters say about the gods. But a subtle equilibrium had been broken. Different ways of thinking about the gods were mixing in new and alarming combinations. Quasi-legal arguments about myth changed how people thought about the Olympians; and, conversely, prominent intellectuals started to be brought to actual court on the grounds that they had insulted the gods. The trials for *asebeia* (impiety) were a clear sign that the Athenians were feeling increasingly anxious about their deities.

Anaxagoras, according to whom the sun-god was a lump of stone, was one of the first to suffer. It seems that at some point during the 430s, he was charged with *asebeia* and exiled from Athens. He settled in Lampsacus (modern Turkey) and remained there for the rest of his life; after his death, the local people set up an altar "to

Mind and Truth" in his honor, no doubt feeling more enlightened than the Athenians. Interestingly, Anaxagoras was accused of Medism (Persian sympathies) in addition to impiety. This charge may have had something to do with Anaxagoras's origins: his native Clazomenae, a Greek city, had sided with the Persians against other Greeks during the Persian Wars. But Anaxagoras had been living in Athens for many years, and the Persians had long become a notional rather than an immediate threat. His "Medism," therefore, might have been a matter of his theories about the gods rather than his international politics: his interest in the stars could have been presented as too close to Eastern astronomical traditions. The timing of Anaxagoras's trial, moreover, betrayed internal rather than international concerns. Anaxagoras was a close friend of Pericles's, and attacking him may have been intended to discredit the politician just at the time when Pericles was at the height of his power. Political considerations of this kind do not, however, indicate a lack of genuine religious anxiety. On the contrary: if, in order to damage Pericles, it was useful to suggest that his friend was impious, then the Athenians were evidently concerned that Anaxagoras (and indeed his friend Pericles) might offend the gods.

The atheist Diagoras was next. He was charged with *asebeia* in 415 BC, the year after the Athenians invaded Melos and killed the entirety of the adult male population. Diagoras himself had been living in Athens peacefully for many years by that point, but all of a sudden its people turned against him, betraying their own moral and religious confusion. The irony was that Diagoras had by then every reason to doubt the existence of the gods. After all, the Melians had trusted that the gods would protect them from Athenian force and had been exterminated as a result. Now Diagoras also faced execution for *not* relying on the gods. The details of his trial are preserved for us in the writings of a medieval Arabic scholar, Mubaššir ibn Fātik, who must have had access to a detailed ancient account, because he reports the exact price the Athenians put on Diagoras's head.[9] Wisely, Diagoras did not wait around to hear the verdict: he fled to Corinth even before the trial took place and lived there for the rest of his life.

As long as troublesome foreign thinkers like Anaxagoras and Diagoras could be isolated and exiled, the Athenians had an easy means of reassuring themselves that all was well with their city and its relationship with the gods. But when Socrates was charged with impiety in 399 BC, his trial shook the entire city. Socrates was a prominent citizen and an Athenian by birth. Intellectually engaged, poor, and brave in battle, he embodied several key values of the Athenian democracy. It is true that he did not take active part in politics and generally irritated people with his incessant questioning about the good life, justice, love, and many other subjects, which tended to seem all the more intractable after he had dealt with them. Still, the Athenians prided themselves on their freedom of speech, and all that Socrates ever did was talk. Why he was executed was a question the Athenians themselves struggled to answer, and it remains a puzzle to this day.

The details of his trial are hard to reconstruct, though he was certainly accused of "not believing in the gods in whom the city believes, introducing new gods, and corrupting the young."[10] Which gods Socrates failed to respect is not stated in the sources, but given the traditional impetus of the charges, it seems safe to assume that at issue were mainly the gods of Olympus. The Olympians dominated the yearly calendar of Athenian festivals, featured on the most important civic monuments, and played important roles in the Homeric poems, which alone were given the honor of regular performances at the Panathenaea, the most important city festival. As for the "new gods" Socrates supposedly introduced, things are less clear. He apparently insisted that "something divine," a *daimonion ti,* spoke to him regularly and urged him to pursue certain courses of action. It was a divine injunction of this kind, for example, that had forbidden him from taking active part in politics. So, whatever new gods (or, more probably, notions of the divine) Socrates championed, they discouraged engagement in the democratic process. Socrates's religion seemed pitched against the duties of a good democrat, and that fact alone must have counted against him in court.

A jury made up of five hundred Athenian men, chosen by lot, found him guilty by the narrowest of margins. Technically, the verdict did not have to lead to Socrates's execution, because his case fell under the category of "assessed trials," in which the state acknowledged that there could be different degrees of guilt. The procedure was simple: If the defendant was found guilty, the prosecutor proposed a penalty, the defendant proposed a lesser counterpenalty, and the jury picked one of the two. Socrates could have gotten away with a fine, but he decided to make a mockery of the whole procedure and demanded, as a penalty, free lunches at public expense for the rest of his life. So the prosecutor's proposal stood: capital punishment.

Plato insists that even after the verdict, Socrates could have easily escaped from Athens and gone into exile, but he chose to abide by the laws of his city. He was a good Athenian, at least in Plato's portrait, and had no intention of leaving. He would stand firm in the face of the verdict, just as he had stood firm when facing the enemy in battle. So, surrounded by his closest friends and followers, the seventy-year-old Socrates drank his cup of hemlock and died. Afterward, nobody could quite understand what had happened. Scores of pamphlets about Socrates were published soon after his death; only the works of Plato and Xenophon survive, but we know that there were dozens of other writers arguing with one another and trying to make sense of the event.

Modern historians suggest that Socrates was tried on trumped-up charges and that the real motives were political rather than religious. But, in fact, it is difficult to distinguish here between politics and religion. The Athenians were worried about their democracy and felt that the gods were turning against them. They had suffered some devastating setbacks in the second half of the fifth century BC: a long war against Sparta that ended in defeat, a typhoid epidemic that

killed at least one-quarter of the population, and two brutal oligarchic coups, one in 411 and the second in 404 BC. Thucydides offered
an unflinching assessment of the war, the epidemic, and their moral
consequences: "People no longer strove to be honorable, because
they doubted they would live long enough to earn a reputation for
honor."[11] Some Athenians fit this description especially well. There
was Alcibiades, famous for his looks, his horses, his wealth, his
drunken excesses—and his on-and-off love affair with Socrates. In
the course of the Peloponnesian War, he had defected to Sparta and
then to Persia before participating in the plot against democracy in
411 BC. And there was Critias, one of the thirty tyrants who seized
power in 404 BC. He set about "purging the city," as Lysias, a contemporary witness, put it.[12] Hundreds of people were sentenced to
death by drinking hemlock, and many more were forced into exile
during the period of oligarchic rule. Critias had also been a close
friend of Socrates.

Democracy was finally restored in 403–402 BC, and only three
years later Socrates was put on trial. It is generally assumed that he
was targeted because he loved and taught the most reviled aristocrats and violent antidemocrats of his time, but religious outrage
might also have been part of the mix. Alcibiades, in particular, was
remembered for having openly mocked religion some fifteen years
earlier. In one of his drunken excesses, he had desecrated the rites of
Demeter at Eleusis and mutilated the herms—heads of the god
Hermes on a pillar body that sported an erect penis. These herms
were revered objects, whose origins harked back to totemic emblems,
marking the possession of territories. In Athens and the surrounding
countryside, herms were placed at crossroads, field boundaries, and
house entrances. Alcibiades had dared to cut off their organs, thinking himself more powerful than those ancestral signs of divine order,
those sacred symbols embedded in the landscape. The Athenians
were horrified, and Alcibiades had been tried and found guilty of
profanation.

Still, the business of the herms, together with Socrates's associa-

A rare example of a herm whose penis survived intact through the ages. This boundary stone comes from the island of Siphnos and dates to about 520 BC. In Athens, Alcibiades mutilated the local herms in an act of sacrilegious vandalism that shocked the city.

tion with Alcibiades and other aristocrats, cannot have been the only reason he was put on trial for impiety. After all, Critias and Alcibiades were both already dead when Socrates was charged, and the Athenians were keen to put the past behind them. After democracy was restored in 403 BC, a general amnesty prohibited trials for political offenses committed before that year. Perhaps the Athenians who found Socrates guilty were more worried about his current followers than about the flamboyant oligarchs he had loved in previous decades. The Cynics ("people who lived like dogs") were gaining prominence at the end of the fifth century BC, and they too claimed Socrates as their teacher. They also made a show of disregarding civil society, masturbated in public, defecated in the streets, and refused to consider themselves citizens. They despised traditional forms of religion and insisted on living according to nature, like animals. The good family fathers who sat on the jury in 399 BC and condemned Socrates to death may have been concerned that their sons too would go to the dogs. That is to say, perhaps they cared precisely about the issues on which the prosecution focused: religion, the safety of the city, and the next generation.

The Olympian gods, like all traditional figures, inspired a sense of security and comfort. They were by no means perfect, of course, but there were ways of managing them. They liked animal sacrifices, libations, votive offerings, festivals, athletic competitions, beautiful poetry, and dancing. If given what they wanted, they would provide their own gifts in return. Traditional exchanges with the gods needed to be fully endorsed and upheld, particularly when Athens was undergoing a difficult crisis. It was not prudent to suggest that the gods did not exist or did not care about how mortals behaved—or, worse still, that a *daimonion ti,* a "something divine," prevented engagement with normal civic duties. The Athenians who survived the war, the plague, and two oligarchic coups were tired. They wanted peace and stability; they needed good politics and the comfort of traditional religion. More important still, they needed to believe that the two things went together: that their democracy was not, in fact, pitched against the gods.

6

Fictions and Fantasies

New dangers awaited the gods of Olympus after the death of Socrates in 399 BC. Plato launched an all-out attack against them, partly no doubt because traditional ideas about the gods had been instrumental in the death of his teacher. A few decades later, Plato's own student Aristotle characterized the Olympians as fictions and fantasies. These two philosophers built on the work of their predecessors, including Xenophanes's criticism of Homer and Hesiod in the sixth century BC, but went far beyond it—in terms of both the depth of their arguments and the influence of their legacies. The gods were now assigned places in complex philosophical systems, where they were defined in relation to both divine truth and human creativity. Plato and Aristotle fundamentally shaped the subsequent history of the Olympian gods, although initially their arguments had little effect on how ordinary Greeks treated their deities.

In classical Athens, people knew, of course, that the gods featured in all sorts of fantastic poems and unlikely tales, but they also thought that those stories revealed fundamental truths about the divine. Poets and artists claimed, for example, that Hermes had stolen Apollo's cattle when he was just a newborn baby—and there was clearly something to their accounts, because Hermes was indeed a useful deity to pray to when it came to thieving or asking for protection from thieves. And when poets described how Artemis had asked her father, Zeus, never to be married, that too sounded plausible. People knew from real life that Artemis needed careful management when it came to holding a wedding. Girls, who were usually wed around the age of fourteen or fifteen, celebrated rituals in honor of Artemis before the nuptials, and it seems that bridegrooms—who were generally much older—also made special offerings to the goddess at that time, hoping to ensure that she would not make too much trouble with her girlish ways at the beginning of the marriage.

One reason Plato and Aristotle failed to change prevailing attitudes was that they took a strictly literary approach to the gods. Plato, in particular, focused exclusively on what the poets said— without considering how mythology gained strength from what worshippers did and felt. As far as he was concerned, feelings were irrelevant. Truth was what mattered, and once that was clear, the intellect would tame the emotions, much as a lion tamer might control a beast. Or so he assumed. Aristotle had greater respect for the emotions, but he too discussed them strictly as part of his theory of poetry, rather than considering their centrality in religious belief and practice. The intellectual approach of these philosophers distanced them from ordinary people and limited the impact they had in their own time. It was only in the course of history—after Christianity drove a wedge between religious experience and pagan literature—that their arguments about the fictionality of the Olympian gods gained common currency.

When Socrates was executed, Plato blamed the rule of the mob and even Socrates himself—who had made a mockery of the democratic process and then abided by its insane verdict. He spent the rest of his life writing dialogues set in the decades preceding Socrates's death and re-creating conversations Socrates had supposedly had with all sorts of different people in the streets of Athens. There is no way of knowing to what extent Plato's dialogues portray the historical Socrates and to what extent they are a conduit for his own ideas; but it seems that Plato differed from his teacher in some crucial ways—not just in his philosophy, but in his life choices, too. Legend has it, for example, that Plato left Athens when Socrates died and traveled as far as Sicily and Egypt, searching for rulers who would listen to philosophers and govern according to their wisdom. When he returned to Athens, he continued to berate his native city, its political system, its poetry, and its prevailing views of the gods. Rather than living amid people and arguing with them in the streets, Plato founded his separate school, the Academy.

In Plato's writings, democracy is a hellish cacophony of voices and a clash of rampant desires. His most influential work, *The Republic,* presents the democratic city as an analogy for the human soul—at an advanced stage of degeneration. Democratic man follows his instincts, enjoys random pleasures, changes views and occupations as the fancy takes him, and abhors all forms of authority, including the rule of the intellect. And poetry, it turns out, is the perfect complement to this depraved creature: it appeals to man's lower impulses and encourages him to be emotional, selfish, and violent. Plato objected particularly to the mixture of entertainment and theological insight that poets provide—that is to say, their insufficiently respectful treatment of the gods. Indeed, his attack on poetry in *The Republic* focuses squarely on the presentation of the Olympians.

Plato made it clear that in his ideal city, Homer and Hesiod would have no place, because their poems spread false and degenerate rumors about the deities. For instance, he presents Hesiod's description of how Kronos castrated his father, and of how Zeus in turn replaced Kronos, as a dangerous lie. In Plato's view, the story is an invitation to violence and insurrection—and since citizens should always subordinate their own desires to the common good, they ought to be shielded from Hesiod's subversive *Theogony.*[1] Homeric epic is equally dangerous, according to Plato. The story of Hera's seduction of Zeus, for example, not only encourages sensuality, but is downright blasphemous. The supreme god could never be distracted by sex, and certainly not to the point of ravishing Hera right there and then on Mount Ida, without even bothering to withdraw to his own bedroom.[2] The story of Ares and Aphrodite trapped in bed is equally ludicrous, and Plato objected especially to its final comic denouement. The gods, he wrote, should not be presented as staring and laughing at the two lovers trapped naked in Hephaistos's chains. "If a poet represents even just worthy men overcome by laughter, we should not approve—far less if he actually depicts the gods in the act of laughing."[3] In short, *The Republic* maintains that the gods are no laughing matter, and they should most certainly not laugh at themselves.

As well as laughter, Plato objected to terror. The gods should never inspire such a powerful emotion. Mothers, in his view, were to blame as much as the poets:

> Mothers should not be persuaded by poets to scare their children with badly told stories, of how the gods go about by night in the likeness of strangers from every land, so that these mothers may not—by one and the same act—slander the gods and foster timidity in their children.[4]

At the heart of Plato's attacks on poetry were the same concerns that motivated the trial of Socrates: the gods, the city, and the next generation. He never tired of attacking Homer and Hesiod for the way in which they portrayed the gods and encouraged irrational behavior. In effect, as a modern critic puts it, his onslaught on poetry amounted to "a wholesale rejection of traditional Greek polytheism."[5]

What Plato offered in its place is the subject of many learned tomes; indeed, for many centuries, it was *the* subject of theological investigation. Among Christians, and later among Muslims, too, thinking about God long meant elaborating on Plato. This makes it extremely difficult, today, to draw a clear line between Plato's own views of the divine and later perceptions of those views, to distinguish between Plato and Platonism. But the main point, at least as far as this history of the Olympian gods is concerned, seems simple enough. Plato's views about the gods of Olympus remain influential, because they were part of a wider argument about the true nature of the divine—which, according to Plato, was single, wholly good, unchangeable, and everlasting. Plato's doctrine may sound Christian and indeed Muslim, but it was rooted in the culture of classical Athens. So many different views passed through that city: that the gods of Olympus did not exist; that they were not what people thought they were; and that the supreme power was a single, divine, higher Intelligence. Some people spoke in earnest, others in jest. Some changed their views depending on the circumstances, others even made *a point* of changing views, in order to show how they could argue for and against any position at all. Plato loathed all that confusion, that double-dealing: he hated the teachers of rhetoric and the way they appealed to the poets to make their points. He was deeply suspicious of arguments based on appearance and circumstance. What he wanted was the truth, firm and unchangeable.

The most fundamental reality, for Plato, was not the world as perceived by the senses, but nonmaterial abstract Forms grasped with the intellect—such as the Form of God, single and perfect. Material reality imitated the Forms, according to Plato, and poetry imitated reality, so it was twice removed from the truth: that was one of the arguments Plato used against the poets. But his theory of *mimēsis*, or "imitation," did not cope well with the gods as depicted in literature. It was hard to know what Homer's Apollo was an imitation *of,* for example. At the beginning of the *Iliad,* he "went like the night," but then he suddenly crouched down, took aim, and shot arrows.[6] Athena, at the beginning of the *Odyssey,* took on the appearance of a foreign visitor in order to talk to Telemachus, but then departed, "shooting upwards in flight like a bird."[7] Mythological monsters posed similar problems. They were intimately linked to the gods of Olympus—indeed, they were often their ancestors or descendants. Did centaurs, sirens, minotaurs, and many-headed monsters like Typhon imitate reality? If so, they did not do it very well.

Plato himself admitted that gods and monsters were not particularly amenable to his theory of literature. In one of his dialogues, he reports an alleged conversation on the topic between Socrates and a young man named Phaedrus. As the two stroll together, this young man asks Socrates whether the wind-god Boreas really once raped a girl, and Socrates answers that perhaps the myth can be seen as a fanciful imitation of reality: maybe a gust of wind once pushed a girl off a cliff, and people then described her as having been abducted by Boreas. But Socrates is clearly not satisfied with that line of argument. "Phaedrus, I believe that explanations of this kind are attractive . . . but require a lot of time and ingenuity," he says: "because after dealing with Boreas, clever fellows would need to set the shape of the Centaur to rights, and again that of the Chimaera, and a mob of other such things—Gorgons and Pegasuses—as hordes of intractable and amazing creatures flock in on them."[8]

The problem lay not in figuring out how people might have come up with mythological monsters: their constituent parts were generally easy to identify. A centaur was half horse and half man; the Chimaera was "a lion in front, a snake at the rear, and a goat in the middle," at least according to Homer's helpful explanation;[9] Gorgons were women with snake hair; and Pegasus was a winged horse. But why were monsters put together in the way they were, and for what purpose? The ingredients alone did not explain the recipe—and descriptions of the creatures differed, in any case, from poem to poem and image to image.

There was, of course, the traditional explanation, in which monsters stemmed from the chaotic times before the rule of Zeus or were the result of mismatched sexual encounters among the gods.

Python, the monster slayed by Apollo, for example, was said to have been born from the Earth goddess, while Pegasus was the offspring of Poseidon and the Gorgon Medusa. And Plato was also familiar with rationalistic accounts of gods and monsters that circulated among intellectual elites—the kind of rather plodding explanations that Socrates makes fun of in the *Phaedrus*. A manual written by one Palaephatus gives a flavor of what those arguments looked like when they were made in earnest: it contains brief summaries of several myths, each followed by the statement "This is incredible" and a prosaic alternative to the story. Bellerophon, it says, never killed a monster called Chimaera, but rather a snake and a lion who lived together on Mount Chimaera in Lycia. Likewise, Odysseus never saw a monster called Scylla; rather, he was attacked by pirates whose ship was named *Scylla* and painted to resemble a doglike monster.

Plato's Socrates maneuvers carefully and seductively between those traditions, accepting neither one but declining to offer an alternative explanation of his own. Instead, he sidesteps the entire question:

> I have no time at all for these mythical creatures, and the reason, my friend, is this. I am not even capable, in accordance with the Delphic inscription, of "knowing myself"; it therefore seems absurd to me that while I am still ignorant on this subject I should inquire into things that have nothing to do with me. So, then, I say goodbye to these creatures, and believe what people generally believe about them. And I inquire—as I said just now—not into these but into myself, to see whether I am actually a beast more complex and more violent than Typhon or both a tamer and a simpler creature, sharing some divine and un-Typhonic portion by nature.[10]

Though he claims to have "no time at all" for stories of monsters, Socrates in the end does offer his own take on Typhon: the creature is allegorized as an image of Socrates's own soul, or rather the most

Composite mythological monsters like Typhon posed a challenge to Plato's theory of imitation. Although their constituent parts were usually recognizable (on this image from an archaic vase, for instance, Typhon sports snake legs and bird wings), the overall composition did not simply imitate reality.

brutish part of it. The mythical monster becomes a figure of speech. It stands for the part of the soul that needs to be tamed by the intellect, which alone shares of the divine. Clearly, poetic fictions are not all bad, in Plato's view; some can be used to enliven philosophical writing.

Plato often reworked traditional myths, adapting them to illustrate his points. Elsewhere in the *Phaedrus,* for example, the soul is compared to a charioteer driving a pair of winged horses—an image modeled on the story of Bellerophon, who tried to fly to heaven on the back of Pegasus and was punished for his arrogance. In Plato's hands, that frightening myth is turned into an uplifting tale: one of the winged horses in his version is wild and tries to drag its charioteer down toward earth, but the good horse pulls the soul upward toward heaven, where it should rightfully aspire to be. In the course of its journey, the soul gets to see the twelve gods "as they feast and banquet," a spectacle that echoes scenes from Homeric poetry. But unlike Homer's all too fallible deities, the gods in *Phaedrus* are good and dutiful. The soul discovers that they feel no jealousy and that they too yearn for the even higher realm of the

Forms: "They feast turning steeply upwards towards the highest heaven."[11] What in Homer was divine entertainment becomes, in Plato, a scene of celestial elevation.

Plato's criticism of epic poetry is thus not simply that poets are far removed from reality—that they imitate an imitation—but that they do so without any sense of responsibility. In many works, including *The Republic,* he insists that traditional poetry needs to be replaced with improving, philosophical myths. His attempts at cultural revolution are extensive. In music, for example, only certain scales should be allowed, those that induce peace of mind or courage in war. Sentimental, seductive, and melancholy tunes should be banned altogether. Likewise, poets should represent only brave, moderate, and modest characters, with no description of "sickness, love, intoxication or misfortune"—that is, precisely the evils that the gods generally inflict on mortals and that make for such good literature.

Poetic visions of the gods could not be more different from Plato's prescriptions. In a play that survives only in fragments, for instance, Euripides adapted the story of Bellerophon, but in ways that drag us down rather than elevate our souls. The plot is simple: Bellerophon notices that evildoers thrive while pious people suffer helplessly. He starts doubting the existence of the gods, so he leaps onto Pegasus and flies up to Olympus to check whether the gods are real and if they care for human justice—a quest that ends with a descent into madness and destruction. On a surface level, Euripides's play makes no sense: as in his *Heracles,* he presents a mythological character paradoxically doubting the truth of his own mythology. (Bellerophon's use of the winged horse sired by Poseidon to look into the gods' potential nonexistence makes the contradiction obvious.) Even more striking than the treatment of myth is the lack of any straightforward moral in Euripides's drama. The original story of Bellerophon was a warning about the dangers of *hybris:* the hero tries to overcome his human limitations, and the gods punish him accordingly. Plato's retelling turns the myth into an uplifting allegory of moral aspiration and divine intelligence. But in Euripides, Bellerophon's story offers no insight at all. The hero sees good people suffer and sets off on a quest for knowledge and justice on his winged horse—and then he falls, for whatever reason.

Reconciling Plato and Euripides seems impossible, yet one man managed to find space for both in his broad vision. Like Plato, Aristotle did not consider traditional depictions of the gods to be believable. But unlike his teacher, he argued that poetry was nonetheless useful, both emotionally and intellectually, and to all people—including philosophers. Aristotle did not try to reform the poets, or suggest that their poetry could be adapted, in order to illustrate new philosophical theories. Instead, he insisted that each type of poetry had a specific function. In the *Poetics,* he argues that the aim of tragedy is "to achieve, through pity and fear, the relief [*katharsis*] of those emotions."[12] According to Aristotle, then, when audiences go to see Euripides's play, they feel with Bellerophon, experience his pity for human suffering and his fear that the gods may not exist or care for justice. And then audiences go home and resume their orderly lives. Poetry helps, not only by providing emotional release, but also by abstracting from daily life and reflecting on the human condition in general, within the self-contained circumstances of the theater. Aristotle insists that poetry is more philosophical than history, opening broader vistas for the mind. It depicts "not what happened, but the kind of thing that could happen, that is to say: what can happen according to probability or necessity."[13]

This is a far more generous view of poetry than Plato's dismissal of it as merely an imitation of an imitation. Yet, like Plato's, Aristotle's theory of literature has great trouble coping with the gods of Olympus. Their descriptions in epic, in particular, seem bound by neither probability nor necessity. Looking for an answer to this problem, Aristotle asserts that "correctness in poetry" is not the same thing as correctness in other fields, such as politics or art.[14] Each endeavor needs to be judged according to its own aims—and if the aim of poetry is emotional impact, then poets may do anything to achieve that, even depict gods in highly improbable ways. The pursuit of *ekplēxis*, "the thrill of shock," justifies the implausibility of Homeric epic.[15] So it is that Athena can look like an ordinary mortal but then fly off in the guise of a bird, and Poseidon can stride down a mountain in three steps and cause an earthquake. Indeed, such thrills are unique to epic poems. (Plays cannot match them. There, the gods are bound by the rules of the stage, and even the deus ex machina is just an actor dangling from some ungainly contraption.) The Homeric gods, in short, come to define what literature alone can do: they become figures of the imagination and indispensable paradigms for later poets and writers.

Aristotle's pupils dutifully organized his theories into an orderly filing system, with neat boxes and labels: actuality, truth, *alētheia*; history, *historia*, a factual report of the truth; fiction, *plasma*, something plausible; and finally, myth and the imagination, *mythos*, *phantasia*. According to Aristotelian theory, the gods of Olympus belonged in that final category. They did not feature in the proper writing of history (Thucydides established that) or in the plausible fictions that imitated real life. They were fantastic. In antiquity, that kind of claim sounded polemical. When Plato attacked poetry for the ways in which it depicted the gods, he was not interested simply in literary criticism; he wanted to dismantle popular conceptions of the divine. When Aristotle suggested that the gods of literature were flights of fancy, which could be pardoned only because they had emotional impact, he failed to acknowledge the very sources of that impact—which had to do with the connections between literature and life. People found the gods of epic convincing because they were linked to ritual experience. Philosophical distinctions failed when dealing with the gods of Olympus: categories and labels were constantly mixed up. Ironically, Aristotle's most famous pupil would be one of the worst offenders in this regard. Truth, fiction, history, and myth all converged in the exploits of Alexander the Great. And the Olympian gods would thrive in the new world he created, expanding their horizons and acquiring yet new identities and powers.

PART III

Travel: Hellenistic Egypt

From the Danube to the Indus, from the Himalayas to the Sahara Desert, Alexander the Great conquered a huge empire in just over a decade (334–323 BC). As he traveled farther and farther away from home, he kept thinking about familiar gods and how he could imitate and even outdo their exploits. He wanted to discover where Dionysos had been and travel farther than he had; and he was determined to complete even greater labors than Heracles. Alexander changed views of himself as quickly as he conquered new lands, and the gods of Olympus changed with him. As he began to think that he was divine—thanks partly to his conquest of Egypt, where pharaohs were regarded as living gods—so the gods began to feel closer to his human experience. Babylonian views also influenced prevailing notions of the Olympians. Astrology flourished in the wake of Alexander the Great, by mixing Greek myth with Eastern astral traditions, and it was at this point that some Olympian deities were systematically identified with the planets.

Amid all these changes, some felt the need to investigate and preserve the origins of Greek culture. In the Library of Alexandria in lower Egypt, poet-scholars started to collect information about early Greek cults, edit the poems of Homer and Hesiod, and distill their own, highly learned forms of poetry. This Hellenistic culture spread through the lands Alexander had conquered. And so it was that knowing about the gods of Olympus became a matter not just of rituals, sacrifices, and live performances, but of reading books.

7

Farther Than Dionysos

In 326 BC, Alexander the Great defeated the Indian ruler Poros by the river Hyphasis, in what is now eastern Punjab. At leisure after the battle, he surveyed the lands stretching eastward beyond the river: they seemed beautiful to him, fertile and grand. He noticed many elephants, more than he had seen in any of the lands he had already conquered. Alexander felt a strong desire to cross the river and continue his conquests, heading farther into India, toward the river Ganges. His troops, however, had different ideas. They had endured relentless marching, constant warring, the dispiriting rains of the monsoon, virulent diseases, homesickness, and an increasing fear of the unknown; they wanted to begin making their way back home. Alexander reacted to their mutinous sentiments with fury. He delivered a resolute speech and then withdrew to his tent. When he emerged some three days later, he gave unexpected orders: His men were to build altars to the twelve Olympian gods on the western bank of the Hyphasis, without crossing it. After that, they were to turn south and begin a long march—first along the Indus, then west toward Babylon, and eventually farther still, all the way back to Macedonia (see map on p. 92).

Alexander never ventured beyond the river Hyphasis, and that, according to our ancient sources, was his first "defeat," the first time his will was thwarted. He stopped because he was facing a mutiny, but perhaps he also had other considerations in mind. Clearly, he had to turn back at some point, and the river Hyphasis offered a good natural border for his empire. The river was also the perfect symbol for his campaign. Having set out to defeat the Persians, Alexander had now reached the easternmost limit of their erstwhile conquests. In the period of their maximum expansion, the Persians too had reached the river, although by the time Alexander defeated them they had already surrendered control of the area. Whatever Alexander's exact motives, all the sources agree on one detail: The last thing he did before embarking on his homeward journey was to set up those altars to the twelve gods of Olympus.[1]

Alexander's gesture mirrored the beginning of his campaign. To

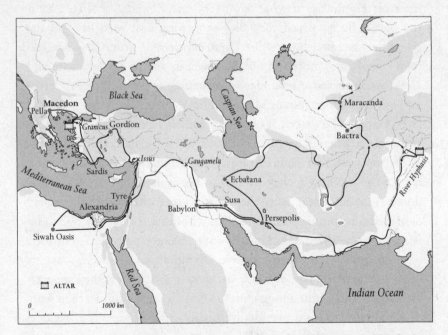

Alexander's journey: Altars to the twelve gods, at the Hellespont and by the river Hyphasis, marked the limits of his Asian campaign.

mark his crossing from Greece into Asia, he had similarly dedicated altars to the twelve gods at the Hellespont (see map on p. 92). The two sets of monuments bookended his campaign. The altars presented Alexander specifically as a *Greek* conqueror over Asia, because it was the Greeks who worshipped a pantheon of twelve.[2] The altars by the Hyphasis can be seen as his way of celebrating and thanking the gods who had helped him all along the way—letting the Olympians enjoy beautiful views of the Indian subcontinent, with its metallic green plains and populous villages. Alexander's impact on the Olympian gods was not limited to expanding their geographic horizons, however. He also changed their personalities, particularly by establishing an unusually close relationship with them: they were relatives and rivals to him, rather than distant deities. To understand what happened to the gods, then, it is necessary to take a step back and consider the life of Alexander, starting with his own first steps in the kingdom of Macedon.

Alexander was born in July 356 BC at Pella, the capital of Macedonia, a Greek-speaking kingdom north of Greece. His mother was Olympias, daughter of the king of the Molossians, a northern Greek tribe, and his father was Philip II, king of Macedonia. The king provided the best possible Greek education for Alexander, even employing Aristotle as the boy's private tutor. He also personally oversaw other crucial aspects of his education, involving the young Alexander in the exercise of power from very early on in his life. When Philip left on a campaign against Byzantium, for example, he entrusted responsibility for the entire kingdom to his sixteen-year-old son (though he took care to surround him with able advisers). Alexander was also given the opportunity to mount an expedition against the Thracians, during which he founded a military colony and—when he was just eighteen—to lead the left wing of the cavalry when Philip defeated a Greek coalition at the Battle of Chaeronea. The close relationship between father and son came to an abrupt end, however, when Philip repudiated Olympias, sending her, together with Alexander, back to the Molossians. In Olympias's place, Philip took a different, Macedonian wife, who soon became pregnant and eventually bore him both a daughter and a son. The exceptionally ambitious Alexander must have hated his father for his ability to deny him a royal future in one single stroke. After diplomats intervened, however, Philip and Olympias were somehow reconciled, so Alexander and his mother returned to Macedonia within a year of being exiled. Still, relationships remained strained.

With his ambitious wife and son back at home, it seems that Philip felt the need to assert his superiority and control. At the wedding of Alexander's sister, for example, he displayed a statue of himself next to images of the twelve Olympian gods, suggesting that he belonged in their number. Ironically, though, it was his mortal nature that became the greatest spectacle at the wedding: during nuptial celebrations held in the theater of Aigai, he was stabbed to death in broad daylight. It is possible that Olympias and Alexander were behind the assassination; after what had happened to them, they had every reason to fear for their position. In any case, whether or not Alexander arranged for his father to be killed, he treated his father's death as an opportunity to purge much of the Macedonian nobility—on the grounds that they had allegedly plotted against Philip—and thus rid himself of potential rivals. He then expanded north all the way to the Danube and, having secured his rear, descended on Greece.

After his victory at the Battle of Chaeronea, Philip had already set up diplomatic relationships in the region in a manner highly advantageous to Macedonia. He had promoted an alliance between Greek city-states on the model of the old Delian League, which had been dissolved in 404 BC. Ostensibly a new pact against the Persians, this league was actually meant as the launching pad for a Macedonian empire in Greece and Asia. Philip had an Athenian adviser, the orator Isocrates, who must have given him a useful perspective based on historical precedent. The friendship between the two men caused much debate in Athens. Demosthenes, in particular, argued forcefully against any form of cooperation with Philip, regarding the Macedonian king as conqueror rather than ally. But while the Athenians traded arguments and insults, they failed to realize one simple thing: that they no longer mattered. Power had moved elsewhere.

After his father's death, Alexander took over as commanding general of the league against the Persians, but Thebes offered resistance. Alexander's response turned out to be characteristic of his style: he razed Thebes to the ground, killed almost all the men, and sold the women and children into slavery. At the same time, according to our ancient sources, he took the opportunity to honor poetry and the gods. He allegedly spared the local priests and the descendants of Pindar, the best Theban poet, whose house was the only one left standing. The story, whether or not factually accurate (exterminating people was labor-intensive in antiquity), says something important about Alexander's reputation: he was brutal—but also versatile. He could engage in mass murder and simultaneously make a show of his own piety and love of poetry. After settling his local affairs in this manner, Alexander led his Greek and Macedonian contingents into Persian territory across the Hellespont. He offered a personal reason for fighting: The Persians, he claimed, were behind the assassination of his father, and he needed to avenge his death.[3] At the same time, like Philip, he presented his mission as a war of reprisal that would punish the Persians for their profanation of Greek temples. The altars to the twelve gods that Alexander set up at the start of his campaign were, in many ways, a formal declaration of war.

After winning a decisive battle in 334 BC near the river Granicus in Turkey, Alexander sent Persian armor and weaponry back to Athens as a votive offering for Athena. An inscription accompanied the gifts: "Alexander, son of Philip, and the Greeks (except for the Spartans) set up these spoils taken from the barbarians dwelling in Asia."[4] The symbolism was clear: the Persians had torched the Athenian acropolis in 480 BC, and now, a century and a half later, Alexander was sending Persian spoils to be stored in the Parthenon. The

Spartans, who had not joined Alexander's expedition, were issued a warning. But although Alexander presented himself as the great avenger of the Greeks and their gods, he also started acting in other capacities. After securing control of the provincial Persian capital of Sardis, he continued south, taking possession of Syria and most of the Levant. Tyre resisted, and Alexander's reputed response again inspired terror: he captured the city, crucified all adult men, and sold women and children into slavery. In Gaza, we are told that he likewise put all men to the sword and enslaved the rest of the population. In Jerusalem, after he had established his reputation, he met with a different attitude. People immediately opened their gates and said that their Book of Daniel had prophesied the arrival of a divinely appointed savior, who had now evidently appeared. Alexander liked this reception; he spared Jerusalem and pushed south into Egypt. There too he was welcomed as a liberator from Persian rule.

The last native pharaoh of Egypt, Nectanebo II, had abandoned the capital—Memphis—in 342 BC, ceding his kingdom to the Persians. Alexander arrived only ten years later and, as he sailed up the Nile toward the ancient city, was greeted as a savior. He was immediately installed in the royal palace, and it is possible that the priests of Memphis crowned him as the new pharaoh. If this is indeed what happened, Egyptians would have come to regard Alexander as a deity. According to local mythology, the god Amun visited the wife of each pharaoh and impregnated her with the new ruler of the kingdom. All pharaohs were therefore divine. We do not know how much of this was explained to Alexander, but it seems that he started to think hard about his identity at around this time and was no longer content to regard himself simply as the son of Philip. He needed a better father, a father who could help explain and legitimize his extraordinary success.

After establishing his rule in Memphis, Alexander sailed down the Nile and explored its delta. Arrian, our most important ancient source on Alexander's expeditions, tells us that Alexander found a place he liked at the delta's western edge: "It struck him that the location was most beautiful for founding a city, and that such a city was bound to flourish. He was seized by enthusiasm for the work and marked out the plan in person, showing where the market-place should be built and which gods should have temples and where. Greek gods were chosen along with the Egyptian Isis. He also established where the city wall should be built."[5] The city in question would be named Alexandria, and it was soon to become the cultural capital of the Mediterranean.

Up to this moment, Alexander's progress was marked by a highly efficient combination of brutality, speed, and foresight. All his actions were perfectly calibrated to achieve the military and political goals he had set for himself. Immediately after laying the foundations of Alexandria, however, he did something stranger and, to my mind, more interesting. He selected a small party to accompany him, took some camels, and struck west. He then bore south into the Libyan desert, heading for the oracle of the god Amun in the oasis of Siwah. The journey across the Sahara was difficult. Salt plains alternated with rocks and sand for hundreds of miles; all water had to be carried. Frequent sandstorms could utterly transform the landscape, while the heat was so intense that travelers could make progress only at night, by the light of the moon. Alexander's party survived the journey, but only just: they were hit by a storm that cost them four days and almost ran out of water. Ancient accounts of Alexander's journey vividly convey an impression of the all-pervading dust, the fear, and the snakes crawling everywhere. They also mention crows, which were a more hopeful sign: the birds knew their way to the oasis. Alexander's guides probably followed their flight.

The oracle of the god Amun had excellent credentials in the ancient world. Egyptians and Libyans regarded it highly, and Greek emigrants who had settled in Africa spread word that Amun—or Ammon, as they called him—was as reliable as Apollo was in Delphi. What is more, they declared that "Ammon" was simply another

name for Zeus. It is not surprising, perhaps, that Alexander decided
to use the oracle to bolster his imperial claims; what is more interesting is that he decided to risk his life in order to travel to Siwah in
person. He could have sent envoys to interrogate the oracle on his
behalf, as pharaohs normally did, but he clearly was on a personal
mission, over which he wanted direct control.

When advice-seeking pilgrims arrived at Siwah, they generally
put their questions to the oracle by specifying two possible alternatives. These were written on potsherds and laid inside a sacred
courtyard, some distance apart from each other. Priests would then
carry aloft an image of the god Amun in a gilded boat and find
themselves swayed in one direction or another by the weight and
apparent impulse of the boat itself. The "nods and tokens" of the
god would point to the answer on one of the potsherds. It seems
that important visitors could put their questions privately to a
priest inside a small sanctuary, instead of having a public ritual; the
priest would then go out, watch the movements of the god in his
boat, and return with an answer. Alexander probably followed this
private procedure, because after his consultation he initially said
only that the response of the oracle had pleased him. People, of
course, speculated about what might have happened at Siwah, and
one rumor became insistent: The god Amun had confirmed that Alexander was his very own son.

To the Egyptians, of course, that rumor would have made perfect sense: all pharaohs were the sons of Amun. To everybody else,
however, the suggestion that Alexander had a god for a father
seemed preposterous. Some Greek heroes boasted a divine parent,
of course, but the times when gods freely mated with mortals were
long gone: Heracles and Achilles belonged to the very distant past.
Aristocratic Greek and Macedonian families sometimes claimed a
god as an ancestor, but they could not countenance the possibility
that Zeus might infiltrate their households and impregnate their
women there and then. Rumors started to spread that Alexander

was a little confused about the basic facts of life. The Greeks hinted that, like the proverbial fool Margites, he did not know how his own parents had made him.[6]

The issue of Alexander's divinity became even more contentious after the fall of his main enemy: Darius III, the Persian King of Kings. Alexander defeated him at the Battle of Gaugamela, in what is now Iraq. The Persian king then fled across the mountains, and Alexander headed toward the great royal residences of his empire: Babylon, Susa, Persepolis, and Pasargadae. Babylon offered no resistance, welcoming Alexander as its new ruler.[7] From Babylon, Alexander marched on Susa and then forced his way to Persepolis, the ceremonial capital of the Persian Empire. At this point, he dismissed his Greek troops and proceeded only with his most reliable and trusted Macedonian soldiers. As it happened, he did not have to kill the Persian king. Bessos, one of Darius's own kinsmen and satrap of Bactria, took care of that.

Alexander immediately exploited the assassination as only he knew how. When Philip, king of Macedon, had been killed, Alexander had used that as a pretext to purge the Macedonian aristocracy and then to attack the Persians. Now he announced his intention to take up the Persian cause and avenge the King of Kings. Darius III was given a magnificent funeral, and insubordinate satraps were issued a clear warning, particularly through the swift execution of Bessos. Alexander now behaved like the loyal, god-appointed heir of Darius III, King of Kings. This sudden shift in Alexander's perspective and rhetoric was not without difficulties, however, particularly when he had to explain it to his own Macedonian troops. Having just fought against the Persian king, they were astonished to find themselves suddenly meant to mourn his death. They expressed their anger in the form of loud complaints about religion. The Persians traditionally prostrated themselves before their Kings of Kings as an act of respect; but the Macedonians refused to perform this ritual for Alexander, choosing to reinterpret it as an act of worship.

Led by Callisthenes, Alexander's own official historian and Aristotle's great-nephew, the soldiers made it clear that as far as they were concerned, Alexander was no god.

It was easier for Alexander the Great to defeat new enemies than to reconcile old ones. And so it was that in 327 BC, he set off on what would be his most impressive and exotic campaign. The aim was to take firm control of the Indian region of Gandhara. As Alexander marched farther and farther away from home, he thought about myths that might unite the different peoples and places he was about to conquer. The god Dionysos, in particular, was on his mind. He was a familiar deity, a favorite of Olympias, Alexander's mother, and he was known to have been born in the East. As they traveled through Afghanistan, Pakistan, and Punjab, Alexander and his soldiers fully expected to see signs of Dionysos's own journeys— and they found them. In the mountains of Afghanistan, for example, they saw some stone burial heaps all covered in ivy, and Alexander confidently declared that these were boundary stones set up by the god himself to mark the territories in his domain.[8] It was the ivy that clinched it: as everybody knew, this plant was sacred to Dionysos. Alexander and his followers carefully noted where it grew, in order to establish the likely itineraries of the god. Sightings of Dionysiac ivy transformed landscapes and situations that were radically strange into something familiar. Indeed, it seems that the farther Alexander and his troops traveled, the more intensely they focused on familiar gods. As they entered Punjab, they noticed ivy all over the trees in the hills east of the river Kunar, and army units were sent to investigate. Up in the hills, they found a natural paradise of the earth: myrtles, box trees, laurels, and roses blooming in an open, sun-filled valley. Their pleasure gave way to excitement when they heard the local people call their main city Nysa, or something like it. The word *Nysa* was dear to Dionysos. Depending on the particular version of the myth, it was either the place where he was born or the name of his wet nurse. In any case, the link was clear! They were certainly following in the footsteps of Dionysos. Alexander organized sacrifices and feasts to celebrate this discovery. The soldiers wove ivy garlands and performed songs and poems in honor of the god.[9]

Dionysos was helpful to Alexander not just as a god, but as a charismatic role model and even a rival. As Arrian put it:

> Alexander was very happy in his heart when he heard the reports from the soldiers, and he wanted to believe the stories about Dionysos's journey. He also wanted to believe that Nysa was founded by Dionysos, because in this case he had already reached the point that Dionysos had reached, and would now go even farther than the god. He thought that his troops would not refuse to join him in still further efforts, if it was in imitation of Dionysos's own achievements.[10]

Alexander also had another role model for his actions: Heracles, son of Zeus and a mortal woman. Here was a hero who, after much traveling and fighting, had actually ascended to Olympus. His story could hardly fail to appeal to Alexander. As with Dionysos, he found confirmation of Heracles's travels in local stories and landscapes. It is possible that his Indian guides helped Alexander to identify Heracles with the god Krishna, who also sported a lion skin; whatever the reason, he convinced himself that Heracles had scaled a particular mountain in the lower Himalayas, and he set out to do the same. The fact that the summit was held by local warriors seemed only to increase his sense of purpose. Ancient sources say that Alexander approached the mountain from the north, filled a deep ravine with stones to enable an ascent, built a bridge using fir trees cut from the mountainside, and finally pulled himself up with ropes to reach the summit. When he got there, the local warriors were already retreating down the southern slopes.[11] At the top of the mountain, Alexander sacrificed to Athena. She was the goddess who had helped Heracles in all his labors, and she was now surely behind his own success. It was soon after this exploit that Alexander reached the river Hyphasis and took stock. It was time to return home, unfortunately; but he would not forget to thank the Olympian gods for their support.

It is difficult to reconstruct the exact details of Alexander's journeys and conquests. The account I have given is based largely on Arrian's *Anabasis of Alexander* and his *Indica,* written in the second century AD. Arrian had at his disposal earlier, eyewitness accounts of Alexander's exploits, but he did not always follow or even understand them. In any case, eyewitnesses were rather confused themselves: those who had accompanied Alexander on his campaigns were not always sure about where they had been or what precisely had happened. Historians have long debated how much trust can be placed in ancient Greek accounts of Alexander's conquests. Still, with the help of Persian, Babylonian, Egyptian, and Jewish sources, a coherent story can be pieced together in broad outline. The archaeological record is also useful: a coin issued by one of Alexander's immediate successors, for example, depicts him with

Early in the third century BC, one of Alexander's successors, Lysimachus, issued a beautiful coin depicting the head of Alexander with the ram horns of Zeus Ammon, his divine father. The other side of the coin bears an image of the goddess Athena.

the ram horns of Zeus Ammon, thus asserting a family resemblance between Alexander and his divine father.

The coin neatly sums up Alexander's own attitudes. Rather than presenting himself to the gods as a humble worshipper, he boldly claimed a place in their number. The consequences of this attitude would emerge only slowly, as his successors grappled with the world that Alexander had created. As for Alexander himself, he hardly had the time to work out the full implications of his claims: by the age of thirty-two, he would be dead.

8

Dead Gods and Divine Planets

When Alexander returned to Babylon after his Indian expedition, the Greeks—who had begun to feel increasingly neglected under Alexander's rule—sent several delegations to draw his attention to Greek affairs. By then they had realized that Alexander expected to be treated like a deity, and they acted accordingly:

> Successive official delegations from Greece presented themselves. The delegates, wearing ceremonial wreaths, solemnly approached Alexander and placed golden chaplets on his head, as if their crowning were a ritual in honor of a god.[1]

Arrian's description of this scene is barbed: the Greeks crowned Alexander *as if* he were a god. But of course he was not divine, because—as Arrian pointedly adds—he died soon afterward. Gods, true gods, did not die, according to the Greeks. They were immortal by definition, *a-thanatoi,* "without death." Clearly, Arrian suggests, the delegates made a categorical error in their worship of Alexander.

Arrian's account, however, does provide enough detail to explain how the Greek delegates might have justified their actions to themselves (even if not to Arrian's satisfaction). They treated Alexander not as a god in general, but more specifically as the cult statue of a god. Greek acts of worship typically included the ritual dressing and decoration of a divine statue, and it seems that this is just what the delegation did with Alexander. There was an element of make-believe in the way Greeks dealt with their cult statues: they perceived that they both were, and were not, divine. And so it was with Alexander. The trend toward illusionistic realism in Greek art must have helped the delegates make sense of what they were doing. The seated statue of Zeus at Olympia, as we have seen, was so lifelike that people imagined it might suddenly stand up and take off the roof of the temple where it was housed. Similarly, Artemis's cult statue on Chios was said to change expression as her worshippers approached and departed.[2] A common term for "statue" in ancient Greek was *zōon,* "living thing." To his delegates in Babylon, Alexander must have looked like an exceptionally convincing *zōon*—even if not for long.

After all his conquests and claims to divinity, the early death of Alexander came as a shock. He fell ill in Babylon, quite unexpectedly; given the circumstances, many suspected that he had been poisoned. A pamphlet later accused Cassander, son of the Macedonian regent Antipater, of assassinating him. The truth is uncertain, but we do know that Cassander arrived in Babylon shortly before Alexander's death and that Alexander treated him with open hostility. Later on, Cassander certainly killed Alexander's wife Roxane and their baby son, Alexander IV—as well as Alexander's mother, Olympias, who led an army against him in 317 BC. Whether or not Alexander was actually murdered, his death came as an interruption. Alleged diaries containing Alexander's "last plans" were published immediately after his burial. Arrian sounds characteristically skeptical about them:

> For my part I cannot determine with certainty what sort of plans
> Alexander had in mind, and I have no intention of guessing; but I
> can say that none was small or petty, and that he would not have

stopped conquering even if he had added Europe to Asia and the Britannic Islands to Europe.[3]

Arrian's vision anticipates the Roman conquests in the north of Europe, but Alexander's immediate successors had other ideas, often contradictory. A colossal struggle for power soon broke out among his generals, governors, wives, relatives, and far-flung subjects, and eventually his empire split into several separate, frequently warring kingdoms.

Those who did not want power for themselves had more time to think—about gods, mortals, and what had happened to them as a result of Alexander's exploits. They allowed themselves time to imagine and write and ended up making more of an impact than many of those who fought to the death over Alexander's inheritance. It would be impossible to survey all the texts, legends, images, and thoughts that Alexander inspired, but we can get a good sense of them from two of the most influential: Euhemerus's *Sacred Register* and the ever-popular *Alexander Romance,* a fantastic account of Alexander's life, which circulated in many different versions.

Very little is known about the Greek travel writer Euhemerus, though it is notable that the *Sacred Register* begins with a dedication to Cassander, the Macedonian ruler accused of killing Alexander the Great. In the book, Euhemerus claims that Cassander sent him on many great missions abroad and that on one of his travels he sailed from Arabia across the Indian Ocean, where he discovered a small archipelago. The *Register* offers a detailed description of that supposed discovery. The archipelago's main island is called Panchaea, Euhemerus tells us, and in its capital city people live in perfect justice "under laws of their own making and with no king ruling over them."[4] Each year they elect three magistrates, who preside over all court cases except capital crimes, which they willingly refer to the local priests. A nearby island produces large quantities of myrrh and incense, and these represent the only foreign exports of the archipelago; they are sold in such abundance "that they suffice for the honors paid to the gods throughout the entire inhabited world." Panchaea is beautiful: "Beyond the plains there are forests of lofty trees, where masses of people like to pass their time in summer, and where countless birds, of many shapes and colors, make their nests, delighting people with their singing." In the middle of this earthly paradise, there is a huge temple of Zeus, "with amazing statues of the gods, exceptionally well made, and much admired for their massiveness."

Inside the temple, Euhemerus discovers an inscription written in hieroglyphics. This is the Sacred Register, and it reveals the true nature of the gods. Zeus himself, we are told, set up this inscription— and it turns out that he was a human king of Crete, rather than an immortal deity. He traveled east to visit his friend Belos (the Greek rendition of Bel, the supreme god of the Babylonians, but a human king in this telling) and sailed to Panchaea on that occasion. There, on that beautiful island, he decided to pay homage to his grandfather Heaven, who had been of great service to humanity. The inscription states that Zeus's grandfather had spent his life "studying the movement of the stars, and had established cults in honor of the celestial gods." Indeed, he was nicknamed "Heaven" precisely because he was such an excellent astronomer. The inscription registers the births and deaths of many other familiar figures—Hera, Poseidon, Hestia, Demeter, Athena, Hermes, Apollo, and Artemis— but we are told that they too were just ordinary mortals, celebrated in Panchaea for their services to humanity. After setting up his inscription, Euhemerus says, King Zeus returned to Crete, where he eventually died and was buried.

Many readers—ancient and modern—describe Euhemerus as an atheist, because he systematically downgrades the Olympian gods to the rank of mortals. But that is not quite accurate, because there are indeed immortal deities in the story: celestial bodies, the stars and planets whose movements Zeus's grandfather was so fond of measuring. Euhemerus draws a clear distinction between "gods who are eternal and indestructible, such as the sun and the moon and the

other stars in heaven, and the winds, and whatever else possesses a
nature similar to them . . . and the other gods, who were once terrestrial beings, but obtained divine honors and fame because of their
great services to mortals."

The *Sacred Register* is a fascinating mix of Greek, Near Eastern,
and Egyptian mythologies. It is difficult to gauge its exact tone and
aims, because it survives only in short quotations, summaries, and
paraphrases, but the separation between terrestrial and heavenly
gods was an important concept in ancient Egyptian religion, as was
the idea that kings are mortal gods. Several other details in the *Sacred
Register* likewise betray Egyptian influences: Panchaea itself, with its
hieroglyphics, monumental buildings, and colossal statues, looks
rather Egyptian. Yet Euhemerus's work also grapples with specifically
Greek questions and problems. Like Plato and Aristotle, he insists
that the gods must be good, not cruel. Like Prodicus, who thought
that primitive people called "god" whatever they found useful, he
suggests that the basic impulse toward deification is gratitude. Like
Anaxagoras, who said that Helios was a blazing stone, he claims that
the gods are stars. And beyond all these correspondences, the nastier
shadow of Alexander the Great lurks in the background of the *Sacred
Register*. Alexander's divine father, Ammon, plays the part of the vil-
lain in Euhemerus's story. Far from being identified with the good
Zeus, Ammon here is a destructive character, particularly prone to
razing cities. It is probably no coincidence that Cassander, Euhemerus's patron, rebuilt the city of Thebes after Alexander had destroyed
it. More generally, Alexander cannot have been a benefactor in Euhemerus's eyes: on his island of Panchaea, there is no need for a king at
all. The people he truly admired were astronomers, artists, and
philosophers—culture heroes rather than conquerors.

For all its fantastical flowers and colorful birds singing in the
trees, Euhemerus's *Sacred Register* has a serious purpose. Like
Thomas More's *Utopia,* it encourages a wide-ranging, imaginative
reflection on how things are and how they could perhaps be better—if
we were prepared to travel far enough, learn, and change our ways.

The *Sacred Register* contains a clear message for those in power: Kings can be worshipped as gods, but only if they act in the interests of humanity. Many other writers of the Hellenistic period (the time between the death of Alexander and the emergence of Rome as a global power) similarly set out to educate the heirs of Alexander the Great. The historian Hecataeus of Abdera, for example, offered an idealized picture of Egypt, based largely on Plato, in the hope of inspiring its new rulers. He had particularly clear ideas about how kings should live (simple diet, regular bedtimes) and what servants they should keep: sons of priests more intelligent and better educated than the kings themselves and willing to speak their mind.[5] It is easy to see that Hecataeus and his fellow authors meant to carve out new roles for themselves, as well as for rulers and gods, in the wake of Alexander.

The new perspectives on power also had implications for how the Olympian gods themselves were conceived and represented. Influenced by Alexander's claims to be a living god, and by writers like Euhemerus who spoke of the Olympians as mortal beings, artists of

Alexander's favorite artist, Lysippus, sculpted this baby Dionysos in the arms of an elderly Silenus. Hellenistic artists became increasingly interested in young and old divine bodies, rather than focusing on perfect adult figures. Just as Alexander started to be treated as a living god, so divine bodies were now seen as subject to aging.

the Hellenistic period increasingly started to show the gods as partaking in human life cycles. Divine bodies became subject to aging: the Olympians could now look old or very young, rather than being depicted in their prime.

Not all responses to Alexander's divinity were as high-minded (or self-serving) as Euhemerus's *Sacred Register* and Hecataeus's *On the Egyptians*. One popular story, in particular, made fun of Alexander's divinity—while nevertheless insisting that he was indeed the true heir of the Egyptian pharaohs. This story originated in the period immediately following Alexander's conquest of Egypt and took inspiration from a long tradition of erotic Egyptian tales about the god Amun. A temple wall at Luxor, for example, featured a picture showing how the royal concubine Mutemwia conceived Pharaoh Amenhotep III (ca. 1388–1350 BC). The text carved around it detailed Amun's technique:

> The god found her as she slept within the innermost part of her palace. She awoke on account of the divine fragrance, and turned towards His Majesty. He went straightaway to her, he was aroused by her. He allowed her to see him in his divine form, after he had come before her, so that she rejoiced at seeing his perfection. His love entered her body.[6]

This kind of bedroom narrative inspired many Hellenistic accounts of Alexander's own conception, though the details became more and more ludicrous as disbelieving Greeks elaborated on them. In the *Alexander Romance* (a text of Hellenistic origins, amplified and reworked throughout antiquity and the Middle Ages), the pharaoh Nectanebo is presented as a great magician and astrologer. He needs no fleet to defend his country, we are told, because whenever the enemy approaches by sea, he fills a basin with water, puts some little wax ships in it, and sinks them. The real ships advancing on Egypt then invariably suffer a corresponding fate. One day, though, the wax ships keep floating despite Nectanebo's best efforts. He quickly grasps the seriousness of the omen: "Being a man experienced in magic and accustomed to talking with his gods, he realizes that the end of his Egyptian kingdom is at hand."[7] So he swiftly decides to leave. He hides plenty of gold under his clothes and flees to Macedonia. There, he sets up shop as a magician and astrologer, quickly establishing his reputation among the local people. Indeed, he becomes so famous that Queen Olympias herself goes to consult him about a problem she has with her husband, Philip II: she is afraid that the king might divorce her, because she has not borne him a son.

Nectanebo takes one look at the beautiful queen and works out a plan that will suit everybody, himself included. He casts a horoscope and tells Olympias that while Philip is on campaign, she will sleep with a god. She will then bear him a son, and that son will avenge her of all she has suffered on account of Philip. Olympias asks which god will inseminate her and what shape he will take; and Nectanebo answers that the god in question is Ammon of Libya and that, as a matter of fact, he looks just like a middle-aged man, but with horns on his forehead. He then offers to take up residence in the royal palace, in order to assist Olympias in her dealings with the god.

A snake, Nectanebo tells the queen, will enter into her chamber, and that will be her cue to dismiss her servants and prepare herself for the god. She should undress, get into bed, and cover her face, so as not to look directly at the deity coming into her bedroom. On the appointed night, Olympias duly sees the snake, climbs into bed, and covers her head. Nectanebo, meanwhile, fixes a pair of horns on his forehead, dresses up in a snake costume, and walks into her chamber, following the real snake he has just released. The queen, of course, steals a look at her lover but sees nothing alarming. The god, we are told, "looks exactly as she was expecting." The next morning, when Nectanebo comes to visit the queen and asks her what happened during the night, she replies: "I am amazed that you do not already know it, prophet. But will the god come to me again? It was a sweet time I had with him." While Philip is away on campaign, Nectanebo goes to visit the queen "as often as she likes." He also performs enough magic tricks on Philip to ensure that on his return, the king accepts Olympias's pregnancy as his own doing, no matter what suspicions he may harbor.

The day comes for Olympias to give birth, and she takes up her position on the birthing stool. Nectanebo stands right beside her, ever ready to assist. He measures the course of the stars and calculates when it would be most auspicious for her child to be born. Like a cautious midwife, he repeatedly tells Olympias to resist the urge to push and to take it slowly, adding that several unlucky planets are just then crossing the heavens:

> Get a grip of yourself, your majesty, and wait for this one. Cancer dominates the horoscope, and there is Kronos [the planet Saturn], who was the victim of a plot by his own children, and who cut off his genitals at the root and hurled them to Poseidon, lord of the sea, and Hades, god of the dead, making way for the majesty of Zeus. If you give birth now, your son will be a eunuch!

Olympias manages, somehow, to slow things down. More planets cross the heavens, but Nectanebo is still unhappy with the baby's potential horoscope. At the appearance of Ares (the planet Mars), he tells Olympias to resist nature a little longer still:

> Ares is a lover of horses and war, but was exhibited naked and unarmed by the Sun on his adulterous bed. So whoever is born at this hour will be a laughingstock!

Olympias further resists the impulse to push. She also waits out the passing of Hermes ("Your son will be a quarrelsome pedant!"), until, at last, Zeus appears in the sky, ready to take on the characteristics of the horned Ammon between the constellations of Aquarius and Pisces. Olympias finally delivers her baby, and there are "claps of thunder and flashes of lightning, so that the whole world is shaken." Zeus Ammon has recognized the newborn king.

The *Alexander Romance* testifies to one of the most amazing developments in the history of the Olympian gods. A new form of astrology had emerged in the wake of Alexander the Great: it combined Greek mythology with Near Eastern astral traditions. The Greeks had long associated the Olympians with the sky, but the systematic pairing of planet and deity was the result of Egyptian and Babylonian influences. Now the planets were named after the Olympian gods, and indeed the Latin versions of their names are still used in English to this day. The goddess Aphrodite was identified with the brightest planet (Venus); Zeus with the largest (Jupiter); Hermes with the swiftest (Mercury); and Ares with the planet Mars, which looks red and therefore fiery and martial. The pairing of planets and gods thus derived from astronomical facts combined with Greek, Near Eastern, and Egyptian myths. Astrology quickly grew into an extremely complex system that combined these several mythological traditions with specific planetary observations and predictions. When Venus and Mars came closest in their orbits, for example, astrologers recalled the two gods' infamous love affair and warned their clients to be on guard against adultery.

Modern horoscopes still work on the same principles, even if the forecasts published in newspapers are more nebulous than Nectanebo's frenzied announcements to Olympias. He, at least, explained the rationale for what he was saying. Kronos castrated Heaven, as we know from Hesiod, and the astrologer announced, "The boy will be a eunuch!" Ares was caught naked in bed with Aphrodite, according to Homer, and Nectanebo warned, "Ridicule!" The fact that Hermes's appearance in the sky indicated that baby Alexander might become a quarrelsome pedant seems strange at first sight, because the Greek god Hermes was lighthearted and mischievous. But the planet Mercury also retained some qualities of Thoth, the Egyptian patron god of academics, and they—to this date—can be rather pedantic and quarrelsome.

After describing Alexander's conception and birth, the *Alexander Romance* recounts many other portents and adventures. In the course of his travels, Alexander meets strange beasts, magical trees and stones, a moving island that turns out to be a whale, the Sirens, the Centaurs, and the Brahmans of India (with whom he has enlightened conversations). He even tries to ascend to heaven in a basket carried by eagles and explores the depths of the ocean in a proto-diving bell. The various versions of the *Alexander Romance* that have reached us testify to a vast tradition of stories that spread through the whole of Europe, the northern coast of Africa, and all the way into central and southern Asia. Each age and place has its own Alexander. The Hebrew tradition turns him into a prophet, the European Middle Ages describe him as a chivalrous knight, for the Persians he is an arch-Satan with horns—or, in other authors, the true son of Darius, King of Kings. In modern Greek folklore, he becomes lord of storms and father of the mermaids. Alexander's heavenward basket journey even features as a carving in the great English cathedrals of Wells and Gloucester.

The ancient Graeco-Egyptian version of the *Alexander Romance* stands at the beginning of all these stories—and the divinity of Alexander is at the core of its concerns. Indeed, both the *Alexander Romance* and Euhemerus's *Sacred Register* turn rulers into gods and vice versa, each in its own fashion. In the *Sacred Register,* Zeus and other Olympians are transformed into mortal benefactors of humanity; in the *Alexander Romance,* the sacred epiphany of a god becomes a ludicrous carnival, as a middle-aged pharaoh sporting fake horns ravishes the queen of Macedonia. In both works, when mortals rob the gods of their earthly privileges, the true, everlasting deities do not cease to exist: they turn out to be planets. Presiding over Alexander's birth in the *Alexander Romance,* Jupiter-Amun-Zeus is still a celestial god, and he duly acknowledges the boy's arrival with a clap of heavenly thunder. But when it comes to the earthly details, Nectanebo is perfectly willing—and able—to perform his own divine duty in Olympias's bed.

9

At Home in Alexandria

People and gods were thoroughly mixed up in the cross-cultural currents created by the passage of Alexander. Sophocles's tragedies were read in the Persian city of Susa; Euripides inspired artists in central Asia; Babylonian astronomy determined the horoscopes of Greeks and Macedonians; and as the edicts of Ashoka reveal, Buddhist precepts reached the Egyptian city of Alexandria in the third century BC. Images traveled even faster than stories, because they could ignore language barriers and freely recombine with local narratives. The magnificent sculptures of the Buddha at Gandhara in northern Pakistan, for example, were partly inspired by naturalistic Greek stone sculptures and terra-cottas of the gods. The Dalai Lama recently invoked them precisely in an attempt to promote a sense of shared heritage that crosses religious boundaries. As he put it, those ancient images simultaneously speak of the "Buddhist goal" and of "western humanism," best represented by the anthropomorphic deities of Olympus.[1]

In the course of time, the Greek gods would go beyond even Gandhara, especially along the Silk Route. In the Kizil Caves of China between the fourth and the seventh centuries AD, for example, artists painted images of wind-gods and a sun-god traveling in

A Greek-style capital with Buddha sitting among acanthus leaves,
dated to the third or fourth century AD. In the wake of Alexander the
Great, new forms of art developed in Gandhara (northern Pakistan
and eastern Afghanistan) that combined the naturalistic impetus of
Hellenistic art with a Buddhist focus on enlightenment.

a chariot, like Alexander. By the Middle Ages, Hellenistic images of
the gods had reached Japan, with the wind-gods receiving an especially enthusiastic reception there. Reinterpreted as local characters,
but retaining their puffed-up cheeks, curly dark hair, and flowing
Greek robes, they became popular figures in the Rimpa-school paintings of the seventeenth to nineteenth centuries.[2]

Such far-flung travels did not make the Greek gods forget their
Mediterranean roots, however, and they found a new home for themselves in Alexandria, the city that Alexander had founded by the
Nile delta. After appointing an architect, outlining the city plan,
and discussing which deities should have their temples set up there,
Alexander had left Alexandria to trek across the desert to Amun's
oracle. He never returned. Ptolemy I, a Macedonian general who
had served under Alexander since the beginning of his campaigns
and accompanied him all the way to India, took control of Egypt

after Alexander's sudden death and set up court in Alexandria. Ptolemy relentlessly promoted Alexander; his account of Alexander's campaigns, though now lost, influenced later histories, including Arrian's. In an amazing coup, Ptolemy even managed to take possession of Alexander's embalmed body as it was being transported from Babylon to the Siwah oasis, where it was meant to rest in the temple of Zeus Ammon. The details of Ptolemy's hijack are murky, but by one means or another he somehow got the body first to Memphis and then to Alexandria, where it became the object of cult. Worship of a divinized Alexander was very much to Ptolemy's liking, since it helped him establish his own legitimacy in Egypt. Claiming divinity soon became a royal tradition: when Ptolemy died, the poet Theocritus claimed that he too had joined Zeus and Alexander on Olympus.[3]

Under the protection of its divinized rulers, the city of Alexandria flourished, and within a hundred years of its foundation, it became the largest city in the ancient Mediterranean. The very rapid growth in population depended on a constant influx of immigrants: Greeks, Egyptians, and Jews all moved there from far-flung places, looking for new opportunities. The son of Ptolemy I, meanwhile, inherited the throne and ruled with great acumen and splendor. After his first wife died, Ptolemy II married his own sister Arsinoe, thus acquiring the Aegean possessions she had obtained through her own first marriage. This move was acceptable according to Egyptian custom: pharaohs regularly married their own sisters. In Greek society, though, such an act was taboo. Again, the poet Theocritus came to the rescue. He pointed out that Zeus had married his own sister Hera and that the Ptolemies were therefore behaving like gods rather than criminals.[4]

Poets clearly had their uses, as Ptolemy II, "the Sibling-Lover," must have appreciated. In all probability, it was he who founded the Museum, an institution devoted entirely, as the name suggests, to the arts of the Muses. The Museum was home of the famous Library of Alexandria, where poet-scholars worked with remarkable commitment and flair. Many of them collected earlier Greek literature, edited it, cataloged it, and took inspiration from it in their own works. The library may also have included works in other languages; their extent is hard to establish, but, as it happens, the earliest surviving source that mentions the library at all is a curious tale from the second century BC about the Hebrew Bible. According to this account—purportedly a letter written (in Greek) by one Aristeas—seventy-two Jewish scholars gathered in the Library of Alexandria under the auspices of Ptolemy II in order to translate the Bible from Hebrew into Greek. Miraculously, although they were working independently of one another, they all chose the exact same words to translate the text, which surely meant that they were divinely inspired. The letter sought to establish the authority of the Greek translation: it was the word of God, just like the Hebrew original. The real extent of the connection between the Septuagint (the "Version of the Seventy," as this translation came to be known) and the Library of Alexandria is doubtful. The Septuagint is written in a lowbrow, Semitic-sounding Greek, and mainstream Greek writers of the period never refer to it, which they surely would have done had it been such a major library project. It seems most likely that the text originated instead among Alexandria's local Graeco-Jewish communities, where it served their needs. Still, the fact that the letter writer was prepared to claim—quite grandly!—that the translation had been created under the direct patronage of Ptolemy II shows that Ptolemy's library was not seen as an exclusively Greek enterprise.

That Ptolemy II was inclusive in his cultural policies is also suggested by his choice of religious festivities. Any self-respecting Greek city offered a rich assortment of public cults and festivals. New colonies usually inherited the religious program of their "mother-city," the place from where its original settlers arrived. But Alexandria was the personal creation of Alexander the Great, and nobody knew what that complex inheritance involved. The Ptolemies took the view that public cults ought to focus on the embalmed Alexander and his successors—that is, the Ptolemies themselves. Accordingly, Ptolemy II established a grand festival in honor of his father. The Ptolemaia, as it was called, began with a procession headed by the wagon of the Morning Star, a well-chosen deity because it was equally relevant to all people living under the sky. The divinized parents of Ptolemy II and his sister-wife followed; again, the choice was inclusive, for everybody had an interest in worshipping the kings. The Evening Star closed the first section of the display. Figures of time, such as a personification of the Year, came next, carrying pharaonic emblems of power. Dionysos and a troupe of actors presenting scenes from his life followed the display of time: here was a god equally at home in the East and the West—a god, moreover, who had inspired Alexander. It was no coincidence that the actors performed Dionysos's return from India, an episode that reminded viewers of Alexander's own greatest exploit. After the divine section of the parade, the Ptolemies displayed many exotic animals—a proliferation of elephants, lions, leopards, panthers, camels, antelopes, ostriches, bears, rhinoceroses, and "camel-leopards" (giraffes). The Ptolemaia was a great success. No matter where they came from or which gods they preferred to worship, everybody could have a good time at the zoo.[5]

Other festivals in Alexandria were more recognizably Greek. The Adoneia, for example, celebrated the liaison between Aphrodite and her teenage lover, Adonis. But even this festival sought to bring different people together. According to Greek myth, Adonis was an Oriental character, so here was a love affair between East and West. Massive crowds attended the festival, and something of the excitement still comes through in a poem by Theocritus. His *Idyll* 15 describes two women meeting up, complaining about their husbands, exchanging compliments on their clothes, and then setting off together through the streets of Alexandria to attend the Adoneia at the royal palace. Although they live in the city, the two friends originally hail from Greek-speaking Sicily: somebody in the crowd makes fun of their broad vowels, but they declare themselves proud of their accent and their origins. They are obviously in high spirits. As they make their way toward the palace, struggling with the motley crowd, they rebuke some soldiers on horseback, complain about Egyptian thieves, and agree that Ptolemy II has done a great job of keeping the streets safe "since his father became immortal." And with this casual little comment, Theocritus once again draws attention to the divinity of the Alexandrian rulers.

While the streets of Alexandria thronged with people, a different atmosphere reigned in the Museum and its great library. It was in this secluded space that the essence of Greek divinity was distilled. Callimachus, the most famous poet-scholar of the third century BC, declared that he hated the crowded road. He hated many things, in fact: promiscuous lovers, bombastic poetry, and grand epic that flowed like "the Assyrian river, carrying much garbage and dirt in its course."[6] A mysterious group called the Telchines, for example, were irksome because they thought they could judge poetry by length.[7] Just who these Telchines were is far from clear, but the general tone of Callimachus's remarks is unmistakable: his work was meant to be exclusive, in every sense of the word. His Muse was slender. He drank only the purest drops of poetic inspiration and spurned his rivals' notions of poetry and culture. In addition to composing verse, Callimachus wrote prose works about nymphs, athletic contests, the foundation myths of Greek islands and cities, winds, marvels, barbarian customs, and assorted names for fish. That last enterprise might seem especially odd, but Callimachus was deeply interested in Greek culture—and then as now, every fishing village had its own local name for different types of fish. In his distant Egyptian library, Callimachus transformed such local knowledge, turning it into a universal encyclopedia and bringing Greece to Alexandria in the process.

His attitude toward religion was, in some respects, not so different from his approach to fish. He collected information about local Greek myths and rituals, cataloged them in prose, and carefully distilled them into poetry. Callimachus's *Aitia,* his most famous poem, discussed "origins" or "explanations" (*aitia* in Greek) of various cities, cults, and festivals. In the course of his exposition, Callimachus offered a telling description of himself. He claimed that he had once celebrated the Attic festival of the Anthesteria— not in Athens, where it originated, but in Alexandria, in the private home of an Athenian friend.[8] Originally a public festival in honor of Dionysos, the Anthesteria was thus transformed into an exclusive, private drinking party in Alexandria. Callimachus shared a reclining couch with a Greek visitor from an island near Thessaly and interrogated him about the mythologies and rituals of his region. The stranger answered with an observation that surely pleased his interlocutor: Callimachus was a lucky man, because he did not need to travel. He could get all the information he wanted right in Alexandria, the new center of the world.

Callimachus was not alone in his determination to pin down Greek culture for his library shelves. Other Alexandrian scholars collected manuscripts of the Homeric poems from many different Greek cities, compiling authoritative editions of the *Iliad* and the *Odyssey*—editions we effectively still use today. In a different but related search for origins, the poet and librarian Apollonius of Rhodes composed the *Argonautica,* an epic set in a period preceding the Trojan War and the other events described in Homer. Theocritus used a similar device in one of his works: he described a young and happy Cyclops in love with a nymph, as yet entirely unaware that Odysseus would one day sail by and blind him.[9]

This fashion for reaching back to a story's remote roots often turned the Olympian gods into children in Alexandrian poetry and art. Surrounded by the far greater antiquity of Egyptian cult, the Greeks constructed for themselves a playful alternative. Callimachus's *Hymn to Zeus,* for example, described at length the childhood of Zeus on the island of Crete. His *Hymn to Artemis* offered an image of the goddess as a little girl sitting on Zeus's lap, charming her father into promising favors and presents. In Apollonius's *Argonautica,* Zeus's thunderbolts are still being made in the workshop of the Cyclopes: the expedition of the Argonauts is set in such a distant past that Zeus himself is not yet in possession of his full powers. Like the Olympian gods, these authors imply, Greek culture itself might have started from childish beginnings but had eventually developed into something tremendously powerful.

Far from being simply nostalgic, the Alexandrians presented themselves as the sophisticated culmination of their complex Greek heritage. They collected all previous cults and myths and created a new, highly learned, and inventive synthesis. Whether this synthesis was addressed primarily to the Greek elites or had a wider appeal is difficult to establish. A contemporary observer described the denizens of the Museum as birds in a cage squabbling with one another, without any regard for the outside world. And the Alexandrian poet-scholars themselves, of course, cultivated precisely such an image of exclusive superiority. In fact, however, they were very aware of the Egyptian realities around them, as Theocritus's carefully drawn parallel between pharaonic habits and the marriage of Zeus and Hera demonstrates. They also realized that new, international elites were keen to learn Greek culture, and they catered to those elites by creating a form of poetry that transformed earlier Hellenic literature into something more accessible to outsiders.

In essence, what the poets and scholars of Alexandria began to do was turn Greece into a place of the mind, a place that could be reached simply by reading books. Callimachus's *Hymns* to the gods of Olympus, for example, were modeled on the *Homeric Hymns* but cunningly included a description of the festival settings in which the hymns were supposedly performed. His word paintings—a temple, a statue, a religious cult—effectively created a ritual frame within the text. There was no need now to be at a real festival and hear an actual performance: the poem itself gave readers all the context they needed. Similarly, the *Aitia* contained a description of Callimachus at a drinking party, a ritual feast at which elegiac poems like the *Aitia* itself were originally performed in early Greece. Theocritus's vignette about the Sicilian women, for its part, included the lyrics of the ritual song performed in honor of Aphrodite and Adonis at the festival. After hearing the words of the ritual song, readers could savor its reception: the two women concurred that the singing was beautiful, then hurried home to make dinner for their husbands, who could be short-tempered, they claimed, before eating. Readers did not need to be in Alexandria to appreciate its atmosphere; they could hear it in the conversation of the two women. Thus accessorized, Greek culture could be appreciated anywhere.

With the spread of Hellenistic culture, Greece became a matter of education. One Hellenistic poet, Meleager of Gadara, remarked, "I'm a Syrian, so what?" and continued with a learned allusion to the *Theogony*, the ultimate Greek poem about origins: "We now live in a united world, and one Chaos bore all mortals."[10] Knowing Hesiod ("From Chaos came Earth . . .") was all that mattered. Across the Mediterranean and the Near East, educated elites now learned about the gods of Olympus from written versions of Homer and Hesiod, together with Alexandrian commentaries on those texts. They absorbed the details of assorted Greek cults from scholarly works and carefully crafted Alexandrian poems like the *Aitia*. Throughout the lands conquered by Alexander, educated people shared these accounts, no matter what other languages they spoke and what local rituals they experienced. And so it was that when the Romans entered the world stage, they encountered people deeply familiar with the Olympian gods wherever they went.

PART IV

Translation: The Roman Empire

After their wide-ranging travels in Greece, Asia, and Africa, the Olympian gods arrived in Rome. This was perhaps their most significant journey, and certainly one of their most mysterious. Today, we tend to take it for granted that the Romans were interested in the Greeks, that they imitated their works, held up Greece as the cradle of civilization, and identified their own gods with those of their Greek subjects. But the choices made by the Romans were, in fact, far from self-evident. Although the practice of equating foreign gods with local ones was widespread in the ancient world, only the Romans systematically devoted themselves to the project of translating—literally, "bringing across"—the entire Greek pantheon.

This translation of gods was part of a much broader enterprise of cultural assimilation: Roman poets imitated Greek ones, Roman sculptors modeled their work on Greek originals, and Roman senators debated Greek philosophy in their beautiful countryside villas. The Romans, in short, acquired a Hellenistic education—and their gods changed accordingly. Traditional Roman religion had focused on the safety of the state and featured rather faceless gods who needed to be carefully managed and appeased. Now, under the influence of Greek culture, the gods acquired complex personalities and specific preferences for individual mortals. Eventually, the most powerful men in Rome, including Caesar and Augustus, claimed to have special relationships with the gods of Olympus. Their might, they said, was a matter of divine favor. The poet Ovid, meanwhile, suggested a different vision: that the gods of Olympus were symbols of human art—beautiful and chaotic—rather than imperial order.

10

The Muses in Rome

The Romans established their rule in the Mediterranean gradually over several hundred years, from the third to the first century BC. Contact with Greek culture accordingly happened in stages. Early Rome started by expanding into the Greek-speaking southern Italy and Sicily. This led to the Punic Wars against Carthage in North Africa, as both sides were fighting for control of the Mediterranean. Rome won: in 146 BC, the Third Punic War ended with Carthage's complete destruction. According to legend, the city was razed to the ground, and salt was plowed into the soil to ensure that nothing would ever grow there again. Meanwhile, conflicts of interest in Illyria, on the eastern coast of the Adriatic, had led to the First Macedonian War, which was fought contemporaneously with the Second Punic War. Ultimately, Rome won again: in 146 BC, the same year that Carthage was destroyed, the Battle of Corinth sealed the Roman conquest of Macedonia and Greece. At that point, the Romans were in a position to conquer all the Hellenistic kingdoms left behind by Alexander the Great. Egypt was the last to fall, capitulating in 30 BC. Cleopatra, its polyglot and multicultural queen, the last of the Ptolemies, refused to contemplate subjugation and committed suicide; her Macedonian, Greek, and Egyptian subjects bowed to the power of Rome.

Given that the Romans so comprehensively defeated the Greeks, it is not immediately obvious why they made so much of their culture—but an answer must be sought, in the first instance, in their determination to expand their empire. The devastating defeat of Greece enabled a light-touch rule. The Romans did not garrison their new conquests, preferring to present themselves as benign rulers and admirers. Adopting Greek culture was useful for maintaining good relations not just in Greece itself, but throughout the Mediterranean. After Alexander the Great, Greek had become the dominant language of the international elites, and Greek mythology provided stories that were widely shared and admired. The Romans used military might to establish their supremacy but also tried to gain consensus by appealing to broadly accepted stories, ideas, and values. In their use of Greek mythology, the Romans were actually not so different from their enemies. Hannibal, the Punic general who crossed the Alps with a herd of elephants, presented himself as the new Heracles, as Alexander the Great had done before him—and so did the Roman generals who fought against him in the Second Punic War. Hannibal equated the Greek Heracles with the Punic Melqart, but both sides appealed to the Greek hero turned god in order to project their local ambitions onto a global stage.

Such attempts to go Greek were not just casual poses, but meticulously planned and managed strategies. Hannibal kept two Greek writers in his retinue to record his deeds for a global audience, and for posterity. (People of the future, it was assumed, would read Greek.) The Romans, for their part, captured the Greek historian Polybius, who went on to memorialize Rome's rise to power. Polybius's work became influential, first in Rome and then in many other cultures. His ideas about the separation of powers in government, for example, is important for many modern constitutions. The Greek writers working for Hannibal, by contrast, fell into oblivion; their work was lost, just as Hannibal himself lost the Second Punic War. Still, they and Polybius shared important life experiences: they all worked as tutors and historians, promoting Greek figures, especially Heracles, as models of behavior for their new masters.

For Roman elites eager to acquire a Hellenistic education, the problem was not so much that of finding suitable teachers—there were plenty of learned Greeks who could be captured or otherwise persuaded to dispense their knowledge—but rather of working out how Greek culture could be accommodated in Rome. It was one thing to imitate Heracles when fighting against Hannibal and quite another to play the role of hero turned god among one's fellow citizens. Traditional Roman religion was not especially welcoming to that kind of fancy; it did not celebrate the stories of individual gods or individual mortals who behaved like them. Early Roman deities, even the greatest of them, did not have distinct personalities. Jupiter, although he shared an ancient etymological connection with Zeus, had developed in a different direction in Rome: he was seen, above all, as a rather impersonal protector of the Roman Republic. The other major Roman gods—including Juno, Mars, Minerva, Venus, and Mercury—were also invested primarily with civic responsibilities and were surrounded by a crowd of minor gods who were even more functional and faceless. There was Imporcitor, for example, "god of ploughing with wide furrows"; Vervactor, "god of turning over fallow land"; and Mantura, "goddess of keeping the wife at home." Clearly, the Romans called on the gods to help them with their daily tasks, but it seems that they did not indulge in much storytelling about them. Greek mythology had developed over time as different Greek communities came together in order to trade, worship, listen to poetry, and compete in athletic games. Travelers who met and exchanged tales gave rise to a complex shared tradition—a tradition of entertainment as well as cult. The Romans were more focused. They knew one simple thing about their gods: that they favored Rome above all other cities. And that

was what mattered. To keep their relationship with the gods in optimal condition, the Romans set up an exceptionally elaborate system
of priestly colleges, tasked with establishing what the gods wanted
and needed—rather than who they were, how they looked, or what
they did to one another, the kinds of questions that deeply fascinated
the Greeks. The Romans had *haruspices*, priests in charge of interpreting freak occurrences; *augures*, responsible for bird omens and
other forms of divine communication; *duoviri*, "two men in charge
of sacred actions," later increased to ten men, *decemviri*; vestal virgins, *pontifices, flamines, fetiales*, and many other groups of religious officers with specific functions and tasks. All of these priestly
colleges had a single overarching aim: to ensure that Rome would
flourish and conquer, with full divine support. There was no clear
division in ancient Rome between sacred and secular power; indeed,
the same men often served as priests, senators, and generals. This
blending of religion and politics was a feature of many other ancient
societies, of course, including Greek ones, but the Roman religious
system was even more closely bound with civic concerns than those
of other peoples.

Given the functional orientation of Roman religion, it may come
as no surprise that the relationship between the Romans and their
gods was rather bureaucratic. When Hannibal threatened to capture Rome in 217 BC, for example, the Romans promised to sacrifice to the gods the whole farming product of one spring season.
They then went on to specify the dates that would constitute "the
spring" and added a clause stating that if any irregularities took
place—if, for example, a farmer hid a piglet or two for private
consumption—the sacrifice would nevertheless count as properly
conducted. The Romans placed great trust in such negotiations
with the gods, but they were also open to other forms of worship—
particularly in times of crisis, when their own standard ways of
doing things did not seem to be working. As Hannibal loomed ever
closer, the desperate Romans introduced a new ritual, presumably
as a form of extra insurance against disaster. Inspired by mythical

Olympian banquets, the *decemviri* brought out twelve statues of the Olympian gods, arranged them in pairs on six couches, and offered them a feast. As far as we know, this was the first time that the Olympians received official recognition in Rome. The pantheon of twelve will have been familiar to the Romans before then, not just through their direct contact with the Greeks, but also because Rome's immediate neighbors, the Etruscans, had long been interested in Greek mythology. Still, it was one thing to know foreign stories about the gods of Olympus and quite another to let them directly affect Rome's own religious practices.

It can be no coincidence that at around the same time, Livius Andronicus—a former Greek slave—translated the *Odyssey* into Latin for the first time. The twelve gods thus entered Rome simultaneously as statues assembled for a ritual meal and as epic characters in a story. Andronicus's translation proved to be hugely important in the history of Latin literature. We do not know what kinds of songs or oral compositions the Romans might have enjoyed before he arrived in Rome, but they had certainly never experienced anything like this poem. As well as producing a version of the *Odyssey* (which now survives only in a handful of clever fragments), he translated and staged several Greek plays. I sometimes imagine that Andronicus's productions might have been as amazing and incongruous as Diaghilev's Ballets Russes touring Texas in 1916, confronting untrained audiences with Stravinsky's music and the finest dancing Europe had to offer. What the Romans made of some of the most sophisticated and powerful plays the world had ever seen we do not know, but Andronicus had a good career. He even secured permission for his troupe of actors to worship together at the temple of Minerva—or, as he and his fellow Greeks will have thought of her, Athena.

As a motley crowd of Hellenic immigrants, poets, teachers, and entertainers settled in Rome, the twelve Olympian gods were systematically identified with major local deities. From a literary point of view, the merging of the Greek and the Roman pantheon was

This massive statue from the first century AD, kept in the Musei Capitolini in Rome, demonstrates that Mars was an important deity in the Roman pantheon. Ares, his Greek "equivalent," was by contrast a marginal deity in Greece. Straightforward-seeming translations of divine names often masked significant differences.

above all a challenge of translation. Today, we are used to thinking that the Greeks and Romans worshipped the same deities; countless school texts and wall charts rehearse for us what seem to be straightforward correspondences. But, in fact, matching them up was not so simple. In the first place, the Romans did not originally recognize a preeminent group of twelve gods; that structure was in itself a foreign import. Second, not all the Olympian gods had viable Roman counterparts. Apollo, for example, had to be imported wholesale from Greece. Dionysos also had no Roman equivalent and came to be known in Rome primarily as Bacchus, an alternative Greek name that was often used in ritual contexts. Even when the Greek gods could be matched up with local Roman deities, such pairings were often misleading. The Greek god Ares, for example, was a crazed, bloodthirsty character despised even by his father, Zeus; the Roman Mars, by contrast, was a central and highly respected deity in the Roman pantheon. And even in the case of the most direct equivalences, such as between Zeus and Jupiter, Greek influences gradually changed Roman perceptions of the gods, making their personalities more complex and well-rounded. The gods acquired new portraits and biographies and also—crucially—new forms of worship.

The most famous of these was the cult of Bacchus, which spread from the south of Italy up the peninsula during the third and early second centuries BC. It promised to reveal great mysteries about life and the afterlife and encouraged the use of wine, sex, and violence as a means of reaching ecstasy. The details of the Bacchic rituals are unclear—they were revealed only to initiates, and we have to reconstruct them from hostile and uninformed ancient sources. It seems, though, that the cult answered needs that traditional Roman religion did not meet: its devotees pursued a personal, even visceral, relationship with the god and sought in the rites an answer to the fear of death. This kind of religion had no respect for the hierarchies of the Roman Republic. Bacchus broke down barriers between citizens and foreigners, men and women, rich and poor, slaves and free, uniting them all in his cult. This proved controversial, and in 186 BC, the Roman Senate crushed the rites of Bacchus with uncommon brutality. Generally, the Romans were tolerant of foreign cults—or, to be more precise, they felt that such cults were not as effective as their own ways of handling the gods and therefore largely let them be—so this state-sanctioned repression was unusual. In part, it seems that the Senate tried to stamp out the rites of Bacchus not so much because devotees were drunken and disruptive, but because they were well organized. Initiates had common funds, leaders, and procedures for membership and thus threatened to create new structures of power within the Roman state. Official propaganda cast the Bacchists as strange members of a foreign sect, but in fact we know that good Roman citizens and matrons were among those sworn into the secret rites of the god, which must have made the Senate feel even more threatened. Bacchus's secret rites destabilized the very principles of traditional Roman religion. The focus was no longer on the welfare of the state, but on a sense of personal and collective liberation.

Outlawing the Bacchists did not prevent Roman culture and religion from changing rapidly in the course of the second century BC. Too many other colorful characters also showed up in the city, spreading strange rumors about the gods. In 168 BC, for example, a famous Homeric scholar—Crates of Mallos—arrived in Rome on a diplomatic embassy from Pergamon, in Asia Minor, and promptly fell into a sewer on the Palatine Hill. His encounter with superior Roman engineering incapacitated him for several months. While recovering, he took the opportunity to lecture the Romans on Homeric poetry, offering striking allegorical interpretations in the tradition of Theagenes: he claimed that the Olympian gods represented human virtues, physical causes, and states of mind. The Romans were amazed. Other visiting lecturers—such as Carneades, a Greek from Cyrene, in North Africa, who arrived in Rome a few years after Crates—fared less well. Carneades was the director of the Academy in Athens, the philosophical school founded by Plato himself, and he lectured on justice. In his first performance, he offered fulsome praise of this virtue and met with applause. In his second lecture, making a rhetorical about-face, he demolished all his previous arguments and presented justice exclusively as an instrument of social control. Cato the Censor—an upright Roman citizen who had appointed himself the moral conscience of the city—was outraged and persuaded the Senate to send Carneades straight back to Athens before he could scrutinize any other virtues.

Today, Crates and Carneades are almost forgotten figures, but they made a huge impression in ancient Rome.[1] Still, even at that time they could not radically change dominant ideas about religion and morality all by themselves. Their unusual views could too easily be dismissed as the fancies of mere *Graeculi,* "little Greeks." It was only when Rome's own senators and generals started to take seriously Greek ideas about the gods that the religious balance of the Roman Republic began to change. By confronting the ways in which the gods were portrayed in Greek plays, epic poems, and philosophical debates, the Romans started to suspect that morality had little to do with the gods. They also began to realize that if the gods had specific personalities, they might favor specific individuals rather than Rome itself.

Ennius, an immigrant from the south of Italy, was largely responsible for teaching the Romans how Greek culture in general—and the Olympian gods in particular—could be used for personal advantage. Messapian by extraction, Oscan by family connection, and Greek by education, Ennius claimed to have three hearts, one for each of the cultures he mastered. After moving to Rome, he eventually became the personal poet of Fulvius Nobilior, a prominent Roman general. It proved to be an influential post: by introducing Hellenistic models of poetry, divinity, patronage, and power, Ennius would fundamentally transform Roman literature and culture.

Among his other works, Ennius composed the *Annales,* an epic poem about Rome that started with Romulus and Remus and ended with Fulvius himself. The whole history of the Roman Republic, as he told it, was bracketed between the personal stories of these individual men, who were especially favored by the gods. The poem began with an invocation to "the Muses who dance on Olympus," and that was the first appearance of these goddesses in Rome. Andronicus, in his version of the *Odyssey,* had translated the Muses as Camenae, thus equating them with some obscure Italian goddesses of fountains (and perhaps inspiration). But Ennius rebelled against that notion. In his view, the Muses did not skulk in local fountains; they were Greek, and the Romans needed to learn their names and celebrate their arrival.

As ever, issues of translation marked larger cultural shifts. Ennius was determined that the Muses, and the Greek arts they represented, had to find proper recognition in Rome. As for the other Olympian gods, Ennius accepted the standard Roman translations of their names but added many Greek details to their portrayals. For example, he offered an apparently straightforward list of the twelve Olympian gods in his *Annales* but hid in it a little Homeric joke for those subtle enough to see it:

Iuno Vesta Minerva Ceres Diana Venus Mars
Mercurius Iovis Neptunus Volcanus Apollo[2]

Ennius carefully placed the goddesses in his first line of poetry and the gods in the second—except that Mars sneaked up and squeezed in next to Venus at the end of the first line, because he wanted to be close to his secret lover. Already in the *Odyssey* he had enjoyed a furtive love affair with her, and now that affair was made into learned literary allusion. Ennius was a master of the sophisticated, bookish culture inaugurated by the Alexandrians. Like the Alexandrians, too, he knew how to use poetry to flatter his patron and enhance his stature.

When Fulvius Nobilior sacked the Greek city of Ambracia in 189 BC, Ennius composed a play celebrating the victory. Fulvius, for his part, decided to take Ennius's project of "bringing across" the Muses literally: he looted nine statues of the goddesses from a local temple in Ambracia and transferred them to his private home in Rome. Cato the Censor, censorious as ever, denounced this move. He claimed that war booty should not become private property and that statues of the gods should never be used as interior decoration.[3] It was imperative, he insisted, to worship and govern together according to traditional Roman principles. It is easy to see where the problem was, in Cato's eyes: Fulvius was using his Greek poet-adviser and his Muses to improve his personal standing, thus disrupting the equilibrium among the elites. Ennius's play about the sack of Ambracia enraged Fulvius's political rivals, but it went down well with the crowds, and the Roman people could grant considerable power to a popular general like Fulvius.

What is more, in addition to composing epic and drama in praise of Fulvius, Ennius translated into Latin Euhemerus's *Sacred Register,* that curious Hellenistic text about the gods as mortal benefactors of humanity. He thus suggested to Fulvius, and the Romans more generally, that the Olympians had once been ordinary people and that succeeding generations, grateful for their services, had deified them. In other words, the people could promote their favorites not just in the political arena, but in the realm of religion. A private friendship between a general and a three-hearted poet was tilting the balance of power away from traditional Roman religion and toward more personal conceptions of the gods. Divinity was becoming a matter of popular appeal.

In the end, Fulvius Nobilior had to yield to political and religious pressure, but he devised an answer to Cato's attacks so cunning that Ennius himself must have been behind it. He removed the nine statues of the Muses from his home and gave them to a public temple near the river Tiber. This temple was then rededicated to "Hercules of the Muses," a title that had no precedent in Roman cult (though it may have featured in southern Italy, Ennius's place of origin). Far from apologizing for the political advantages he had gained from Ennius, Fulvius Nobilior thus turned his Greek Muses and his relationship with the poet into a public affair. As a general and patron of literature, Fulvius himself was, of course, the most perfect "Hercules of the Muses," and his donation became another act of self-promotion. Over the following centuries, many powerful men in Rome would imitate the Hellenistic trick that Ennius popularized and start to portray themselves as gods. The temple of Hercules and the Muses, meanwhile, became a meeting place for poets and artists for generations to come. They created a new, hybrid Graeco-Roman culture, over which the nine pillaged Muses of Ambracia presided.

11

Ancestors, Allies, and Alter Egos

The military successes of the second century BC utterly transformed Rome. The elites, who had become immensely rich, invested much of their wealth in land, using the vast numbers of slaves captured in a century of warring to farm it. Roman peasants, meanwhile, felt increasingly drawn to the city, where men of influence were distributing favors in return for votes. The imperial capital grew into a metropolis: a few decades before the birth of Jesus, it contained an estimated one million inhabitants, a European record that would be broken only by industrial London.[1] But prosperity did not bring stability. Indeed, as the empire continued to grow through conquests in the east and west, tensions among the powerful increased. Volatile alliances between ruling elites, fraught relationships between generals and their armies, controversial agrarian reforms, numerous slave revolts (of which Spartacus's was the most famous), and frequent uprisings throughout Italy and the provinces—all of these helped fan the flames of successive civil wars, which eventually brought an end to the Roman Republic itself.

The gods of Olympus were thoroughly entangled in all these developments. As a recognizable band of characters, they made themselves useful, to begin with, as international facilitators, helping the Romans make sense of the world as they marched forward and conquered it. When Caesar invaded Gaul, for example, he immediately identified familiar gods in what must have been a radically unfamiliar landscape. His *De bello gallico* includes the following observations about local deities:

> Among the gods, the Gauls worship Mercury in particular. There are numerous images of him; they claim that he is the inventor of all crafts, the guide for all roads and journeys; they consider that he has special power over money-making and trade. After him, they worship Apollo, Mars, Jupiter, and Minerva. On these deities they have roughly the same views as all the other nations—that Apollo dispels sickness, that Minerva bestows the principles of arts and crafts, that Jupiter holds sway in heaven, that Mars controls wars.[2]

Caesar's identifications are breezy, even slapdash. Mercury, roughly speaking, can be matched up with the Gallic Teutates, Apollo with Belen, Ares with Esus, and Zeus with Taranis—but we have no idea what local equivalent Caesar had in mind for Minerva, for example. He seems, in any case, to have been supremely uninterested in the details. What he wanted to suggest, above all to his Roman readers, was that the same international gods held sway everywhere—and that they supported Rome. He implied that the Gauls were a little unclear about proper divine hierarchies; it was odd, and perhaps a little weak of them, to privilege Mercury over Apollo and Mars, let alone Jupiter. But apart from that local quirk, which in any case boded well for commerce, there was nothing interesting to report about local religion. Indeed, Caesar blithely concluded, the Gauls had "roughly the same views" about the gods as everybody else. This is not how the Romans treated the Greeks, of course. Every description of the gods in Greek literature, art, and philosophy was carefully scrutinized, and internalized in Rome. The characteristics that Caesar attributed to Mercury, Apollo, Mars, Jupiter, and Minerva thus exactly matched Greek stories about Hermes, Apollo, Ares, Zeus, and Athena. Indeed, it was because the Greek and Roman gods had been systematically merged that Caesar could make grand claims about "all nations."

In reality, as might be expected, religious beliefs varied radically across the Roman Empire. But conquered people had few options when presenting their gods to the Romans. They could claim that they worshipped their own unique deities—but then the Romans had no reason to care about the bizarre gods of the defeated. Alternatively, they could insist that their gods were actually the same as the Olympians, in which case the Romans already knew everything they needed to know about them. The final result was the same in either case: distinctive local traditions were submerged, while broadly Graeco-Roman views of the gods spread across the empire. To be sure, some foreign gods did manage to command respect and even worship among the Romans. Cybele, an Eastern Earth Mother, enjoyed remarkable success in Rome; the Persian god Mithras became popular among the Roman legionnaires; and the Egyptian goddess Isis spread her influence along the coast of Africa, then across Gibraltar to Spain and Gaul. But even Cybele, Mithras, and Isis entered the Roman world from the Hellenized East, which gave them respectable Greek credentials. Without a Hellenic passport of some kind, it was difficult indeed for conquered gods to make any impact in Rome.

The assumption that the Olympians were universal gods informed religious attitudes throughout the Roman Empire, from northern Europe to Africa and Asia. For example, Varro, a contemporary of Caesar's, claimed that the Jews worshipped Jupiter. To us, the idea of a Jewish Jupiter may seem preposterous, but it was probably meant as a sign of respect. Varro admired the Jews for worshipping only one deity, and from his perspective the supreme god had to be Jupiter. Interestingly, the Jews themselves seemed to share his views, at least up to a point: they also thought that their God was the same deity who had granted victory to the Romans. When Pompey captured Jerusalem and desecrated its Temple in 63 BC, the Jewish scriptures presented this as a sign of divine anger. God had helped the foreign conquerors, they said, in order to punish his people for their wickedness.

The conquered Gauls and Jews were not the only ones whose theology was affected by the Roman conquests: the conquerors themselves were transformed, too. As the military campaigns of Caesar and Pompey rolled on, seemingly unstoppable—Pompey sweeping across the Mediterranean and the Near East, Caesar subduing much of western Europe and briefly invading Britain—both men began to boast about their divinity. Julius Caesar insisted that because he belonged to the family line known as the *gens Julia,* he was a descendant of Venus herself. It was Venus who gave birth to Aeneas, who begat Iulus, who gave his name to Caesar's family. At some level, everybody in Rome already knew that, but now Caesar made sure that this fact was not overlooked. To that end, he dedicated a temple to Venus *Genetrix,* "the Ancestor." The name was carefully calculated: the goddess was the ancestor of Romulus and Remus and therefore of all the Romans, but Caesar also emphasized that she was more specifically *his* ancestor. The story of Aeneas, Venus's son, also became particularly popular around this time, no doubt because it was useful to Caesar and his followers.

Meanwhile, Pompey styled himself as the new Alexander. He insisted on being called Pompeius Magnus, "Pompey the Great," and demanded several divine honors, particularly in the Greek East. On the Aegean island of Mytilene, for example, a whole month was named after him, although months were usually devoted to the gods. On the island of Delos—the birthplace of Apollo and Artemis!—Pompey enjoyed a personal cult, complete with specially appointed priests known as the *Pompeiastai.* It is hard to know what ordinary Greek people made of Pompey's claims to divinity. Perhaps they felt that worshipping him was simply their best option under the circumstances, or perhaps they thought that his overwhelming power truly was, at least on some level, divine. One tiny piece of evidence suggests that some Greeks, at least, were ambivalent about Pompey. A graffito scratched on an Athenian wall politely advised him: "The more you know you are a man, the more you become a god."[3]

Whether Pompey paid much attention to such wisdom of the streets is doubtful. In Greece, he could do as he pleased. It was in Rome that he needed to be careful. In the capital there were time-honored ways of handling the relationship between gods and mortals, and straying too far from those could endanger the extraordinary divine support that Rome enjoyed. Pompey needed to respect Roman tradition—and this he did, with some crucial twists. For example, he modified a key Roman ritual, the triumph, to suggest the idea of his divinity to his fellow citizens. Traditionally, after a significant victory the Senate granted the returning general the right to perform a grand entrance into the city. The general drove through a special triumphal gate at the head of his army, making a display of war prisoners, spoils, exotic animals, and other marvels he had gathered on campaign. The procession followed a specific ritual route through the city, ending up in front of the temple of Jupiter on the Capitoline Hill. There, the general laid wreaths of laurel on the lap of the red-painted cult statue, formally thanking the supreme god for his victory. During a triumph, the victorious general himself also wore a laurel wreath, dressed in red, and had his face made up in red, mimicking the appearance of the Jupiter statue. For one day, in other words, the general and Jupiter mirrored each other, but then the man laid his wreath in the lap of the god and resumed his normal appearance. Not so with Pompey: after the fall of Jerusalem, the Senate granted him not only the right to celebrate a triumph, but permission to wear his Jupiter costume and makeup whenever he went to the Circus Maximus. The Roman public would thus see Pompey looking exactly like the Capitoline Jupiter whenever he made an official appearance at the popular stadium.

In practice, it seems that Pompey dared do this only once, but he certainly set an example for his rival, Caesar. By the 40s BC, the world no longer seemed large enough to contain them both—as they fought for control of the republic, Pompey was killed in Egypt by the Ptolemies, who presented his severed head to Caesar, literally, on a silver platter. After Caesar returned to Rome, he felt no constraint in behaving like a god. He insisted on the right to wear the Jupiter costume on all public occasions; the laurel wreath, part of the divine attire, became a distinctive attribute in his portraits. As befitted his new status, Caesar also made some telling adjustments to his home, adding a triangular pediment to the front of his house that made it look like a temple. He then appointed a priest to attend to his personal cult and renamed a month after himself. (Unlike the month that Pompey named for himself in Mytilene, Julius Caesar's month—July—bears his name to this day.) In short, rather than limiting his more extravagant divine manifestations to the Greek world, Caesar insisted on being worshipped as a god in Rome itself.

Unsurprisingly, such behavior bred resentment—and Caesar's opponents found ammunition not only in his deviation from traditional Roman conduct, but also in Hellenistic philosophy. In the mid–first century BC, the Roman poet Lucretius had insisted on asking what it actually meant to be a god, opening up a line of inquiry that would soon have obvious relevance to Caesar's claims. As Lucretius saw it, what happened in our world depended only on physical causes, specifically the movement of atoms, and on human will. The Olympians, according to Lucretius, had no influence on human affairs at all. They lived in utter contentment in their own separate realm, appearing to mortals only as images and visions, *simulacra*. At the same time, Lucretius insisted that ordinary mortals could become like gods: all they needed to do was relinquish their terror of death and start enjoying themselves. The Greek thinker Epicurus, he said, had showed the way. The Epicurean philosophy, which posited simple pleasures as the highest goal in life, was a guide to perfect happiness. Lucretius could not praise Epicurus highly enough. He was greater than Bacchus, bringer of wine, and Ceres, provider of corn; he was stronger than Hercules, slayer of monsters, because he defeated the fears and sorrows that plague our lives.

As far as Lucretius was concerned, Epicurus was the true savior of humanity. In order to publicize Epicurean philosophy in Rome, he wrote a passionate and rigorously argued poem called *On the Nature of Things*, outlining his view of the universe and explaining how to make human life not just bearable, but blissful. Lucretius succeeded, up to a point: reading his poem is still a great, uplifting pleasure. On the Olympian gods, he left many questions unanswered. What were these *simulacra*, these divine images that commanded the attention of mortals? Were the gods, as Euhemerus argued in the *Sacred Register*, visions of real people (like Epicurus) who had helped humanity? Did the same laws of physics govern the movements and combinations of atoms in the divine realm the gods inhabited? Lucretius knew that he needed to explain the gods and the astonishing endurance of their power, and he promised to tackle the issue in his poem—but never got around to writing the relevant section. It is possible that he died before finishing *On the Nature of Things*. Like Simonides, he may have discovered that a single human life is too short to capture the essence of the divine.

After Caesar began to act like a god, people turned to Lucretius's work with a renewed sense of urgency. Who or what was a god, really? How did a god act in the world? Could a god die? And if so, did he survive only as a mental image or as an actual power shaping the future course of events? These questions now became of interest not just to philosopher-poets like Lucretius, but to politicians, too. Cicero, a prominent Roman senator and statesman, wrote an extensive treatise called *On the Nature of the Gods*—because, he claimed, it was in the interests of the state that he do so. Besides, he added, he had plenty of free time, since Caesar had taken sole control of politics:

> If someone asks me why I decided to write about the nature of the gods . . . I can explain my decision easily. I had nothing else to do:

the state of public affairs was such that an autocratic form of government had become inevitable.[4]

For Cicero, thinking about the nature of the gods was a logical response to Caesar's dictatorship. Given Caesar's pretension to divine status, he saw it as his civic duty to investigate what such claims might mean. In his treatise, Cicero considered the possibility that there were no gods at all, but then pointed out that all people throughout the world believed that the gods existed—and there had to be some truth to such widespread views. After starting from this universal perspective, the argument then quickly homed in on Rome. Cicero structured his work as a conversation among high-ranking Roman officers: he described them having a leisurely conversation al fresco, in a beautiful Roman garden, discussing the nature of the gods, exploring different theories—that the divine was providential, as the Stoics maintained, or that it was unconcerned with human life, as the Epicureans argued—and ultimately reaching no conclusions at all.

Formally, this made Cicero an academic skeptic, somebody who examined all theories and espoused none. Just how he maintained a skeptical position toward the gods while remaining true to his duties as senator and priest—which included interpreting the will of the gods and advising the Roman Senate on it—has been much debated. Some argue that Cicero kept his roles separate: that when he served as a Roman priest he conformed to Roman conceptions of the gods, and when he wrote philosophy he followed his Greek sources. I disagree—not because I believe that Cicero ever worked out an entirely coherent position for himself, but because he wrote philosophy precisely as a form of politics. He developed into a philosopher in the Greek tradition *because* he was a Roman senator and priest. It is no coincidence that when Caesar started monopolizing state religion by suggesting that he was a god, Cicero offered an extensive, skeptical treatment of divinity. He was using the imported science of Greek philosophy for his own, Roman ends.

The classicist Mary Beard compares Cicero in this regard with a tribal witch doctor trying to adapt Western medicine in order to retain some of his traditional power.[5] The comparison is apt, in many ways: it captures something of the confusion, the inner conflict, and the creative response to foreign ideas. But it also plays down a fundamental difference between Cicero and a tribesman from a colonized African village. Rome was not a backwater settlement—it was a global, imperial capital. Likewise, Cicero was not turning to the methods of the colonizers in a desperate attempt to retain some of his local power. He belonged to an imperial elite and was taking his cues from the vanquished, subjugated Greeks. So was Caesar, for that matter. Despite their differences, both men were adapting Hellenistic ideas about the gods to their urgent Roman needs—Caesar was hinting at the possibility that rulers might be gods, while Cicero philosophically questioned such claims.

The mystery and fascination of ancient Rome lies in this creative reworking of Greek culture. Uniquely, here, the victors were forging opportunities for themselves by adapting to the views of the defeated. As Horace put it, "Captive Greece conquered its conquerors."[6] And the result of this cultural conquest was not a beautiful, well-balanced Graeco-Roman synthesis of the kind we might picture today, but a fierce clash of people and perspectives. Most of the chief protagonists of the late Roman Republic met with a violent death. Caesar was assassinated less than four years after Pompey's decapitation, and Cicero was murdered (by Caesar's supporters) less than two years after that. His hands and head were publicly pinned to the Rostra, the platform from which he had delivered so many of his speeches.

Scattered body parts marked the end of the Roman Republic: Pompey's head in Alexandria; Caesar's mutilated corpse in the theater of Pompey; Cicero's head and hands on public display. The Olympians, meanwhile, delighted in the confusion. As ancestors, allies, and alter egos of the most prominent men in Rome, they instigated a bloody revolution. Tacitus summarized the late Roman

Republic in one devastating sentence: "The gods no longer cared for our safety, but only for our punishment."[7]

Punishment or, more precisely, revenge—*ultio,* in Latin. The term described personal feuds: god against god, man against man, faction against faction. Violent personalities tore Rome apart, until Caesar's successor charted an unlikely route toward peace. Under his rule, philosophical speculation about the gods lost all momentum. The possibility that the gods existed, or did not exist, or existed but took no part in human affairs; the idea that the gods had to be immortal beings, or human generals, or perhaps thinkers like Epicurus, bent on pleasure rather than political power—the new emperor disliked such stark alternatives and preferred a more accommodating style of thinking about the gods, one that allowed different ideas to coexist and blend. He encouraged poets and artists rather than argumentative philosophers. Their visions of the gods, he hoped, might keep everyone happy—not just with the gods, but with him, the new ruler of Rome.

12

Mutants

When Julius Caesar's will was opened after his death in 44 BC, it was found to contain a few surprises. Most dramatically, it named Octavius, one of his adopted sons, as his principal heir. The choice would prove to be an inspired one, but at the time Octavius hardly seemed a natural successor to Caesar. To claim his inheritance, he would have to deal not only with the senators who had killed his adoptive father, but with Caesar's own power-hungry allies, of whom Marc Antony was the most important. Octavius was only eighteen years old; he was away on campaign and probably did not even know the contents of Caesar's will. When he found out about it, however, he acted swiftly. He insisted, first of all, on being called Julius Caesar like his father (though modern historians instead call him "Octavian" in this period of his life, to avoid confusion with the earlier Caesar). When he was refused a consulship, he crossed the Rubicon, as Caesar had famously done before him, and marched on Rome.

Having thus firmly established himself as following in Caesar's footsteps, Octavian orchestrated the deification of his father. In 42 BC, a public decree officially granted Julius Caesar the status of a god. It seems that Marc Antony was not enthusiastic about that plan. As a god, Julius Caesar was bound to support his son and heir above all other men in Rome. Antony was right to be worried. Relying on the dead Caesar as his only unquestioning ally, Octavian quickly neutralized the Republicans and gained control of the army. Along the way, he wiped out much of the senatorial class, confiscated their property, and handed it over to the army. He quickly acquired a reputation for extreme violence. Rumors spread that Octavian was capable of plucking out people's eyes with his bare hands.

Brutality, however, was not his main resource—for one thing, it was in plentiful supply among his enemies, too. What distinguished Octavian was his ability to adapt and transform his basis of power. Outwardly, he restored many republican institutions after Caesar's dictatorship, but in practice he kept control of the empire firmly in his own hands. Such a maneuver required, of course, a very careful handling of the gods. Octavian made a show of returning to traditional Roman forms of piety, emphasizing the link between proper religious behavior and the safety of Rome. In religion as in politics, though, he kept personal control, rather than relying on the advice and insights of priests. The gods were united in their support of Rome, he insisted, and that actually meant that they were united in their support of Octavian himself.

It was not easy to make this sound convincing, because Octavian's main rivals also had strong claims to divine support. Marc Antony cultivated a close relationship with Hercules—indeed, he even tried to suggest a family resemblance. Hercules was usually depicted wearing minimal clothing, the better to show off his muscles; he often had a heavy cloak or a lion skin on his shoulders and a large club or a sword in his hand. And this was just how Marc Antony presented himself in the streets of Rome, according to his ancient biographer Plutarch:

> Marc Antony had a shapely beard, a broad forehead, and an aqui-
> line nose that were thought to show a virile resemblance with the

portraits and statues of Heracles. There was an ancient tradition that the Antonii were descendants of Heracles and that their forefather Anton was a son of Heracles. Antony thought that the shape of his body confirmed that tradition, and he emphasized it with his attire too. Whenever he was going to be seen by many people, he always wore his tunic hitched up to his thigh, a large sword hung at his side, and a heavy cloak enveloped him.[1]

Just as Alexander the Great had used anthropomorphic art to enhance his own claims of divinity in the Hellenistic period, so Antony now meant to use his resemblance to Hercules to increase his authority in Rome. Political circumstance, however, eventually forced Antony to shift his basis of power from Rome to Greece and Asia, where he chose a different role model for himself: the god Dionysos. Some said that playing the part of Dionysos was simply an excuse for Antony to pursue excessive drinking and sex, but as long as those excesses were liberally shared, there was little objection. "People hailed Antony as Dionysos Giver of Joy and Beneficent," Plutarch reported, though in the end, "for most people he proved to be Dionysos Carnivorous and Savage."[2]

Whether he was presenting himself as Dionysos or Hercules, for Antony the point of divinity was its glorifying pageantry. Queen Cleopatra—who had been Caesar's lover—shared that perspective. When Antony summoned her after Caesar's death, the official reason was that he wanted to question her loyalty, since she had allegedly given funds to Cassius, one of Caesar's murderers. Cleopatra, however, used the occasion to stage a breathtaking encounter between gods. She sailed to Tarsus, the city in southern Turkey where Antony was stationed, in a barge with a gilded bow, purple sails, and a crew plying silver oars to the sound of music. The scene was so dazzling, Plutarch said, that "a rumor spread on every land that Aphrodite had arrived to revel with Bacchus for the good of Asia."[3] This divine spectacle had a practical aim: Cleopatra was in search of new political and personal allies. As Caesar's mistress and the mother of his son, she had few options but to side with an avenger of Caesar, and Antony was on her doorstep. Their union gave them unprecedented military and economic power, while acting like gods further enhanced their charisma. It is no wonder that, back in Rome, Octavian decided that he too needed an Olympian alter ego. He chose Apollo, god of beauty and order, and even promised to build a temple for him right next to his own home on the Palatine Hill.

The battle lines were becoming clear, on Olympus and on earth. Octavian and Apollo were on one side; Antony, Cleopatra, and the sensual deities that supported them were arrayed on the other. That particular lineup suited Octavian just fine. It helped him present himself as an upright officer determined to uphold traditional Roman values of duty and moderation. To be sure, Apollo was Greek in name and origin, but he had long resided in Rome, and he was compatible with the image of obedient piety that Octavian wanted to project. As the historian Ronald Syme put it, "There was no harm, but every advantage, in invoking the better sort of Greek deities."[4] Still, the prospect of strife among Olympian gods was far from reassuring to the Romans. Accordingly, Octavian did everything he could to suggest that *all* the gods actually supported him and that he was, in fact, not engaged in a civil war at all. He persuaded the Senate to declare war on Cleopatra alone, reducing Marc Antony to a minor player—a good Roman soldier led astray by a seductive queen.

As part of this reframing, Cleopatra herself was made to undergo a significant transformation. The Greek-Macedonian mother of Julius Caesar's son was now cast as a native Egyptian who worshipped strange, animal-like deities—"the barking Anubis and a whole progeny of grotesque gods," as Virgil put it.[5] That description was tendentious, to say the least. It is true that Cleopatra, unlike her Ptolemaic predecessors, had made a point of learning Egyptian, but the Olympian gods were still her gods, just as they had been the gods of Alexander and Ptolemy I, her ancestor. Still, history is written by the victors—and in 31 BC, Octavian's forces decisively defeated Antony and Cleopatra at the Battle of Actium. So the exotic Cleopatra, Octavian's creation, lives on in the popular imagination. Virgil, Shakespeare, Liz Taylor, and countless others through the ages have presented Cleopatra as a ravishing Egyptian beauty, though the portraits made during her lifetime suggest a different picture: in those she looks Roman and quite bland.

After vanquishing his rivals, Octavian continued to evolve. When he had first marched on Rome, he had called himself Caesar, like his adoptive father; now, as Rome's emperor, he changed his name again, taking on the title of Augustus. This new designation had an aura of religious authority: it meant something like "the Holy One," though its precise import was vague. The details mattered less, though, than the overall message of divine authority. In the highly volatile circumstances of the period, it was vital for a ruler to present the right kind of image, accompanied by the most appropriate myth.

Indeed, according to contemporary poets, Augustus's most urgent need was for an epic poem that would explain the past, present, and future of Rome—and his own place in it. The poets insist that he desired this poem more than anything else in the world. We may doubt their testimony, but it is true that he started demanding an epic remarkably early in his career, long before he had become emperor. Horace refused to write one; he self-deprecatingly claimed to be too short and fat for such an elevated task and kept to his favorite topics—wine, women, and friends. (When he grew older, he even wrote philosophical poems about how to say no to power and still maintain comfortable living standards.) It was Horace's friend Virgil who took up the task of writing an epic for Rome, even though he had every reason to resent Augustus, who had been responsible for the loss of the poet's land and home during the period of confiscations. The *Aeneid* was the result, and it pleased the emperor.

The poem tells the story of Aeneas, who survives the sack of

Troy and, after many trials, settles in Italy. It is set in the mythical past but reaches forward into Rome's present and its future. Jupiter explains how Aeneas will beget a great dynasty; how his descendant Romulus will found the city of Rome; and how Romulus's descendant Julius Caesar (that is, the emperor Augustus) will establish an "empire without end."[6] From the perspective of the *Aeneid*, Augustus's ascent to power is not just what happens, it is what *has* to happen. The *Aeneid* is influenced by Stoic philosophy: Jupiter's will is providential, as the Stoics maintained it was. But Virgil does not offer a simple, triumphalist story of Roman success. There are further voices in the *Aeneid*—of melancholy and even of despair. Aeneas himself feels impossibly burdened by the weight of destiny. He carries his father on his shoulders as he flees from Troy and, when his father dies, travels on by himself, weighed down by a future even heavier than his past. Aeneas is lonely, dutiful—and exceptionally violent. Augustus must have identified with him: the loneliness, the savagery, the absolute commitment to the future, were all his own.

Virgil too must have felt implicated in his own fateful description of Roman supremacy. Perhaps he viewed the *Aeneid* itself as his own burden of duty, an exercise in commitment and self-denial. After Virgil's death, some said that he had wanted to destroy his masterpiece. Virgil knew about loss, and he described it with particular poignancy in the figure of Dido, the African queen who hosted Aeneas during his travels and fell in love with him. She wanted him to stay with her, enjoy his share of happiness, and forget his obscure duties to the gods, guardians of Rome's future glory. Dido was an Epicurean at heart: she wanted happiness and was convinced that the gods did not care about human affairs. She was wrong about that. The gods did care, only not about her.

Human suffering is real and puzzling in the *Aeneid,* and so are the gods. There is no straightforward route to human happiness. Right at the beginning of the poem, Virgil introduces Aeneas, describes his trials, and asks why Juno treated him so viciously. How can there be such cruelty against a pious man; how can heavenly minds have such anger? *Tantaene animis caelestibus irae?* Virgil never answers his own questions, nor does he explain the nature of Juno's power. Of course, at one level she is the familiar Olympian goddess, who ever since the judgment of Paris has wanted to see Troy and the Trojans destroyed. At another level, Virgil identifies Juno with the African goddess Tanit, supporter of the Carthaginians. Simultaneously, he associates her with air (following the dominant etymology of her Greek name, Hera): Juno does not just send a storm at the beginning of the *Aeneid;* she somehow *is* the storm that almost wrecks Aeneas. Sketching out all these different possibilities, Virgil couples them with a promise that whatever Juno is, she will one day become a champion of Rome. There will be peace on Olympus and on earth, and Augustus will rule the world. In the words of Jupiter, "Even the spiteful Juno shall join me in fostering the cause of the Romans, the people with togas, the lords of creation."[7] Domestic and cosmic visions of peace all come together in this prophecy, perfectly summarizing the reach of Augustus's ambition.

Eager to suggest that all the Olympians had united behind him, Augustus must have wanted to picture the gods much as they appeared on the central section of the Parthenon frieze: a well-ordered family. Art historians have shown that Augustus favored classical sculpture rather than the later Hellenistic style, and that makes good sense. Classical images suggested balance and harmony, harking back to a pure and glorious Greece, before the Eastern excesses of Alexander the Great, the Ptolemies, Cleopatra, and her lover Marc Antony. But Augustus was never exclusive in his preferences: he could play Alexander, too, when it suited him. The idea of building a temple to Apollo right next to his own home was Alexandrian, as was the notion of adding a library to that temple, allowing poets and scholars to work there together. In art, Augustus was equally eclectic. His forum was broadly classical in style, but between its perfectly symmetrical, classical columns there were images of Zeus Ammon, that compound Greek-African deity so dear to Alexander. Just as Augustus's approach to government changed depending on time and circumstance, so did his style and his engagement with the gods.

This hybrid, changeable nature of power was so striking an aspect of the Augustan age that one poet decided to take it as his subject, on a grand scale. Ovid's *Metamorphoses* catalogs a huge range of divine and human transformations and is itself a poem in flux: both epic and resisting the conventions of epic, both stable and shifting, both Greek and Roman, the poem is Augustan and yet a piece of flippant subversion. Within the *Metamorphoses*, the story of Arachne offers, perhaps, Ovid's most straightforward commentary on his own enterprise. In his telling, Arachne is a Lydian girl "famous neither for her origins nor for her family, but for her art alone."[8] She can weave so well that she fancies she might be better than the goddess Minerva herself. The goddess predictably takes offense at that suggestion and challenges Arachne to a contest. Woman and goddess work tirelessly at their looms for many hours, each producing the best of her art. Minerva creates an image of the twelve Olympian gods, with Jupiter ruling over them all; each god is faithfully depicted and instantly recognizable. In the center of her composition, Minerva places herself in the act of winning a contest: she shows how she offered the Athenians the gift of the olive tree, beating Neptune's inferior gift of the horse. To teach an even clearer lesson to poor Arachne, Minerva decorates each corner of her tapestry with images of various arrogant mortals punished by gods.

At her own loom, meanwhile, Arachne weaves a very different picture: she displays the gods taking on all sorts of different shapes in order to satisfy their sexual urges. On her tapestry, Zeus is no stately patriarch surrounded by his family; he is a bull about to rape Europa, a swan in pursuit of Leda, a satyr after Antiope, an eagle grasping Asteria. Willful and disobedient, Arachne in her own way nevertheless produces perfect art. Not even Minerva can actually

Diego Velázquez's *Las Hilanderas* (ca. 1657) takes inspiration from the story of Arachne in Ovid's *Metamorphoses*. In the foreground, Minerva (disguised as an old woman) and Arachne compete in spinning. Their finished tapestries are displayed in the background, on a raised platform.

find fault with her work when she inspects it. But the goddess punishes the poor girl regardless: she hits her three times over the head and turns her into a spider.

That Minerva's tapestry depicts a scene of Augustan classicism is something that Ovid explicitly points out. The twelve Olympians, he says, appear there in *augusta gravitate,* in all their august majesty. Everything in Minerva's composition is arranged so as to demonstrate her power and to match image to reality. The twelve Olympian gods appear just as they are. And Minerva portrays herself, too, just as she is: victorious. Arachne, by contrast, weaves a portrait of deceptive gods, and her art is deceptive in its own right: "You would think that her image of Jupiter really was a bull," Ovid remarks.[9] Yet while Minerva is meant to embody justice, ultimately she needs no justification at all. She can strike down Arachne even though the girl's work is universally acknowledged to be faultless.

What did this portend for Ovid himself? The *Metamorphoses* included precisely the kinds of myths and transformations that feature on Arachne's masterpiece, and Arachne in general feels very much like Ovid's representative in this episode. Indeed, the portrait had prophetic power: just as Arachne was punished by Minerva, so Ovid eventually was punished by Augustus. When Ovid composed the *Metamorphoses* he was one of the most fashionable and admired poets in Rome, but given his subversive energy, it is not too surprising that he eventually fell afoul of the emperor. In AD 8, Augustus banished Ovid to Tomis on the Black Sea, where he died some ten years later. The reasons for Ovid's exile are notoriously unclear: the poet laconically stated that it all happened because of "a poem and an error."[10] The poem may have been the *Ars Amatoria,* which taught the Romans how to seduce married women precisely while Augustus was passing laws against adultery. And the error may have had something to do with Augustus's granddaughter Julia, who broke the laws against adultery and was exiled at the same time as Ovid. Her restless, mobile ways could not be tolerated while her grandfather was asserting his stately, timeless, Olympian authority.

The competition between Minerva and Arachne in the *Metamorphoses* stands for a broader conflict between classicism and Hellenistic innovation, morality and deception, the power of the emperor and the different truth of art. Of course, the two sides in those debates were never exact opposites of each other. Minerva and Arachne are both excellent weavers. They both have a truth to tell—and they both lie in the process. Arachne deceives herself above all: she thinks that the competition is about artistic merit, whereas it is decided on sheer power. But she is also right about the gods, because they do act to satisfy their lust. In real life, meanwhile, Augustus and Ovid also mirrored each other. Augustus had the emperor's ability to enforce law and morality as he saw fit; but Ovid had the unstoppable power to expose the emperor's vanity and his reliance on brute force. As for the gods, both of the tapestries reveal something about them. The Olympians do indeed take on different disguises in pursuit of their selfish goals. Yet they also remain a stable, and instantly recognizable, family of twelve.

PART V

Disguise: Christianity and Islam

Christianity and Islam dealt a fatal blow to pagan religion—but the Olympian gods managed to survive. Their last worshippers hid their statues in cellars and wells, covered up mythological mosaics, and moved cult objects to the countryside, where they could still use them undetected. These determined pagans played a crucial part in the history of the Olympian gods, because in later ages archaeologists would uncover what they had hidden and thus revive classical sculptures of the gods. Christian and Muslim scholars also played an important role in the gods' history, though not always in the way they intended. The Church Fathers, for example, argued tirelessly against the pagan deities and thereby made them sound powerful and important.

Denied the status of gods, the Olympians gradually reinvented themselves as demons, temptations, fictions, and other pernicious powers. In the Arab world, meanwhile, they haunted those who studied Greek philosophy and science, dominating their explanations of dreams, humors, atoms, and celestial bodies. Through astrology, in particular, they continued to affect the human mind. Religiously bankrupt, the gods of Olympus found ever more creative ways to exert their power in the Middle Ages—and eventually, after a long identity crisis, they emerged victorious.

13

Human Like You

It is hard to believe that Jesus was born only a few years after the sophisticated and scandalous Ovid; they seem to belong to entirely different eras. Yet while Ovid was enjoying the high life in Rome, planning his *Metamorphoses,* and reflecting about the power of human art, the pregnant Mary—according to the Gospels—was making her way to Bethlehem. Her child, born to poverty and oppression, hardly seemed likely to inspire millions of people, but he would soon do just that. Christianity spread with astonishing rapidity in the ancient world. At first it was repressed, but eventually the tide turned against the worshippers of the ancient gods. Now it was they who could practice their rites only in secret, as "private citizens" or "rustics" (for that is what the term *pagani* originally meant).

The sudden rise and lasting success of Christianity can be interpreted in many different ways, depending in large measure on our own religious beliefs and consequent ideas about what might count as an explanation. In his celebrated *History of the Decline and Fall of the Roman Empire* (1776–1788), Edward Gibbon distinguishes, polemically, between theology and history in a famous passage: "The theologian may indulge the pleasing task of describing Religion as she descended from Heaven, arrayed in her native purity. A more melancholy duty is imposed on the historian. He must discover the inevitable mixture of error and corruption which she contracted in a long residence upon Earth, among a weak and degenerate race of beings."[1] Gibbon's own melancholy view is that Christianity spread because it was inflexible, promised life after death, made good use of alleged miracles, promoted "pure and austere morals," and was exceptionally well organized. Unsympathetic though he is, this analysis has considerable merit.

That the early Christians were inflexible is confirmed by the reactions they inspired: from the beginning, they met with a most unusual degree of hostility. The official repressions curbed their influence for a while, but they also gave prominence to the Christian faith and suggested that it was special. Roman authorities were known to tolerate a wide variety of religious cults and beliefs—yet they not only approved the execution of Jesus, but actively persecuted his followers. When a fire broke out in Rome in AD 64, for example, the emperor Nero sought to pin it on the Christians. Faced with accusations that he had started the conflagration himself in order to clear some space for his magnificent villa, Nero needed to find alternative culprits—and the Christians, widely known and generally disliked, suited his purpose ideally. According to Christian sources of the third century AD, the apostles Peter and Paul were among Nero's victims. Whether or not those reports can be trusted (and there is considerable contradiction in what they claim), it is apparent that within a few decades of Jesus's death, Christians were visible in Rome and regarded as easy targets. Tacitus, who lived through the fire, offers firsthand evidence for this. His description of the events is so hostile to the first Christian martyrs that it commands trust as a historical source:

> To end the rumor that he had started the fire himself, Nero sub-
> stituted as the guilty party—and punished with the choicest
> penalties—those hated for their vices, popularly called Christians.

The originator of their name, one Christus, had been executed in the Principate of Tiberius by the governor Pontius Pilate. The deadly superstition he inspired was checked for a time, but broke out again, not only in Judaea, the origin of the evil, but even in the capital. . . . Those killed were made an object of mockery: they were nailed to crosses, or covered with animal skins and torn to pieces by dogs; when daylight failed, they were set alight as torches, to lighten the darkness.[2]

Although there are some uncertainties about Tacitus's exact wording at the end of this passage, Nero clearly tortured and killed Christians with perverse inventiveness. Only the number of deaths remains uncertain: ancient sources are silent on that score. As a result, scholars tend to reveal more about themselves than about history when they offer their estimates. Generally speaking, the less sympathetic historians are to the Christian faith, the lower the number of martyrs they will admit.

The dedication of the early Christians to their cause comes through in many different accounts, both Christian and pagan. The Acts of the Martyrs, a collection of early Christian testimonies, describes in detail how professions of faith—and ensuing persecutions—broke apart families and communities. Husbands were set against wives, daughters against fathers, brothers against sisters. Today Christianity is sometimes associated with traditional family values, but in its early history it ripped through the fabric of society, and sought to create alternative structures. Christians called one another "brother" and "sister," acknowledged no difference in class or rank, and accepted even slaves in their number. It seems that they adapted the language of Athenian democracy to describe their own new institutions: *ekklēsia* (church, but also the ancient Athenian assembly), *leitourgia* (liturgy, service, Mass; but also public service in ancient Athens), *episkopos* (bishop, but also "overseer" in the Athenian imperial administration). At a practical level, they used the formidable infrastructure of the Roman

Empire—well-built roads and functional postal services—to reach
potential converts everywhere from Africa and the Near East to the
far north of Europe. In short, early Christian missionaries were
building an entirely new community. They were *edifying*, in the literal sense of the word.

The rewards they promised were enormous: the resurrection of
the body and the life ever after. Miracles offered a crucial form of
testimony, but it was the Christian message that won over new
believers. People suddenly felt that they mattered, that they were
loved, and that they would be saved. The emphasis on life after
death and on communion with God answered urgent needs. Traditional Roman religion scored badly precisely in those areas where
Christians were making the greatest promises: it had nothing
encouraging to say about death or the underworld and offered no
intimate, loving relationship with the gods. In origin, Roman religion was not about individuals at all, but about keeping the relationship between the gods and the state in optimal condition. To be
sure, the greatest men in Rome eventually forged connections to the
gods of Olympus, but those connections only emphasized the distance between ordinary people and the great gods and emperors who
ruled over them. Christianity was different: it promised a God who
paid personal attention to every person, however lowly. "Blessed are
the meek," preached Jesus, according to Matthew, "because they
will inherit the earth."[3]

Other cults, in the years before and after the birth of Christ,
also seemed to respond to needs that traditional Roman religion
had failed to meet. Bacchism, as already mentioned, promoted its
own intimate relationship with the god of wine and madness and
initiated people into "mysteries" that supposedly eased their transition from life to death. Indeed, Jesus and Bacchus could look similar from a certain angle. Both had a divine father and a mortal
mother; both could turn water into wine; both encouraged feast-
ing as a form of communion and brought together radically different people—men and women, slaves and free, rich and poor, Roman

citizens and their subjects. Some have argued that the Gospels and the Acts of the Apostles even deliberately allude to the Bacchic mysteries. That is hard to prove, in my view, but it would not be too surprising.[4] The apostle Paul, for one, was a Hellenized Jew from Tarsus, a flourishing center of Greek education. He must have known Euripides's *Bacchae* and may have been familiar with the Bacchic mysteries as well. Given that his mission was addressed mainly to Greek communities, he could well have made use of the language of Dionysos.

There were, of course, crucial differences between Bacchism and early Christianity—not just in terms of beliefs, but also in the practices that these cults promoted. Though we do not know the details of the "mysteries," it is fairly clear that sex, violence, and wine brought people close to Bacchus. Christianity, by contrast, promoted self-denial; an ascetic streak concerning meat, drink, sex, and luxury developed early on in the history of the faith. Some have argued that personal discipline was in itself a reason for the success of Christianity: "Disciplining causes people to achieve," as one rather stern scholar of ancient religion put it.[5] Nevertheless, Christian and Bacchic practices may not have looked so different to outsiders. Tacitus, for instance, spoke of "Christian vices." He may have understood the Mass as some mock cannibalistic feast or, more generally (and correctly), seen Christian converts as a threat to the traditional structures of family and society.

It was difficult for early Christian preachers to articulate the differences between their own religion and the cults practiced all around them. One problem was that they were pushing against a long-standing habit of translation and accommodation. People were used to identifying their own gods with those of their neighbors—or were content to keep their views and practices to themselves, in order to live more peacefully with those around them. Christian missionaries despised both attitudes. Like the Jews, they refused to sacrifice to the emperor; unlike them, they wanted to convert the entire world. This attitude proved to be too great a challenge for the Roman authorities. Christian worshippers were ordered to perform traditional sacrifices and faced torture and death if they refused to do so. Sacrifice thus quickly became the most contentious issue in the clashes between Christian converts and the wider community.[6]

It was so central, in fact, that it still colors modern perceptions of the ancient world. Historians tend to describe Greek and Roman religion as a matter of *practices* rather than beliefs. Because persecutions focused on sacrifice (what people did or refused to do), it is tempting to conclude that all that mattered to pagan communities was ritual performance. In fact, of course, practices went together with deeply held commitments and explanations. Christian converts refused to sacrifice not only because the act was incompatible with their own beliefs, but because they wanted to challenge the beliefs of the people around them. They disputed the whole system of sacrifices, propitiations, and divinations—together with the bargaining and pleading with the gods that went with it. The problem, they soon discovered, was that it was difficult to shake off people's beliefs in the ancient deities. Pagan religion was extremely flexible, and the gods of Olympus, in particular, could adapt to all sorts of different circumstances. When put under pressure, they could even appear in the guise of Christian apostles.

A passage in the Acts of the Apostles illustrates this particular feat. When Paul and Barnabas traveled to the city of Lystra, in southern Turkey, they healed a cripple "lame from his mother's womb."[7] Impressed with this miracle, local people immediately concluded that the two visitors were gods disguised in human form and proceeded to identify them forthwith: "Barnabas they called Zeus, and Paul they called Hermes, because he was the chief speaker." The crowd wanted to make sacrifices to Zeus and Hermes and thus acknowledge their divinity, but the apostles acted swiftly to forestall this. They tore off their clothes and rushed into the crowd, shouting that they were only men, "human like you." Then, once they had prevented the infamous sacrifice, they started to preach, offering the good news about the living God. They insisted that "in the past, he let all nations go their own way, but did not leave himself without testimony: he showed kindness by giving you rain from heaven and crops in their seasons." Even with their sermon, however, they had difficulty preventing their own deification.

Biblical scholars have dismissed this whole episode as a fiction. The argument is that the author of the Acts did not accompany Paul and Barnabas to Lystra, and because he had no actual information about that visit, he made up the story of the sacrifice as a piece of literary embellishment. Indeed, some readers have seen in this passage an allusion to Ovid's *Metamorphoses*. This last suggestion seems very far-fetched to me, however. The identity of the author of the Acts is unknown, but it is unlikely that he was familiar with the details of Ovid's poetry and inclined to use them to make up stories about St. Paul.[8] The narrative in the Acts was not a playful literary game; it was an all-out attack on ancient practices and beliefs. The author of the Acts offered a scene of stunned confusion and rapid—even instant—translation. Confronted with a miracle, local people reached out for what they thought they knew about the gods, assuming their universality, anthropomorphism, ability to manifest themselves as ordinary mortals, and need of sacrifices.

We do not know, of course, what really happened in Lystra. One of the most influential modern commentators on the Acts plays down the whole episode and finds the reaction of the local people exaggerated: "It is highly improbable that the pagan priest would immediately believe that the two wonder-workers were Zeus and Hermes, quite apart from the fact that the animals had first to be brought from the pasture, and the garlands woven."[9] In this prosaic interpretation, the two miracle workers begin to look like tinkers who straighten out tools and pots rather than the limbs of a living cripple. The people in Lystra are expected to remain calm and rational even when confronted with something they cannot possibly explain. It seems better to interpret the moment on its own terms. Whatever actually took place, and whatever Paul and Barnabas reported about their visit, the author of the Acts described a scene of amazement. People, we are told, spoke to one another in Lycaonian; Paul and Barnabas presumably did not understand their language but were quickly offered an explanation in Greek. The Olympian gods appeared precisely at that moment of translation from one language into another: Zeus and Hermes, or Jupiter and Mercury (in subsequent Latin versions of the Bible), thus acted in their usual capacity, as international mediators. They were trying to help people make sense of one another, but this time their services were squarely refused. The apostles insisted that people would henceforth unite only in the name of the true God.

The general message is clear, even if some details in the performance of the apostles may still seem puzzling. It is not immediately obvious, for example, why Barnabas and Paul decided to tear off their clothes to prove their humanity. After all, the gods of Olympus were generally represented in the form of naked human statues. Perhaps the bodies of the two apostles did not look divine. In any case, the decision to strip represented a direct attack on anthropomorphic visions of the gods. Raphael, in his interpretation of the scene, understood this precisely. When he illustrated the sacrifice at Lystra for the Sistine Chapel, he placed a naked statue of Hermes at the vanishing point on the horizon, showing just what the apostles were trying to chase away.

Despite their intransigence, even Christians had to accept that there were some similarities between their own beliefs and those of the people they were trying to convert. In Lystra, for example, Paul insisted that the Christian God was responsible for rain and crops, thus evoking Zeus the thunderer, who had a particular association with agriculture in local cult. And, of course, Zeus resembled the Christian God in other respects, too—as father figure and ruler of fate, for example. Other aspects of his personality, however, seemed objectionable: Zeus was a serial rapist, a violent king, and a deceptive shape-changer, among many other vices. For these reasons, Augustine of Hippo vigorously argued, in the fifth century AD, against identifying Jupiter with the Christian God. He did not object to the ancient

Raphael's *The Sacrifice at Lystra* (ca. 1657) illustrates a famous episode from the Acts of the Apostles. When confronted with a miracle, people in Lystra tried to sacrifice to Paul and Barnabas, thinking that they were Hermes and Zeus.

practice of translating divine names, but he worried that it might lead to entirely wrong notions:

> If Jupiter is God—the God who controls all the causes of events, and of all substances, and of all things in nature—then people should stop slandering him with scandalous stories. They should replace Jupiter with some fictional character as the protagonist of those stories. This would be far better than saying that Jupiter is both the thunderer and an adulterer, the ruler of the universe and a drunkard, controlling the highest causes of all substances and all things in nature, and yet acting with the vilest intentions himself.[10]

Unlike the author of the Acts, Augustine knew Ovid's *Metamorphoses* very well. His polemic alludes to a passage where Jupiter transforms himself into a bull in order to rape Europa—a metamorphosis of which Ovid had remarked that "love and dignity do not go well together."[11] Augustine, a brilliant reader of ancient literature, pounced on this insight to articulate his own position. Christian love and dignity did in fact go well together, he insisted; the problem with Jupiter was his animal lust. The differences between the ancient poet and the Christian saint were made clear. Ovid wanted to show how Jupiter united contradictory impulses, how he could be both a majestic Olympian ruler and a randy bull, how he could mix, transform, confuse, and damage and still reign. Augustine, by contrast, wanted to keep things separate. If Jupiter was God, then he would be no bull, and most certainly no rapist. And since all poets agreed that Zeus did transform himself and rape, then he was not God. Such distinctions became fundamental to Christian theological thought, but they brought to the surface an awkward question: If the pagan gods were not gods, then what were they?

Demons

The most important, and unexpected, event in the history of Christianity was the conversion of the emperor Constantine in the early fourth century AD. Historians speculate about what might have happened had Constantine not converted; some suggest that without strong imperial endorsement, Christianity would have died out, like many other cults that were once popular in late antiquity. Whether or not that is true, Constantine certainly had a profound influence on the history of Christianity, and consequently on the history of the Olympian gods.

At the time he converted, the gods of Olympus were on display everywhere. They dominated city landscapes from Africa to northern Europe, from Asia to Spain: their statues stood in temples, overlooked town squares, watched over crossroads, peeped from fountains and archways, and took pride of place in many wealthy villas. Nobody could imagine a city without them—not even Constantine himself. And so it was that when he founded his new imperial capital in AD 324, he filled it with the most beautiful statues of the gods, looted from all over the Roman Empire. As Jerome put it, Constantinople "was dedicated upon the nudity of all other cities."[1] This description was as double-edged as Constantine's own

actions: divine nudes were brought into Constantinople from far
and wide, and thereby other cities were left nude, stripped of their
gods. Why was the Christian emperor Constantine filling his capital
with pagan statues? Eusebius, bishop of Caesarea, tried hard to give
an answer to this question in his biography of Constantine, written
in the fourth century AD. He argued that the sanctuaries of the
other cities were denuded so that people in Constantinople could
more easily insult the dethroned gods. This was a valiant defense
of the first Christian emperor, but it hardly sounds convincing.
Whatever the pagan statues were doing in Constantinople, they
were not meant to be abused. The effort required to transport them
and the way in which they were then proudly displayed in the city all
indicate that they were valued—though exactly why is harder to
untangle.

To understand Constantine's puzzling attitudes toward the
Olympian gods, it helps to consider the broader context in which he
lived and ruled. He grew up in what is now Turkey, at the court of
Diocletian, one of the four emperors who ruled the Roman Empire.
The imperial court was a lively, multicultural environment. The
young Constantine probably attended lectures by both pagan and
Christian scholars and met people coming from all over the empire.
Above all, he learned early that religious authority and imperial
power needed to be closely aligned. That was a fundamental insight
of Roman religion—and it never deserted Constantine. In 303,
Diocletian instigated the most far-reaching and vicious persecutions yet against the Christians, probably in response to increasing
anxieties about the unity of the empire. Constantine did nothing to
prevent those persecutions (a fact that later became a liability for
him), perhaps because he too considered that Christian preachers
were weakening and dividing the empire—but more probably
because, at that point in time, he was more worried about his own
safety and success than about the Christian Church. His father,
Constantius, was the emperor in charge of the western portion of
the Roman Empire; Diocletian, in the east, kept Constantine at his

court almost as a hostage to ensure his father's good behavior. When Diocletian died, the situation became even more dangerous for Constantine. Eventually, he managed to leave Turkey and join his father in Britain, where he was campaigning against the Picts. Constantius died in Eboracum (modern York) in 306, and the troops immediately proclaimed Constantine as his successor. Their proclamation did not quite settle the issue. Emperors were not necessarily appointed by their troops, nor did emperors' sons necessarily inherit their fathers' titles. Over the following years, Constantine hacked his way toward total control of the Roman Empire. He moved from Britain to Trier in Germany, then marched on Rome.

Before the decisive battle at the Milvian Bridge, north of Rome, he had a dream—or a vision—that changed the course of history. Exactly what Constantine saw remains unclear. Apparently, the sun-god Apollo appeared to him in the company of Victory, or so Constantine initially claimed. Eventually, it also transpired that he had seen a cross above the sun and had heard the injunction "Conquer by this." Whatever the exact details, Constantine concluded that he should send his soldiers into battle with a new symbol, the Chi-Rho: the first two Greek letters of Christ's name, intertwined as ☧. The soldiers no doubt carried other symbols, too, but Constantine recognized in their victory the hand of the Christian God and wanted to secure the favor of such a powerful ally for the empire and himself. Only a year after the Battle of the Milvian Bridge, he passed the Edict of Milan, which guaranteed religious freedom for all people. In the following years, he undertook a massive program of church building. In Rome, he provided a basilica near the city walls, now known as St. John Lateran, and oversaw the foundation of St. Peter's, south of the Tiber.

Yet despite his massive investment in churches, when he founded Constantinople a few years later, he also set up numerous statues of the Olympian gods. The most prominent was a bronze likeness of Apollo-the-Sun, which stood on top of a great column in the forum and represented the emperor himself; legend had it that it had been looted from Phrygia. Famous statues were removed from many other places and cities, too. In front of the Senate, Constantine placed a statue of Zeus from Dodona, in western Greece, and one of Athena from the city of Lindos, on the island of Rhodes. Inside it he housed the nine Muses, taken from Mount Helicon (where Hesiod had allegedly once met them). Dozens of statues adorned the baths of Zeuxippus; a tedious poem preserved in the *Palatine Anthology* lists them all.[2] Most of them represented heroes of mythology, but there were also poets, orators, philosophers—and gods.

Whatever Constantine was doing by importing those statues, the trend did not stop when he died. A great collection was assembled in the palace of Lausus, a eunuch who worked as a chamberlain in the imperial court. It included the famous statue of Zeus from Olympia (one of the Seven Wonders of the World), a Lindian Athena made entirely of emerald, the Cnidian Aphrodite by Praxiteles, and a celebrated Hera from the island of Samos. Clearly, these statues were valued for their beauty, and the Lausus collection had something in common with a museum. (Indeed, it is a terrible loss for modern museums that all the statues assembled in Constantinople eventually crumbled or were destroyed. Not one of them survives, and the Louvre and the British Museum make do with mere Roman copies of those great masterpieces of Greek art.) But the value of the statues in the fourth century was not simply artistic. Some people in the city may still have regarded them as images of true gods. Many, certainly, continued to worship the emperor as represented by Apollo's statue: this was a cult that Constantine did nothing to squash.

When Constantine had his famous dream, Christians represented only a minority in the Roman Empire. Estimates are notoriously difficult to make, but they seem to have accounted for about 10 percent of the population.[3] Although Constantine decided to throw in his lot with the Christian God, most of his subjects, and even his administration, still worshipped the ancient deities. They made sacrifices at temples, relied on divination, and honored the gods by participating in athletic and artistic competitions. Accordingly, when he set up his new capital, Constantine did not just import statues of the gods, but went as far as allowing the restoration of old temples (Constantinople was founded on the site of the ancient city of Byzantium) and even financed a new temple of Victory. We may choose to interpret Constantine's building program as a concession to his ministers and advisers, or a sign of hypocrisy, or a token of his broad religious inclusiveness. All these explanations have been suggested, but for my part I favor a simpler account for his actions: In the fourth century AD, all imperial cities included statues and temples of the Olympian gods. That is simply how cities looked—and Constantine did not rethink the whole urban landscape. It is no accident that the great churches he built in Rome, including the basilicas of St. John Lateran and St. Peter, were in the periphery. The city center still belonged to the gods of Olympus.

It was only gradually that people started to feel discomfort, and even hostility, toward images of the pagan gods. Eusebius's argument—that the emperor filled his capital "with brazen statues of the most exquisite workmanship . . . so that they could be held up to the ridicule and sport of all beholders"—sounds rather muddled: he recognized "exquisite workmanship" while encouraging "ridicule" as a response.[4] He was not alone in expressing such conflicting feelings. In the fourth century AD, fascination with antique statues and anxiety about them were widespread indeed. The Old Testament was clear on the subject of worshipping idols, and Paul categorically insisted that the Greeks "sacrificed to demons, and not to God."[5] The notion thus spread that demons inhabited statues representing the gods of Olympus.

Classical art suffered greatly as a result of this notion—and not just in Constantinople. In Gaza, for example, there was a nude figure of Aphrodite that was a particular favorite among local women. As early as 402, though, Bishop Porphyry confronted that statue, accompanied by a crowd of Christians bearing crosses. We are told that "the demon who inhabited the statue, being unable to contemplate the terrible sign, departed from the marble with great

Two men topple the statue of a pagan god. This fourth-century painting decorated a catacomb in Rome, one of the many underground tunnels where early Christians buried their dead.

tumult, and, as he did so, threw the statue down and broke it into many pieces."[6] I doubt that the wreckage was altogether spontaneous, but the belief that demons had to be cast out of ancient cult statues was strong in late antiquity. For centuries, Christian preachers went around the countryside expelling "the demon Jupiter" or "the devil Mercury" from the rustic haunts where they still lingered. The lives of saints are full of such encounters. When St. Benedict climbed Monte Cassino, for example, he smashed a local statue of Apollo and converted his temple into an oratory of St. John. The evicted god, we're told, then started to torment the saint, appearing to him as a black monster with flaming eyes.[7] Apollo, god of measure and beauty, had turned into a medieval dragon.

Like pagans, Christians had trouble treating cult statues simply as objects; they seemed too powerful, too full of life. Yet some people did start trying to detach representations of the gods from their religious significance. Cult statues were often removed from temples and placed in what we would call "secular" locations, such as market squares or public baths. By supervising such relocations, Christian officers acknowledged the beauty of ancient statuary while denying its religious value. The risk was that a statue could continue to attract worshippers even when it was removed from its sacred contexts; in some places that led to further relocations, in others to outright destruction. Meanwhile, the pagans were also considering their options. Faced with increasing threats to their cults, they tried to protect their gods by hiding or burying the statues. There was devotion in what they did, but sometimes also a more secular desire to preserve objects of beauty. Zosimos, a pagan historian of the late fifth century, noted that the statues of Zeus and Athena in front of the Senate house in Constantinople fortunately remained intact when a fire broke out and thus continued to give pleasure to the "more cultivated" people in the city.[8] Pagan admirers of the statues did not necessarily present themselves as devout worshippers of idols, but as connoisseurs of art.

Archaeological evidence is crucial for piecing together what happened to Olympian statuary in the course of late antiquity and the Middle Ages—and the picture that emerges is extremely complex.[9] Practices varied considerably from region to region and from period to period. In some parts of the Roman Empire statues were left to decay gradually; in others they were viciously mutilated or destroyed altogether. In some cities cult images were repeatedly moved from place to place, while in others they were carefully buried. The trouble with archaeology, however, is that it gives no direct access to what people thought. The slowly decaying statues, for example, may yet have exerted their fascination even while they fell into disrepair. Written sources suggest that as statues deteriorated, the demons inside them underwent a subtle change of personality. Initially seen as extremely dangerous, they eventually became only mildly sinister, and some of them even turned out to be demonically useful. Statues of Athena, in particular, often fulfilled the role of talismans, averting minor calamities such as rat infestations or heat waves. Other demons living in ancient statues offered more specific services. Theophylact Simocatta, writing in the seventh century, included a few interesting observations about demons in his work.[10]

He claimed that when the emperor Maurice was assassinated in Constantinople in 602, some demons immediately reported the news in the city of Alexandria. Several statues, he said, slid down from their pedestals and walked right up to a calligrapher who was returning home late at night after a party and told him what had happened to the poor emperor, leaving him stunned and anxious. Nine days later, official human messengers arrived in Alexandria and confirmed the news. Demons could travel quickly and thereby learn about events that had taken place very far away. They often tried to pass off their speed as foreknowledge, but that, Simocatta insisted, was not a gift they actually possessed.

Just as demons could be useful, so could ancient culture more generally. To explain their relationship with pagan antiquity, early Christian writers often invoked the Jewish exodus from Egypt. According to the Bible, when the Hebrew people returned home after their captivity, they carried away many gold and silver vessels belonging to the Egyptians in order to use them for their own rituals. Just so, the writers said, Christians should plunder the riches of the Greek and Roman past to the greater glory of God. It was on the strength of this argument that much classical culture was appropriated and preserved. Ancient literature became part of ecclesiastical schooling, ancient temples were converted into churches, and ancient philosophy was mined for arguments in support of the Christian God.

It was in this fashion, as looted goods, that the Olympian gods managed to survive into the Christian age. Even after most of their statues had been destroyed or buried, they continued to live on in stories: classical poetry, brimming full of gods, remained the cornerstone of a good education right through the Middle Ages. Homer was a central text in Byzantine culture, while Virgil and Ovid were widely read in the West. And to help account for the presence of pagan deities in the educational curriculum, Christian scholars again applied the plundering-Egyptian-silver approach, mining ancient sources for information about what these gods were or represented (given that they could not actually be divine). Many Greek and Roman texts quoted in earlier chapters of this book, from Xenophanes to Varro, have reached us only through the polemics of Christian authors, who used them to explain the nature of the pagan gods.

One idea that the Christians picked up from ancient sources was that the Olympian deities might have been real people who got treated as gods by their gullible contemporaries. Euhemerus, in the third century BC, had suggested that the Olympians were originally benefactors of humanity; and Arnobius, in the third century AD, adapted that notion with a twist, arguing that the gods had been deified for their crimes rather than their good services. "Venus was a courtesan and Cinyras, king of Cyprus, worshipped her," Arnobius claimed with typical vigor.[11] Jupiter, he said, had been some wicked man who enjoyed the ballet, the theater, athletic competitions, and "looking at horses running to no purpose."[12] There could be no true holiness in a god who spent his time watching sports. And in any case, it was absurd to project divinity onto real flesh-and-blood people. As a Christian, Arnobius was particularly sensitive to what it meant for God to take on human form, to the vulnerability and pain that a real body implied—and he found the anthropomorphic portrayal of the Olympians to be completely unconvincing. Should we imagine, Arnobius asked, that the Olympian gods needed to shave? Did they have divine barbers on Olympus, keeping them trim and tidy?[13] Predictably, he also attacked divine sex, though what worried Arnobius was not so much its indecency as its sheer randomness. Was it really imaginable that Jupiter, ruler of the universe, might never have been born but for some chance attraction between primordial deities? It was inconceivable, he said, that "without degrading pleasures and sensual embraces, there may never have been a ruler of the universe; and even to this day the gods would have no king, and heaven would stand without its lord."[14] Arnobius cunningly projected onto Jupiter that very human anxiety about our own origins, about the chance embrace that stands at the beginning of every human life. Surely, he argued, the true God was different: eternal, not begotten.

Among pagan authors, Arnobius's favorite was Plato—not so much because of Plato's views on spiritual immortality and divine transcendence (which were of fundamental importance for other early Christian authors), but because he had criticized poetry and questioned the truth of epic. Like Plato, Arnobius was suspicious of allegory as a means of justifying poetry and its amazing claims. He argued that allegory revealed more about the mind of the interpreter than the true nature of the gods. Perhaps the union between Jupiter and Ceres could indeed be interpreted as "rain falling into the bosom of the earth," Arnobius admitted, but then there was no knowing whether some other explanation might not be equally valid: "All that allegory, as it is called, is taken from narratives that have been made obscure on purpose, and allows everyone to read whatever meaning he likes."[15] Arnobius himself preferred down-to-earth, literal interpretations whenever possible. Confronted with Zeus's metamorphosis into a bull to rape Europa, he invited readers to go ahead and imagine the scene: "Jupiter, father of the gods, ruler of the universe, adorned with the horns of an ox, shaking his hairy ears, with his feet contracted into hoofs, chewing green grass, and having behind him a tail and hind legs smeared over with soft excrement."[16] And then he delivered his punch line: Were Christian beliefs really so strange, so very unlikely, in comparison with this pagan nonsense?

Arnobius fought a losing battle against allegory. Despite his best efforts, it proved to be too attractive and convenient a solution to the problem of the gods in classical literature. And it had excellent Christian credentials: after all, Jesus himself had spoken in parables. More important, allegory seemed necessary in order to reinterpret the Old Testament in light of the New. The Bible was, as one scholar put it, "only slightly more amenable to automatic Christianization than Ovid's *Metamorphoses*."[17] Christianity sought new meaning in ancient stories, separating itself from both the Jewish and the classical tradition. Allegory and metaphor were crucial tools in that enterprise. Christian writers, carrying looted culture across the Red Sea, were transporting ancient wisdom—and the Greek for "transport" is *metaphor*.

Together with the notion that ancient poets spoke allegorically went a stealthy admiration for their imagination. How could they look at rain falling on dry land and describe it as sex between Jupiter and Ceres? That required a lively mind and permission to speak it. Early medieval writers were uneasy about such poetic license, and not only because it was often licentious. Even apart from the inventive sex scenes, the lying, cheating, adultery, and general silliness on Olympus, there was a more fundamental danger in ancient poetry. It made people imagine things—even gods—that did not actually exist, and it did not give a clear indication of where the line was between reality and the imagination. Lactantius, one of Arnobius's pupils (and later a teacher of Constantine's son), was concerned with the absence of a sure way to distinguish between truth and tale. "People do not know what the limit of poetic license is, or to what extent it is permissible to proceed in fictionising," he wrote. But he also admitted that "the poet's function consists precisely in this: transferring, with gracefulness, what actually happened into some other appearance by figurative language."[18] In the end, Lactantius tended to hold readers, rather than authors, responsible. Poets were doing only what they were supposed to do when they blurred the line between reality and figure of speech; it was the readers' task to draw the correct conclusions. Ancient literature was therefore acceptable, as long as it was accompanied by a good Christian education.

The gods as demons, as real people, as products of the imagination: These different theories were not entirely compatible, of course, but they all had their roots in antiquity. In origin, the Greek gods had been both real and metaphorical at the same time; it was precisely that mixture that had made them so powerful. But Christian thinkers took a more rigid approach: either the Olympians were evildoers or they were figures of speech. Both strategies cut them down to size. As a real-life adulterer, Jupiter could not be as impressive as his mythological persona. And if, on the other hand, he was just an allegory, a figure of speech, then there was no real power to him at all. The problem was to decide upon one single strategy against the Olympian gods and abide by it.

It was Augustine who took on that challenge and attempted to put together an all-encompassing Christian theory of the pagan gods. In his *City of God Against the Pagans,* he presented the ancient deities as malign fantasies with no real truth to them—which made them demons, ultimately, because the devil was an illusionist, whereas God was Truth. Moreover, he said, because they were demons, the pagan gods could also take on the appearance of real people. In this way, Augustine found space for Euhemerus-style explanations as well. In fact, he rather liked the idea of gods as mistakenly deified mortals, because it accounted for the very human appearance of the gods of Olympus and the literary detail of their personalities. Allegorical interpretations often seemed rather abstract, Augustine noted: "A far more credible account of the gods is given, when people say that they were once human beings—and that each was worshipped according to his personality, manners, deeds and circumstances."[19] Jupiter, for example, was probably some vicious young prince who wanted to kill his father, Saturn; or else he was not vicious himself but was obliged to fight against an evil parent. Whatever the historical details (and Augustine wisely admitted he could not be sure about them), they made better sense than clever allegories, because they could accommodate the textual richness of the gods as characters.

Augustine was a sensitive reader of poetry, and his explanations proved to be influential. Even so, the gods were never tamed into a coherent theory. For many centuries, they would feature both in works of history (often in the guise of ancient kings and queens) and in complex allegorical explanations (of abstract qualities such as virtues and passions). The two traditions, historical and allegorical, flourished side by side right through the Middle Ages and beyond. In historical narratives, the gods often looked like ordinary medieval characters, such as damsels with pointy hats and knights in shining armor. In one manuscript, for example, Jupiter is depicted in the guise of a crusader killing Saturn, with a medieval city labeled "Crete" in the background. That label traces a route all the way back to Euhemerus and, ultimately, to Hesiod's *Theogony*, composed more than two thousand years earlier. Ovid's *Metamorphoses*, meanwhile, seemed to inspire ever more elaborate allegorical interpretations, such as the anonymous *Ovide moralisé* and Pierre Bersuire's *Ovidius moralizatus*, both from the fourteenth century. These works argued that Ovid had deliberately concealed profound theological truths under a veil of allegory, to protect them from the

In this French illuminated manuscript, Jupiter confronts his father, Saturn. A medieval city labeled "Crete" can be seen in the background, while the two gods look rather like crusaders.

gaze of the profane. But, of course, it was also possible to reject such arguments altogether. If Ovid needed to be moralized, then perhaps he was not moral in the first place. It was that ambiguity, that allegorical double-dealing, that preserved ancient literature through the centuries and betrayed its vitality.

Over time, ancient stories gave birth to new ones. Chaucer, for instance, was inspired by Bersuire and other Ovidian moralizers, and his *Canterbury Tales* contained frequent references to Ovid's *Metamorphoses*. Most famously, Chaucer's "Manciple's Tale" included a retelling of the myth of Apollo and Coronis (a mortal lover of Apollo who had dared betray him), turning it into a warning against the dangers of gossip. Chaucer was also inspired by Boccaccio, the most exuberant storyteller in fourteenth-century Italy—and Boccaccio himself was under the spell of the Olympian gods. Toward the end of his life, he systematically collected stories about them for his encyclopedic *On the Genealogy of the Gentile Gods,* which presented both historical and allegorizing explanations for the ancient myths. When Boccaccio told the story of Zeus's love affair with Semele, for example, he explained that the combustion of the poor woman had resulted from a mixing of hot air (represented allegorically by the jealous Juno) and fire (the thunderous Jupiter). In the same breath, though, he could also describe Jupiter as a real-life, lustful king of Crete.

Boccaccio's fluctuating interpretations are emblematic of a broader, long-lasting ambivalence about the gods. Christian readers needed to explain the gods away yet wanted to celebrate the stories in which they appeared. They recognized the rampant vitality of ancient literature, yet also felt the need to tame the gods of Olympus. There was, after all, still something suspect about these pagan deities and about the literary enterprises they inspired. Throughout the Middle Ages, Olympian storytelling continued to smell—however faintly—of sulfur.

15

Sackcloth and Scimitars

By the seventh century AD, the western part of the Roman Empire had split into many unstable kingdoms. The Eastern Roman Empire, by contrast, was thriving; indeed, it seemed set to reconquer western Europe—except that the rise of Islam suddenly reconfigured the entire political landscape. Like Christianity, this new religion of the book cast itself as a return to an original and true faith. It was attractive and vigorous, and it had extraordinary military success. Within a century, the Arabs had reached the borders of India and the Atlantic coast of Spain. The Eastern Roman Empire—the Byzantine Empire, as we now call it—survived for another eight hundred years, but its place in the world was dramatically changed. The Arab conquest was a key factor in making "Europe" into a distinct cultural space. The regions of the southern Mediterranean no longer belonged to the Eastern Roman Empire and were thus cut off from the influence of their former capital, Constantinople. Meanwhile, the capital itself increasingly came under attack from the Islamic south—and also from the Christian west. The Fourth Crusade of 1204 was one of the worst episodes in the history of Christianity. Originally launched to liberate Jerusalem from Muslim control, it was derailed by the Venetians, who led the whole expedition against Constantinople instead. From then on, the city declined significantly, until it fell to the Turks in 1453.

The Muslims, in accordance with their tolerant attitudes toward "the people of the book," did not destroy Christian academies and parochial schools when they conquered the southern Mediterranean in the seventh century, and in these a version of the Hellenistic syllabus continued to be taught. The first caliphal dynasty, residing in Damascus, had relatively little exchange with these centers of Christian learning. However, the second dynasty, the ʿAbbāsids, showed much more interest in classical culture, particularly because it became clear that engaging with Greek philosophy could help articulate the intellectual foundations of Islam and justify its structures of power. The ʿAbbāsids founded a new capital, Baghdad, and the caliph al-Maʾmūn (who ruled at the beginning of the ninth century AD) is even said to have sponsored a "House of Wisdom" there, devoted to the study of "the ancients"—by which Muslim scholars, just like their Christian colleagues, meant the Greeks.

According to legend, Aristotle himself appeared to the caliph al-Maʾmūn in a dream and had a philosophical conversation with him. "What is the good?" asked the caliph; "Whatever is good according to intellect," answered the philosopher. "Then what?" asked the caliph; "Whatever is good according to religious law," replied Aristotle.[1] This dream encounter was credited with enormous cultural significance. Some medieval Arabic sources suggest that it inspired the entire vast project of translating works from the Greek over which al-Maʾmūn presided. In fact, engagement with classical culture must have predated and indeed inspired the dream: al-Maʾmūn was actively leveraging the authority of Aristotle in order to support his struggles against charismatic Muslim leaders. Still, even if the dream was the effect rather than the cause of Greek studies in Baghdad, it nevertheless confirms the prestige that Aristotle enjoyed in the city.

Homer's works, by contrast, remained largely unknown under the ʿAbbāsids, and thus a major source of information about the gods of Olympus remained untapped. This lack of engagement with Homer might seem surprising, given that his poems were the cornerstone of a classical education, but there were both literary and theological reasons why Homeric epic was sidelined in Baghdad. For one thing, there was a widespread belief that poetry was untranslatable. The ninth-century scholar al-Jāḥiẓ, for example, argued that "poems do not lend themselves to translation and ought not to be translated. When they are translated, their poetic structure is rent; the metre is no longer correct; poetic beauty disappears and nothing worthy of admiration remains in the poems."[2] Accordingly, he and many other Muslim scholars focused primarily on philosophy and science. Ancient theories *about* poetry, however, did attract great interest in Baghdad; Aristotle's *Poetics* was translated no fewer than three times, and through it Homer's fame was preserved—even though his poems were generally not in circulation. Aristotle said that Homer was the best Greek poet, and that assessment was generally taken on trust.

The paradox of Homer in the Arabic world—simultaneously admired and unread—is reflected in the life and work of Ḥunayn ibn Isḥāq, the most influential translator in Baghdad. He was a Nestorian Christian born in Hira who moved to Baghdad in the first decades of the ninth century to study with the greatest physician of his day, Yūḥannā ibn Māsawayh. However, he asked too many questions, irritated his teacher, and was expelled from class. Disheartened but by no means defeated, Ḥunayn left Baghdad for several years. We do not know where he went, but upon his return he was supposedly able to recite from memory the complete medical works of Galen as well as the Homeric epics, all in the original Greek. The story goes that his teacher, impressed, took him back, and Ḥunayn went on to become the greatest scholar of his time. It is hard to distinguish fact from fiction in the many anecdotes about Ḥunayn. His Homeric and Galenic performances seem especially unlikely, for it would take weeks, if not months, to recite the entire works of those two authors. But Ḥunayn certainly did learn Greek, knew the Homeric poems well, and was even acquainted with some ancient scholarship on them. It has been suggested that he had traveled all the way to Byzantium to acquire such high-level expertise, and that seems plausible. Ḥunayn was clearly prepared to go to great lengths for the sake of learning.[3]

Wherever he learned his Greek, though, the fact remains that Ḥunayn never translated Homer, even though he had sufficient knowledge to do so. He may, of course, simply have had different priorities, but one detail suggests that he perhaps also had a specific problem with the Greek gods. When commenting on the works of Galen, Ḥunayn wrote a note about the mythical Paean, explaining that he was a "prophet and role model for doctors."[4] This was a deceptive little comment. It deliberately obscured Paean's divinity and his role as "physician of the gods" in Homeric epic. Ḥunayn did not mention the story of how Paean had cured the god Ares himself on Olympus, for example, although it had made for such an effective conclusion to the fifth book of the *Iliad*. This was not just a matter of sweeping divine physicians under the not-so-magic carpet of Arabic science; it was a maneuver designed to sidestep religious controversy.

One of Ḥunayn's pupils, the Christian scholar Qusṭā ibn Lūqā, was more forthcoming in using Homer for the purposes of theological discussion. A Muslim scholar, Ibn al-Munajjim, once sent to both Qusṭā and Ḥunayn an earnest and open-minded letter where he tried to prove the truth of Islam by using Aristotelian logic. Was his reasoning flawed? he asked. Would his Christian colleagues please review it? Ḥunayn answered briefly, but Qusṭā sent a long and learned reply. Among the positions that Qusṭā rebutted was the notion that the Koran was divinely inspired because it was beyond all imitation. Qusṭā pointed out that according to Aristotle, Homer's style was also inimitable, yet he was a pagan poet with no religious insight at all.[5] It seems that when confronted with the revered yet alarmingly pagan Homer, people in Europe and the Arab world alike were beginning to recognize the power of human—rather than divine—inspiration.

Still, without being translated, Greek poetry could not make much of an impact on Arabic culture. The Olympian gods, in any case, found other ways of infiltrating the Muslim world. If science was what mattered, then it was through science they would make their presence felt. Besides medicine, Arabic scholars were assiduous students of mathematics, astronomy, and astrology. Indeed, they regarded all those enterprises as connected, because the stars and planets were thought to have a direct influence on the human body. Ptolemy's *Almagest,* a monumental Greek textbook of astronomy, was translated early into Arabic, and that translation became extremely influential. (Notably, the name under which we now know the book in English derives from the Arabic version of its Greek title. Originally the work was simply called "Mathematical Treatise"; then it became known as "The Greatest Mathematical Treatise," *Hē Megistē Mathēmatikē Syntaxis* in Greek; and that superlative title, *Hē Megistē,* became *al-majisṭī* in Arabic, hence our *Almagest.*) And along with the theoretical *Almagest,* Arabic scholars translated Ptolemy's *Tetrabiblos* (*The Four Books*), which explained how the positions of stars and planets affected human life on earth.

As in antiquity, the practice of astrology in the Arab world required both scientific expertise and mythological flair. The positions and movements of celestial bodies had to be measured, understood, and predicted—and then they were interpreted as encounters and clashes between mythical personalities. Arab scholars were deeply interested in both these different aspects of astrology. Abū al-Saqr al-Qabīsī, a tenth-century scholar known in medieval Europe as Alchabitius, argued that the best astrologers not only knew facts about the movements of planets, but could also *prove* them. Empirical observation was of crucial importance, and valuable information could be gleaned from a variety of astral traditions. After all, the sky was accessible to everybody, so insights into celestial movements could be gathered from anyone who cared to observe it. Such intense and far-reaching exploration helped the Olympian gods to broaden their range, but they also lost some of their more specifically Greek features.

Arabic versions of Ptolemy's work carefully recorded the positions of celestial bodies but were much more free when it came to their mythological representations. In Greek astronomy, groups of stars were named after mythological characters and were meant to look like them. The Gemini constellation, for example, was said to represent the Dioskouroi, the twin sons of Zeus and the mortal woman Leda. Likewise, the stars in the Heracles constellation were supposed to draw a picture of the muscular hero in the sky. However, lacking access to classical poems or pictures that explained how Heracles was supposed to look, Muslim artists used their own imagination when illuminating astronomical texts. And so it was that Heracles lost his club and lion skin and acquired a turban and a scimitar. Other changes could be traced more directly to linguistic difficulties. Thanks to an ambiguous translation, for example, Hermes suddenly found himself holding a surprising implement in his hand: a penis, rather than his traditional staff. (The term that the Arabic translator had used could refer to either item.)[6] It was pure coincidence that this error evoked the herms, those ancient roadside markers that had long been mutilated or buried.

As the Greek gods gained new prominence through Arabic astronomy and astrology, the Babylonian gods also experienced a revival. Of course, Greek and Babylonian deities had already mingled in the Hellenistic period—but now they came together again, in new combinations. Exactly how the Babylonian gods suddenly surfaced in Arabic science is a matter of some debate, but clearly some very ancient local traditions had stayed alive, because the Arabic planetary deities at times resembled their Babylonian ancestors more closely than their Greek cousins. In isolated districts of Mesopotamia, people must have continued to worship and study the stars, relatively sheltered from Greek, Roman, Christian, and Islamic influences.[7] And now the

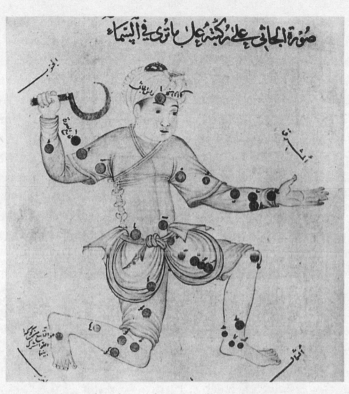

An Arabic Heracles, with turban and scimitar, illustrating the work of the Persian astronomer ʿAbd al-Raḥmān al-Ṣūfī (tenth century). The large dots are the stars that make up the constellation of Hercules.

ancient Babylonian gods were making their way into Arabic treatises. The Arab Mercury, for example, turned out to be a scholarly type, rather like the Babylonian Nabu: he had little in common with the playful, thievish, irreverent Greek Hermes. The Arabic Jupiter likewise shared some features with the Babylonian Marduk: he was portrayed as a judge, for example, a role that the Greek Zeus played only rarely. The planetary gods of Arabic science thus mixed with Babylonian as well as Greek and other deities. They were, in fact, as wideranging as the scholars who studied them.

These mixed-up planetary gods eventually made their way to Europe, where they still decorate castles and cathedrals, looking down on us from their lofty perches and living on incognito. The details of their convoluted routes are uncertain, but the main stages of their journey to Europe can still be reconstructed. In the first place, it must be noted that astrology never truly died out in the Christian world. If nothing else, it belonged to the Christmas story: the three wise men from the East predicted the birth of Jesus on the basis of a star, so planetary observation could not, from a Christian perspective, be entirely wrong. Yet it was difficult to reconcile astrology with the omnipotence of God and the free will of human beings on earth. One Church Father, in a rather desperate attempt to arbitrate between astrological determinism and Christian free will, claimed that planets and stars had provided a useful means of knowledge up to the birth of Jesus but no longer worked after that: from AD 1 onward, it had become impossible to determine the future on the basis of Saturn, Mars, and other "dead gods."[8]

The Church's repeated efforts to stamp out astrology never quite succeeded, but up to the twelfth century, European would-be astrologers had very few books on which to draw. It was only in the later Middle Ages that ancient astronomical and astrological knowledge became more widely available. Partly as a result of the Crusades, contact with Arab scholars increased and, while the soldiers fought, more contemplative types exchanged ideas about the stars. Arabic texts were translated into Latin (often by Jews) and made their way into Sicily, Spain, and eventually the rest of Europe. Ptolemy's *Almagest* and *Tetrabiblos* now entered Western consciousness, enriched by having passed through the hands of scholars like al-Qabīṣī. The result was an extraordinary increase in the prestige of astrology. Between the twelfth and the fourteenth centuries, it experienced a veritable boom.

The career of Michael Scot exemplifies the increased intellectual traffic of this time. Born in Scotland around 1175—his name literally means Michael the Scotsman—he studied first at the cathedral school of Durham and then in Oxford and Paris. Not content with that, he moved farther south to Bologna and eventually wound up

in Palermo, at the court of Frederick II. From Sicily he moved to
Toledo in central Spain, and there he learned Arabic, thus gaining
access to many ancient Greek works in Arabic translation, together
with scholarly additions, corrections, and commentaries. Michael
communicated what he had learned through his own, often allegorical interpretations of planetary science; his work, and the illustrations that accompanied it, brought to Europe some distinctly
Near Eastern visions of the gods. Michael himself did not fare too
well with posterity as a result: he gained a reputation for magic and
duly found a place in Dante's *Inferno*.[9] But his mixed-up gods flourished. Mercury-Nabu, the planetary patron of scholars, appeared on
a beautiful capital in Venice, topping a column in the Doge's Palace. He also made an appearance in the Cappella degli Spagnoli in
Florence and in the choir of the Eremitani in Padua. He did not
necessarily look Oriental—indeed, he often took on the appearance
of a bishop—but his provenance was ultimately Near Eastern: the
Greek Hermes had never shown much interest in formal learning,
whereas Nabu was a great scholar.

For me, the most amazing disguise is the one adopted by Jupiter
on Giotto's campanile in Florence. There, right at the heart of the
city, decorating the bell tower of the cathedral itself, is the supreme
pagan deity—looking, astonishingly, like a Christian monk. Gone
is Jupiter's reputation for serial seduction, adultery, and rape. Gone
is his awesome classical body. He now appears in the guise of a
rather portly friar in humble sackcloth, holding a chalice in one
hand and a crucifix in the other. Yet we know this must be Jupiter,
because he is surrounded by all the other planetary gods.

How could the supreme ruler of Olympus possibly have come to
appear in this perfectly Christian guise? The answer lies buried, surprisingly, in an Arabic text: the *Ġāyat al-Ḥakīm*, a manual of magic
written in the eleventh century but containing much earlier Greek
and Babylonian lore. The manual was translated from Arabic into
Spanish and then into Latin. Under the mysterious title *Picatrix* (possibly a corruption of the name of Hippocrates, the Greek doctor), it

Jupiter in the guise of a monk on the bell tower of Santa Maria del Fiore, Florence (late 1330s).

circulated widely in the Middle Ages, telling would-be magicians how to propitiate the planetary gods and thus secure their services. Each planet was said to preside over a specific region of the earth. Saturn, for example, was in charge of India, which is why in some manuscripts he was drawn as an Indian sage. Jupiter's allotted domain was western Europe, and he was thought to be the patron planet of Christians.

Applying the principles of sympathetic magic, the *Gāyat* insisted that worshippers adopt the manner of Westerners when praying to Jupiter. They would need to "be humble and modest, dress in the manner of monks . . . and act in every way as the Christians do, wearing their costume: a yellow mantle, a girdle, and a cross."[10] On the bell tower of Santa Maria del Fiore, right at the heart of the beautiful city of Florence, Jupiter thus sports a monk's costume— his appearance complying perfectly with the instructions given by an Arabic magic manual. This does not mean that Giotto (or Andrea Pisano, who was responsible for the design of the planetary gods on the campanile) read this specific manual and drew pictures directly from it. But artists and architects are shaped by the culture around them, and as Graeco-Arabic astrology spread far and wide, it found expression (through channels of transmission we can no longer trace in detail) in the great works of Western art.

Clearly, the Olympian gods had to go to extraordinary lengths to survive under Christianity and Islam. Their statues were smashed, their temples ruined, and their worshippers seduced by other, more righteous visions of God. It seems misguided to claim (as some historians do) that ancient paganism carried on unperturbed well into the Middle Ages; instead, its character changed radically.[11] Worship of the Olympian gods became a secret thing, a practice that could survive only in the most sheltered circumstances. Far from being the cornerstone of civic life, it became a rustic superstition, a matter for isolated *pagani*. Yet the gods themselves, astonishingly, managed to survive the demise of their worshippers. That they continued to attract interest and speculation—even without the aid of religious belief or practice—is one of the most extraordinary facts in the history of classical civilization.

If the Olympian gods continued to flourish, it was because people valued the ancient cultures they inhabited. From the borders of India to the British Isles, diverse societies continued to engage with ancient philosophy, literature, art, and science and thus constantly met up with the gods of Olympus. These encounters were electrifying and often challenging. The gods as demons, or fictions, or real people, or planets—the wide range of competing theories about the Olympians testifies to the intensity of the clash between ancient and medieval perspectives on the world. Some thought that the gods were best grouped under the twelve months (our March is still called after Mars), others that they might be associated with the seven liberal arts—the so-called trivium of grammar, logic, and rhetoric and the quadrivium of arithmetic, music, geometry, and astronomy, each organized under a presiding planetary deity. As pupils moved up the curriculum, so they reached out into the spheres of the more distant planets.[12] The whole effort of medieval scholasticism was devoted to organizing a universal system of knowledge, and the ancient gods were supposed to be slotted into it. But the gods of Olympus proved too unruly for that. They kept swapping labels and disguises and eventually started rattling the whole sacred edifice of medieval knowledge. Indeed, their disturbing behavior impelled history onward, into the Renaissance and toward modernity.

PART VI

Born Again: The Renaissance

Ancient literature and art became a major focus of attention in Italy during the fourteenth and fifteenth centuries. Scholars, poets, artists, and architects vied with one another in their attempts to revive ancient culture, and they encountered the gods of Olympus at every turn. In dealing with these gods, they repeated arguments that had already been made in the Middle Ages but gave them a new inflection. If the Olympians were just human creations, figments of the imagination—then how powerful that imagination! How impressive that ability to create! Having started life as deities, the gods of Olympus emerged in the Italian Renaissance as ambassadors of a new belief in humanity.

This transformation was, in part, cast as a revival. In archaic Greece, after all, discussing the gods had already involved a critical appreciation of poetry and art, while in classical Athens the gods had featured in debates about human power and the ability of ordinary people to govern themselves. In the Hellenistic period, the gods of Olympus had mingled with the deities of Persia, Egypt, Babylon, and India—and now again, as Italian captains sailed across the Atlantic, they met old gods in a new world. Mexican deities joined the company of Olympians in the pages of mythological handbooks. Everywhere, it seemed, human creativity shone through most clearly when picturing the gods.

16

Petrarch Paints the Gods

In the Middle Ages, people did not think of themselves as inhabiting a dark and oppressive period between antiquity and the Renaissance. In fact, they perceived no definite break between the ancient world and their own, except on the crucial issue of faith. Their greatest efforts were devoted to organizing all culture according to Christian doctrine—and in the Mediterranean, that generally meant a profound engagement with the culture of the Greeks and Romans.

A work like Dante's *Divine Comedy* (written between 1308 and 1321), for example, was a supreme feat of systematization, devoted to finding the right place for everybody, and for all eternity. Given the poem's emphasis on the relationship between Dante and his pagan predecessor, the poet Virgil, deciding what to do with the ancient gods was inevitably part of such a project. Dante's approach allowed ancient myths to have both metaphorical meaning and historical reality: pagan deities featured in the poem as human characters, variously condemned, but also as powerful Christian symbols. So it was that Dante could ask Apollo for inspiration at the beginning of his *Paradiso*, treating him as the Holy Spirit. He even referred to Jesus Christ as "the highest Jupiter," *il sommo Giove*.[1] Boccaccio, as

we have seen, would adopt a similarly ambidextrous attitude in the
years immediately after Dante. In the centuries that followed, both
styles of interpretation would continue to thrive, with poets often
presenting the Olympians as Christian allegories while historians
insisted that they had been real people. In 1483, for example, the
universal chronicle of Giacomo da Bergamo discussed the reign of
King Jupiter of Crete, before moving on to other historical figures:
Joseph, Mary, Apollo, Bacchus, and Vulcan.

Given this degree of continuity, we may well ask whether the
gods of Olympus actually experienced a "new birth" in the Renaissance, for they never abandoned their medieval guises. Indeed, in
recent years this question has been asked repeatedly and in a much
more general form—for the issue, ultimately, concerns not just the
gods of Olympus, but our very conception of history. What was the
Renaissance? Would it not perhaps make more sense to talk about
many different Renaissances? And why parcel up human history in
distinct periods at all? At one level, it is easy to argue that the Renaissance is an artificial invention. Just as people of the Middle Ages did
not know that they were living in medieval times, so nobody living
in the fourteenth, fifteenth, or sixteenth century would have recognized "the Renaissance" as a label. Italian humanists did sometimes
talk about a *rinascita* of classical culture, but our conception of the
Renaissance, in all its breadth and significance, would have been
alien to them.

The term was introduced only in the middle of the nineteenth
century, by the French historian Jules Michelet, who argued that
men like Columbus, Copernicus, and Galileo redefined the universe
and the place of humanity in it. Michelet saw the Renaissance simultaneously as a historical period and a human attitude—an attitude
that for him was somehow quintessentially French (which is one
reason he defined the Renaissance as the sixteenth century, indeed a
good period for France). A few decades after Michelet, the Swiss
scholar Jacob Burckhardt reconfigured the Renaissance as an Italian achievement of the fourteenth and fifteenth centuries. It was at

that time, he argued, that the revival of classical antiquity, the dis-covery of the wider world, and growing criticism of the Church led people to think of themselves, for the first time, as independent, self-governing individuals. In describing "the Renaissance man," Burckhardt offered influential portraits of figures like Leon Baltista Alberti and Leonardo da Vinci, but he also revealed something of himself: there was a distinctly Protestant, republican, Swiss tinge to his vision of Renaissance Italy.

Shortly after the publication of Burckhardt's work, Walter Pater, an Oxford aesthete, focused the discussion more specifically on art. His 1873 book, *The Renaissance,* sidelined the question of political and scientific advances, celebrating instead the senses and the imag-ination. For Pater, the Renaissance was all about art for art's sake— and it was thanks to him that the gods of Olympus, who served as the inspiration for many artists, became emblematic of the period. Pater's work was influential and problematic from the start, and it remains so to this day. His contemporaries considered him decadent and irreligious; more recently, critics have denounced his vision as a barely disguised argument for Europe's cultural—and hence politi-cal and economic—superiority.[2] It is certainly no coincidence that Pater's *Renaissance* was born precisely at a time when Europe, through its colonies and empires, dominated the rest of the world.

Perhaps, then, there never was a "rebirth" of antiquity, impelling Europe onward to its specific, and aggressive, form of modernity. Maybe the Renaissance was just a nineteenth-century myth, and a self-serving one at that? Even in the early twentieth century, before postcolonial reassessments of history, some scholars began to ques-tion the meaning and significance of "the Renaissance" as a period. Johan Huizinga's *The Waning of the Middle Ages* argued persua-sively that many qualities attributed to the Renaissance were actually the product of the late Middle Ages. And Jean Seznec's influential *The Survival of the Pagan Gods* made a more specific argument about the gods of Olympus: he showed that they had been around continuously from antiquity to the fourteenth century and that it was therefore misleading to talk about their "rebirth." Noting that the gods had traveled through Asia and Africa as well as Europe, Seznec's work emphasized the many and varied routes of divine survival.

Seznec's intuition that the gods of Olympus never died, and were in any case never exclusively European, remains crucial to any understanding of their history. But even Seznec had to concede that something peculiar happened to the gods in the period we now call the Italian Renaissance. Most obviously, their appearance changed. All of a sudden, rather than looking like medieval monks, kings, damsels, demons, sultans, and scholars, they started to resemble ancient statues. Curiously, this visual transformation was initiated in part not by a painter or a sculptor, but by a fourteenth-century poet: Francesco Petrarca, known in English as Petrarch. Today, Petrarch is remembered principally for his sonnets, written in a beautiful, pure, pared-down Italian; but it was the *Africa,* a massive epic poem in Latin, that sealed his fame during his lifetime. The *Africa* was never finished—Petrarch had a habit of working on several projects at once, interrupting and restarting them in a lifelong struggle to keep up with his own ideas—but some passages from it circulated early on as stand-alone extracts. And it was through the *Africa* that the Olympian gods dropped their medieval garb and began to look like their old selves.

Petrarch's epic was modeled on Virgil's *Aeneid* and intended as its sequel. Just as Virgil had taken as his subject Aeneas, the founder of Rome, so Petrarch wanted to compose a poem about Scipio, the general who had defeated Hannibal in the Second Punic War and established Rome as the republican capital of a world empire. It was Petrarch's ardent desire that Rome might one day be restored to its ancient glory—though in the fourteenth century this was a rather quixotic notion. Dilapidated, infested by criminals, and run by feuding families, the Eternal City was not a hopeful prospect. Even the pope had left for Avignon, and a general atmosphere of violence and decay hung over the city. Petrarch had every opportunity to see how far Rome had fallen from any standard of decent behavior (he was once captured by brigands as he tried to leave the city), but his utopian vision for the city never faltered. Rome was the heart of both Christianity and classical culture, the center of the world.

Because the *Africa* was meant to provide a link between Rome's illustrious past and its glorious future, the Olympian gods represented a difficult problem for Petrarch. He did not want to suggest that a horde of pagan deities had once ruled over the Eternal City. On the other hand, if he wanted his poem to imitate Virgil's *Aeneid*, he could not leave the Olympian gods out of the epic entirely. As a compromise, Petrarch tried offering just one scene set on Olympus: a passage where two matrons, allegories of Rome and Carthage, ascend to heaven and ask Jupiter to arbitrate between them.[3]

During the arbitration, Madame Carthage claims that she enjoys Juno's support, but the goddess herself never confirms this. Indeed, she never appears at all, leaving open the question of whether she really is an active force in the poem. Jupiter, for his part, presents himself as a Christian allegory; he even announces that he is about to be reincarnated in Jesus Christ and nursed at the soothing breast of the Virgin Mary. Coming from Jupiter, this eager anticipation of Mary's breast sounds rather alarming. But I doubt that Petrarch wanted to evoke the numerous incidents when Jupiter enjoyed raping a virgin. What he tried to do was offer an Olympian scene that affirmed the supremacy of the Christian God. And in this, he failed. Dante could get away with presenting Jesus Christ as Jupiter, but only because he kept his entire *Divine Comedy* within a strictly Christian and allegorical framework. Because Petrarch wrote a historical poem and followed the conventions of Roman epic, the whole idea of a Christian Jupiter started to seem anachronistic and absurd.

If the episode on Olympus was a flop, another scene in the *Africa* demonstrated a much more successful approach to including the Olympian gods in a modern poem. Rather than resorting to allegory, or presenting the gods as historical kings and queens, Petrarch took a different approach entirely: he placed the Olympians inside a picture.[4] The palace of the African king Syphax, he claimed, was decorated with images of the Olympian gods. Within the poem, the Roman ambassador Lelius visited the African court and thus provided the perfect opportunity for Petrarch to describe the gods at leisure, without having to account for them.

Jupiter is, predictably, the first god mentioned in Petrarch's catalog: he is "proud in his august throne, sceptre in hand, standing before the other gods, and brandishing a thunderbolt." Next to him is a miserable Saturn, an old and defeated father; then comes Neptune, holding a trident and surrounded by sea monsters. Farther along in the picture, a beautiful Apollo plays the lyre, while his younger brother Mercury approaches him "with a mischievous expression," holding a staff with intertwined snakes. The lame Vulcan is depicted as an object of ridicule, a divine laughingstock ever since his wife, Venus, betrayed him with Mars. Petrarch's Juno has her head encircled in a colored cloud, a rainbow: the association between the goddess and moist air endures, even though the Greek pun on which it is based has long been forgotten. Minerva, born out of Jupiter's head, stands proud in Petrarch's description, with a long spear in her hand and a crested helmet on her head. She mocks Venus for having been shamefully born out of castrated genitals; the goddess of love is depicted naked on a shell floating on the sea. Nearby, three nude Graces intertwine their arms in a circle: "The first girl is turned away, but the other two fix their gaze on us," Petrarch says, describing what would become a favorite pose in Renaissance art. Cupid stands in position, meanwhile, ready to shoot an arrow. Diana follows, surrounded by creatures of the woods—nymphs, fauns, and satyrs. And last, in Petrarch's description, comes Cybele: this Anatonian Earth Mother is depicted as "an aged, massive, seated goddess." Petrarch helpfully explains that "according to the ancients, Cybele bore all the gods, including the Thunderer himself."

This description of the gods in the *Africa* proved to be immensely popular. It was one of only two passages from the poem that circulated widely before Petrarch was crowned poet laureate, and which thus justified his coronation. Everybody wanted to know what the gods of Olympus looked like, without being burdened with long-winded allegorical explanations of who or what they were supposed to represent. Petrarch's brief, vivid portraits of the deities—a painting in words, rather than a lengthy philosophical discussion—answered that desire perfectly. By placing the Olympians in ancient Africa, within a picture, the poem framed the gods, setting them up at a safe distance for readers to admire. There is some evidence that Petrarch wrote this description of the gods even before deciding where to place it within the narrative of the *Africa*: that is how keen he was to paint the Olympian pantheon and how certain that the scene would please his readers.

The other passage from the poem that circulated widely and helped establish Petrarch's reputation was a speech delivered by Mago, Hannibal's brother, shortly before dying.[5] Mago remembered all the great ambitions he had when he was young, realized he would not be able to fulfill them because he was about to perish in a shipwreck, and felt the deepest regret. (In Italian, *magone* actually means "regret"; the etymology of the word is probably linked to the German *Magen*, "stomach"—a sorrow felt in the guts—but many Italians believe that the word derives from Mago's speech: to experience *magone* is to feel like Petrarch's Mago.) Some of Petrarch's contemporaries complained that Mago's sentiments were too noble for an African pagan, but Petrarch replied that Mago was voicing feelings common to all human beings, *humanum omniumque gentium comune*.[6] Antiquity was helping Petrarch articulate what it meant to be human—and he saw that it had something do with aspiration, with yearning to accomplish worthy things. In Petrarch's view, all people—no matter who they were, when they existed, where they lived, or which gods they worshipped—could experience Mago's feelings.

These two passages from the *Africa* announced major cultural developments. Petrarch's defense of Mago contained the seeds of what we now call Renaissance humanism; his description of the gods in Syphax's palace, meanwhile, marked the beginning of a long-lasting visual interest in the Olympians. Petrarch's word painting inspired the writing of iconographic manuals, and those manuals in turn inspired artists, who now deliberately attempted to depict the gods *all'antica*—as they had appeared in ancient times. Initially, these depictions were heavily dependent on written accounts; aside from occasional coins and carved gemstones, few ancient artifacts were readily available. As the artists' work attracted increasing attention, though, antiquarians began to look for Roman statues, and as soon as they investigated ancient ruins, they started to find them. In half-buried buildings they even discovered ancient murals—*grottesche,* they called them, "motifs found in caves." Soon, artists were arranging to be lowered down into the "caves" on the Esquiline Hill in Rome (actually the remains of Nero's extravagant palace) in order to copy the decorations on the walls.

Together with this interest in ancient art came the desire to read and rediscover classical literature, in both Latin and Greek. Petrarch was a pioneer in this enterprise, too. He looked for ancient manuscripts in dusty libraries, edited the texts he discovered, and took inspiration from them in his work. For example, he recovered Cicero's letters and used them as a model for his own. He also worked hard for years to get his hands on a copy of the *Iliad* and then to find someone to translate it and teach him the language—knowledge of Greek was rare in the West. In a letter that Petrarch penned to Homer himself, he addressed the ancient poet as a long-lost friend: "I had given up all hope because, except for some few beginnings of your books—from which I had caught a glimpse of your flashing eye-brows, and your flowing hair—I could read nothing of yours in Latin."

Eventually, with the help of his friend Boccaccio, Petrarch managed to get in touch with Leontius Pilatus, a Greek speaker from southern Italy who claimed great Byzantine erudition (and indeed possessed some). Initially, things went well. Leontius started to translate the *Iliad* and to teach Petrarch Greek along the way, and Petrarch's enthusiasm soared to new heights. Boccaccio and Petrarch even managed to convince the Florentine city fathers to endow the first chair of Greek in western Europe, and Leontius triumphantly arrived in Florence to take up his new post. Then events took a bad turn. Distraught letters between Petrarch and Boccaccio convey something of the impression Leontius made: "gloomy," "stubborn," "vain," "volatile," "badly dressed," "head as hard as a stone," "intractable."[7] Students did not take to this professor. More generally, the relationship between Italian humanists and Byzantine scholars was marked by rivalry and mistrust. The whole project of spreading knowledge of Greek was delayed by several decades.

When Petrarch died, there were no students of Greek in Florence, the pope was still in Avignon, and the *Africa* lay unfinished. But eventually his work bore fruit. Greek manuscripts slowly found their way to Italy; scholars learned how to read them; and their editions and translations inspired new poems and paintings, contributing to a general revival of ancient culture. In some ways, Botticelli's *Birth of Venus*—the ultimate expression of the Renaissance, as Walter Pater saw it—can be seen as the culmination of Petrarch's work. Greek manuscripts containing the *Homeric Hymns,* including the short *Hymn to Aphrodite,* reached Italy in the fifteenth century. Inspired by the description of Venus's birth in that hymn, the scholar Politian included a version of the story in one of his own poems—a piece written in honor of Simonetta Vespucci, beauty queen of Florence, and her champion Giuliano de' Medici. Following Petrarch's example in the *Africa,* Politian turned Homeric epic into a fictional image: he imagined an artwork showing the birth of Venus and gave a description of it in his poem. A few years later, inspired by both Politian's poem and Simonetta herself, Botticelli delivered the real thing.

There are, of course, ways of interpreting Botticelli's *Venus* as a Christian allegory. A Grace stands near her, ready to wrap her up in

Sandro Botticelli's *The Birth of Venus* (1486) was inspired by ancient art and poetry, especially the shorter *Homeric Hymn to Aphrodite*, and by Simonetta Vespucci, beauty queen of Florence. Simultaneously, the composition recalled the iconography of a baptism.

a pink robe, and the composition resembles the scene of a baptism: countless paintings depict Jesus coming out of the water and accepting a similarly pink towel from John the Baptist. Other details also invite viewers to look at the scene with Christian eyes. Venus's pink robe, for instance, is studded with cornflowers, symbols of Our Lady, Queen of Heaven. The painting can thus be seen as an image of celestial love, an important Christian and Platonic notion—but it does not *have* to be viewed that way. Pictures do not dictate their interpretation in the same way as texts; allegorical narratives can accompany them, but these can just as easily be dismissed. There is always the option, for viewers, to enjoy the obvious—that Simonetta is beautiful and naked.

I am sure that in the backlash against such growing permissiveness, Savonarola would have burned Botticelli's painting in his 1497 Bonfire of the Vanities, had he been able to lay his hands on it. The fact that he did not suggests that *The Birth of Venus* was tucked away in some countryside villa belonging to the Medici. And this, in turn, implies that there was not yet any obvious public function for the painting; its vision was a fantasy shared only by select scholars, artists, and their patrons. Still, this fantasy had considerable powers of attraction and would become ever more influential in the course of time. From the pages of dusty manuscripts, from the remains of half-broken statues, the gods were emerging and beginning to resemble their old selves.

The process entailed a new appreciation of the gods' distant origins. Those dazzling creatures were not part of the Christian world: they were mysterious, ancient, exotic. Medieval thinkers had devoted extraordinary energy to constructing a single, unified world out of Christian religion and pagan culture, using liberal amounts of allegorical glue in the process. But now their construction was falling apart. Suddenly, antiquity was one thing and its Christian revival quite another. And while "the Middle Ages" and "the Renaissance" might be nineteenth-century inventions designed to prove the superiority of Europe, already in the fourteenth century Petrarch was proclaiming that a period of benighted ignorance separated him from his beloved ancients. He admired what the people of antiquity achieved "through toil and talent" and deeply regretted that later generations had erased their efforts "through shameless neglect."[8]

As Theodor E. Mommsen points out, Petrarch boldly reversed the Christian language of light and darkness. Jesus Christ was "the Light of the World," yet Petrarch denounced the dark Christian centuries that lay between him and the bright achievements of pagan antiquity.[9] He did not, in any sense, condemn Christianity, but he could not bear ignorance or anything that might hamper human inspiration. Indeed, he boldly stated that he was determined to learn from "exceptional men of all countries and all times."[10] And the Olympian gods played a key role in helping Petrarch define his range and vision. No longer seen as fallen idols, they now came to stand precisely for the human toil and talent that he valued so highly.

17

A Cosmopolitan
Carnival of Deities

Over the course of the Renaissance, the Olympian gods steadily gained ground—even if not as quickly as is often assumed. We may imagine that Renaissance artists and their patrons devoted a great deal of energy and wealth to resuscitating ancient culture, but this was not the case. Indeed, as one art historian points out, until the seventeenth century, "the proportion of dated paintings devoted to mythological themes in any one year rarely rose above 2 per cent."[1] This sobering statistic suggests that we should revise some commonly held views of the period, particularly when we consider that many of the paintings in that narrow 2 percent are known to have remained in the homes and studies of the artists themselves, presumably because they had found no buyer. There was, to put it bluntly, no great demand for the gods of Olympus. Artists often painted the gods as a way of honing skills and comparing themselves with the masters of antiquity, but their work was not immediately marketable.

Slowly, though, the gods began to find new roles for themselves. At first, their appearances seemed flirty and ephemeral. In the winter of 1406, for example, when unusually abundant snow fell on the city of Florence, locals immediately built a giant snowman in the shape of Hercules. Clearly, the classical hunk was on their minds, particularly when they went out to play. The gods of Olympus also provided inspiration for carnival costumes and floats. Like the snowman Hercules, these were relatively spontaneous fancies but also required a degree of communal effort. By the middle of the fifteenth century, it was clear that the ancient gods had taken charge of street parties; their appeal was undeniable.

Perhaps the most striking street appearance was a massive Olympian display that Pope Paul II organized in 1466 to celebrate his victory over the counts of Anguillara, who had been threatening him from their base north of Rome. He began the festivities by releasing a large flock of birds from his window, and these were followed by trumpets, firecrackers, and a naked Cupid who sang the pope's praises while taking aim at him with flaming arrows. (Here was truly a new way of staging love for the pontiff.) After Cupid's song came a lengthy procession of giant floats, carrying the Olympian gods seated together and enjoying a banquet. The goddess Diana followed on a white horse, with plenty of skimpily dressed nymphs in her train. Stopping just below the pope's balcony, she declared that she, all her virgin nymphs, and the whole wide world would gladly submit to his rule. The ancient defeat of the pagan gods was thus transformed into a massive display of the pope's power. Paul II's army had triumphed over the counts of Anguillara, who would now yield to him—just as the Olympians had yielded to Christianity.

Alongside such public occasions, the gods also made themselves increasingly at home in more private settings, providing incidental decoration in the form of tableware, medals, gems, brooches, embroidery, and cakes. Banquets frequently had an Olympian theme, while wedding trunks would often display Venus, Cupid, and amorous scenes loosely based on Ovid. In short, the gods were in fashion, and it is by studying their often trivial apparitions in the fifteenth century that we begin to understand how they marked out new human endeavors. Clearly, they were not replacing Christianity with a new (or ancient) form of religion. What they did, rather, was to colonize whole areas of human experience where Christianity seemed to have little to offer.

Sex was one. The gods increasingly appeared in drawings that were, frankly, pornographic, while classical texts supplied explicit details that could ignite even the dullest sexual imagination. Venus, of course, had always inspired action in the bedroom, but now the entire Olympian pantheon seemed devoted to the task. An ancient Roman visitor time traveling to fifteenth-century Italy would have been amazed by the amount of nudity in the portrayal of the gods. Even Diana happily appeared with no clothes on, though in antiquity she usually dressed like a modest maiden. Actaeon had learned at great cost how bad it could be to chance upon Diana in the nude—but now, in the fifteenth century, she was fully exposed for all to see, and nobody seemed to become a stag or get torn apart by dogs as a result. Myth had become a celebration of healthy, beautiful human bodies and everything they inspired. This included homosexuality, of course: the story of Zeus's affair with the adolescent Ganymede was a particular favorite.

Nature and the love of nature often went together with this celebration of the senses. In Renaissance art, the gods of Olympus tended to appear in lush settings: fresh meadows, riverbanks, shady woods, the seaside. In that respect too they were exploiting a gap in the market, for Christianity was essentially a city religion. Artists could, of course, depict Adam and Eve in the Garden of Eden, or St. Francis surrounded by birds, but on the whole Christian scriptures offered few opportunities to celebrate the open air. For that very reason, the classical gods rushed out into the countryside, naked and beautiful. It is partly because of their affinity with nature that one of the great breakthroughs of Renaissance art—the use of perspective—hardly features in mythological paintings. Natural backgrounds are usually flatter than the buildings, streets, and arches that typically frame scenes from the Gospels or the lives of the saints. Thus, although the study of perspective was directly inspired by classical art, it found its most effective expression in the depiction of Christian subjects rather than Olympian scenes.

In lieu of sophisticated perspective, mythological painting afforded other joys—relaxation, above all. Christian art could be emotionally demanding: it inspired worship, humility, horror, gratitude, sadness, ecstasy. Beautiful naked nymphs dancing in the woods were much easier, not only on the eye but on the heart as well. It was all right simply to sit back and enjoy them without asking too many questions. Those nymphs did not matter much, after all. Unlike suffering martyrs or the Holy Virgin, they did not even exist.

Together with sensuality, ease, and beauty, the gods of Olympus offered positive images of secular human power—which were also hard to come by in the Christian scriptures. The popes themselves were quick to take advantage of this. Pope Paul II, as we have seen, had Cupid, Diana, and the whole Olympian pantheon celebrate his military victory over the counts of Anguillara. But secular rulers could also marshal the gods of Olympus to celebrate their successes. It was Sigismondo Malatesta, the "Wolf of Rimini," who most fully realized the potential for exploiting the gods as ambassadors of earthly power—and put himself on a collision course with the papacy as a result.

The illegitimate son of a warlord, Malatesta was no stranger to conflict and controversy. He had begun by challenging the most powerful members of his own family: by the age of fifteen, with several battlefield experiences to his credit, he had established himself as the sole ruler of Rimini. He would spend the rest of his life fighting on behalf of whoever could pay the best wage, trying meanwhile to acquire lands, security, and prestige for his own small state on the coast of the Adriatic. Generally, he had few scruples when it came to advancing his own interests. When he became smitten with a twelve-year-old girl after glimpsing her through a window, for example, it surprised few onlookers that both the girl's father and Malatesta's wife died soon thereafter, leaving the two of them free to wed.

Overall, Malatesta's reputation could hardly be worse, and the accusations that he faced in Rome in 1461 reflect the rumors that circulated about him:

> He raped virgins who had vowed themselves to God as well as Jewesses, killed young girls, and had young boys who rebelled against him brutally whipped. He committed adultery with many women whose children he had held at baptism, and murdered their husbands. His cruelty was greater than any barbarian's, and he inflicted fearful tortures on guilty and innocent alike with his own bloody hands. He rarely told the truth, was a master of patience and dissimulation, a traitor and perjurer who never kept his word.[2]

Those were serious charges, but it must be said that crimes of violence, sex, and duplicity were widespread, not least among the clergy. It was the next allegation that was unique: Malatesta was charged with having turned a church into a temple full of images of the Olympian gods. In other words, as one account puts it, "the most heinous accusation against Sigismondo Malatesta was architectural."[3] The pope chose to describe this Tempio Malatestiano in rather medieval terms: Malatesta, he said, had "filled the building with so many pagan works that it was plainly a temple for infidel worshippers of demons, and not for Christians."[4]

Why and how the Wolf of Rimini decided to build his temple is a matter of some interest, because it reveals precisely the kinds of enterprises that the Olympian gods were beginning to inspire in the fifteenth century. Malatesta, bastard and soldier of fortune, craved respectability. And he knew that he could get it only through his own accomplishments: the religious and secular establishment would hardly champion an illegitimate man like him unless he could prove his worth. It was as an individual of talent, then, that he needed to advertise himself. Even Malatesta's enemies quickly acknowledged him as the most daring and crafty military commander of his time. But he also wanted to suggest that he was a man of letters, writing passionate love poems, conversing with humanists, and supporting their work. (It was as a patron of the arts that he would be remembered in Ezra Pound's *Cantos*.) Malatesta's combination of military power and artistic ambition had ancient roots: his cultural advisers specifically encouraged him to think about antiquity and take inspiration from ancient models. Roman emperors had, after all, conquered the world without needing any blessing from the pope. It was the Olympian gods who had inspired them and made them feel strong. And it was through poetry and art that the emperors had managed their public images.

In 1446, Malatesta commissioned Matteo de' Pasti, a fine artist, to cast a series of medals that bore his image in profile in the manner of a Roman emperor. Not satisfied with the medals alone, he soon turned his attention to grander projects. He had a fortress built, the Castel Sismondo, where he could live in proper imperial style. Next, he tackled the modest chapel of St. Francis, where members of the Malatesta family had been buried for centuries. Matteo de' Pasti initially took charge of that project, too, reworking the building piece by piece. He added new chapels and decorations to the original medieval structure. While officially dedicated to saints, these new accretions were actually very far from Christian in intent. In the sacristy, where the very objects of the Mass were kept, a portrait of Malatesta now took center stage. He was, to be sure, kneeling in front of his patron saint—but the saint was shoved into a corner of the picture, while Malatesta dominated the composition, flaunting, as ever, his imperial profile. Near the altar, a chapel celebrated the liberal arts, represented by the Muses; their translucent clothes revealed all. On the other side of the altar, yet another chapel extolled the planetary gods, whom the pope would later find particularly provoking.

By and by, the old Gothic chapel was clothed in new classical garments: Corinthian columns, cornices, putti riding dolphins, acanthus and laurel leaves, sacred courtesans, sibyls, and, of course, the Olympian gods themselves. The planetary deities Diana, Mercury,

Venus, Apollo, Mars, Jupiter, and Saturn were not new to churches
and other sacred buildings; as we have seen, they decorated Giotto's
campanile in Florence, among other structures. But there was something startling and sacrilegious about their use in Malatesta's visions.
Here, Venus's nudity, Diana's diaphanous dress, and Apollo's biceps
spoke of human, earthly pleasures. These gods had little in common
with the grave and dignified allegorical figures in Florence, who

Jupiter, in the Tempio Malatestiano (ca. 1450). The figure displays Greek, Roman,
and Near Eastern features. Pope Pius II condemned it as demonic, but the Olympian
gods, in the guise of planetary deities, still decorate Malatesta's temple, which
today serves as Rimini's cathedral.

were wrapped in heavy robes or thick sackcloth. Malatesta's marble marvels had no edifying purpose, no didactic intent. Instead, the entire Tempio Malatestiano was a monument to Malatesta's power—and the talent of the artists and humanists who worked for him.

Malatesta's temple is now considered a landmark of the Italian Renaissance, but it must be said that its gods are far from purely classical. Jupiter, with a sheaf of wheat in one hand and a whip in the other, has a mixed Egyptian and Syrian provenance, as described in the Latin author Macrobius.[5] Apollo, with his overabundance of props—the lyre, the laurel, and three miniature Graces in one hand, a bow and arrow in the other, a globe beneath his feet, and a raven and a swan to his side—represents the whole solar system, as explained by Porphyry when commenting on the Egyptian cult of Osiris. As for Mercury, he is depicted as a peculiar magus with a pointy cap, a mixture of the Greek Hermes (who leads the souls to the underworld) and the Egyptian Thoth (who teaches souls how to elevate themselves by degrees to divine knowledge). Art historians have often criticized these Malatestian figures for their exuberance of detail and lack of balance—and they do indeed seem, to borrow Nietzsche's phrase, "a cosmopolitan carnival of deities."[6] But their hodgepodge variety is easily explained. The figures in the Tempio Malatestiano represent an attempt at translating what was still largely a textual and allegorical tradition—a tradition rich in detail and wide-ranging in its influences—into an effective visual language.

Soon after work on the temple had started, Malatesta invited a new architect to oversee it. It seems that he trusted Leon Battista Alberti as soon as he met him and perhaps felt a sense of personal connection with him. Like Malatesta, Alberti was the illegitimate son of a noble family, and he too was ambitious and proud of his physical strength: according to an anonymous account of his life (most probably written by Alberti himself), he could jump over a man's head with his feet together. More important, his views on architecture matched Malatesta's visions. Alberti preached a return to antiquity: he used the only surviving ancient manual on building, Vitruvius's *De architectura*, and simultaneously took inspiration from actual ancient ruins. Indeed, he claimed that the remains of ancient theaters and temples could "teach as much as any professor."[7] In his time, such ruins were mostly the hovels of beggars and thieves, and Alberti was shocked and horrified by their degradation. Still, just by looking at them, he could picture beautiful ancient cities filled with statues, and future buildings erected on their model; he was so deep in conversation with the past that in his architectural writings, he referred to churches as temples. Alberti was just the man to translate Malatesta's secular dreams of power into an actual building. Conversely, Malatesta's money could translate Alberti's theories into a marble reality. It was a partnership made on Olympus.

De' Pasti celebrated the arrival of Alberti with a new medal. On one side, as usual, there was a portrait of Malatesta in profile, while the other featured an image of Alberti's plan for the church of St. Francis with a daring inscription: "The famous temple of Rimini." Both words and image established the identity of the building as a

This medal, designed by Matteo de' Pasti in 1450, depicts Sigismondo Malatesta as a Roman emperor and, on the obverse, a building described in the caption as "the famous temple of Rimini." The medal gives the best available indication of how Leon Battista Alberti planned to structure his temple, because the building was never completed.

modern "temple." The plan clearly showed a facade modeled on the Roman triumphal arch, thus adding for the first time this symbol of imperial power to a Christian structure. It also featured a beautiful dome, similar to that of the Pantheon in Rome—an ancient temple devoted, literally, to "all the gods," which had been converted into a church in the seventh century. Alberti's project was meant to follow the opposite route, turning a church into a temple. Sadly, though, the medal remained the closest realization of his intentions, because the actual Tempio Malatestiano was never completed. The arched facade remained unfinished, and the dome was barely started at all: Malatesta ran out of money. The Wolf of Rimini had to face the pope's charges in Rome and never recovered his power after his excommunication. Alberti was dismissed and must have been devastated—not perhaps so much on account of Malatesta's misfortunes, but because of the unfinished work. For Alberti, beauty was a matter of perfect proportions, of each part relating to the whole, but all he had managed to achieve was a stump of a building. It was no better, in fact, than an ancient ruin.

Still, even this incomplete temple, this modern ruin, proved to be significant: it announced to the whole world that the gods of Olympus had escaped papal control. When the pope denounced the Tempio Malatestiano for being filled with "demons," the issue, clearly, was not that the pagan gods had entered a Christian building for the first time; as planetary deities, they had done so many times before. The problem was that Malatesta had used them to advertise his own secular power rather than that of God. It was all a matter of intent and interpretation—and the whole project of turning a humble chapel of St. Francis into a "famous temple" was a downright provocation.

The pope who excommunicated Malatesta, Pius II, knew that ancient models needed to be used with care, for he was none other than Enea Silvio Piccolomini, well-known man of letters, diplomat, and libertine. When, after an adventurous life, he had been (surprisingly) made pope, he had chosen the name Pius in honor of Virgil's *pius Aeneas,* playing on the Latin version of his own secular name: he needed to suggest that he had indeed become pious even while remaining Enea. His love of classical literature provided a form of continuity, as did his long-lasting admiration for mythological art. In short, this pope could not very well argue against the Olympian gods in general; his objections were aimed much more specifically at Malatesta's arrogance in using them as symbols of his personal wealth and power. Malatesta was a treacherous upstart, a bastard, and a mercenary, determined to carve out his own state of Rimini too close to that of the pope. That would not do. Nor would it do to line up the Olympian gods as allies. As far as the Church was concerned, they were meant to side with God.

From where we stand today, the Olympian deities seem unlikely champions of Christianity. But we must remember that classical

Correggio's *The Punishment of Juno* (1519) decorated the entrance of a convent of nuns in Parma. One ecclesiastical commentator claimed that the painting was meant as a warning to novices tempted to forsake their vows. Juno had, after all, learned to her own cost how terrible it could be to have sex, even with one's own husband: the *Iliad* told that story.

literature was central to a Christian education; ecclesiastical teachers had spent many centuries dealing with the gods of Olympus by presenting them as moral allegories and warnings, and this tradition continued to flourish in the Renaissance. We may be surprised, for example, to find a naked Juno hanging from chains in a convent of nuns—but Correggio's painting, based on the "deception of Jupiter" episode in the *Iliad,* was supposedly meant to warn novices against forsaking their vows.[8] In Homer's story, after Juno seduced her husband, Jupiter, in order to help her beloved Greeks against the Trojans, he angrily reprimanded her. He reminded Juno that he had once tortured her for a previous infraction by suspending her from chains and threatened to do so again if she ever tried to repeat such a seduction trick. The myth could be seen as a powerful warning against lascivious behavior, even within marriage. The lesson was simple: Nuns should at all costs avoid behaving like Juno. The gods of Olympus were suitable subjects for Christian eyes, then, as long as their images were accompanied by the right form of explanation.

The trouble was that in the Renaissance, such explanation was no longer in the sole hands of the Church. Scholars and artists started to wield considerable power: they could interpret the gods and make them useful to a variety of different patrons in different contexts. Alberti himself worked as a secretary to the papal court, but he could also take commissions from people like Malatesta. Other humanists and artists went further still and offered their services to the Ottoman sultan himself. Their decision to work for the archenemy of Christianity neatly sums up how much the study of antiquity in the Renaissance was emancipating itself from Christian control.

Traditional accounts of the Renaissance insist that it was the fall of Constantinople in 1453 that precipitated the revival of Greek antiquity in the Latin West. According to that story, Byzantine scholars fleeing in terror brought with them valuable manuscripts of ancient authors, which ignited the imagination of Italian scholars, poets, and artists. Like most clichés, this version of events contains some truth. Although manuscripts had started traveling west long before the fall of Constantinople, the Turkish invasion certainly terrorized Byzantine people, and refugees from the East did play a key role in the revival of classical antiquity. Mehmet II, "the Conqueror," was famous for his cruelty. Everybody living in Constantinople before 1453 knew that the sultan enjoyed watching people die slowly and painfully. Indeed, he used this reputation to unnerve his enemies. Sometimes he would arrange for a stake to be driven through the body of an opponent, from the anus to the shoulder, avoiding major organs, and then wait for days while the impaled man gradually succumbed; or he would have people skinned alive and hung by their feet, to ensure prolonged, intolerable pain. When Mehmet II finally captured Constantinople, fear had already defeated its people—and that was before churches were sacked, altars defiled, nuns raped, monks tortured and killed.

Some of the Christians who survived and escaped indeed brought precious ancient manuscripts and knowledge to the West (though their collaboration with Westerners was seldom straightforward). But that was not the only way in which Mehmet II contributed to the Italian Renaissance. He soon started patronizing Western humanists. He wanted to conquer Rome, too, and to that end it was useful to present himself as a universal, modern ruler. He appealed to people who cared more for secular than divine power. Malatesta, for example, once sent his friend Matteo de' Pasti, the maker of fine medals, to the sultan with a Latin treatise on war machinery. The ruler of Rimini rightly saw that antiquity could provide a common language, a shared culture, on which to base an effective secular alliance. His gift was well chosen, but it never reached its intended recipient. Papal emissaries intercepted de' Pasti on the island of Crete—a fact that did not help Malatesta's case in Rome.

The fifteenth century, then, was a period of confusing crosscurrents for the gods of Olympus. They could still be used as Christian allegories, but they also began to appeal to people who challenged the supremacy of the Church. Indeed, their threat to Christian authority sometimes appeared to be quite direct. In 1468, for example, Paul II—the very pope who just a couple of years before had arranged for Cupid to serenade him—was enjoying the Fat Tuesday carnival celebrations from his papal perch when a man "dressed as a philosopher" approached and warned him of great danger. Several humanists were soon arrested and taken to the papal prison of Castel Sant'Angelo in Rome. It was unclear whether they had actually conspired to kill the pope, but they were accused of sympathizing with the sultan and of being pagans—that is, of worshipping the gods of Olympus.[9]

Among those arrested were the humanist Bartolomeo Platina, who promoted himself as an expert on love, and his colleague Pomponio Leto, who had barely escaped trial for sodomy in Venice only to find himself now accused of paganism in Rome. The two crimes went together, as Leto's own poetry testified. While working as a tutor in Venice, he had praised one of his charges—the son of a noble family—by comparing him with the adolescent Ganymede, beloved of Zeus. It was a shame, Leto suggested, that the Venetian boy did not live in the golden age of the gods, for otherwise Zeus would surely have ravished him rather than the Trojan Ganymede, who could not have been as pretty. The tutor went further in his praise: "Happy is he to whom the stars have given a pretty arse; the arse seduces Cupid. Riches and honors are showered on the arse; and kind fate favors a magnificent bottom."[10] It is no wonder that he eventually got into trouble, even before being charged in Rome. And apart from appreciating boys' bottoms, Leto showed an alarming interest in learning Arabic. Ostensibly his goal was to study classical Islamic thought, but it is possible that he was also courting the Ottoman sultan for patronage. The pope, at any rate, insisted it was the sultan himself, together with the arrested devotees of the ancient gods, who wanted him murdered.

Eventually, the humanists were released, and some of them even went on to work for the pope—apparently managing to put behind

them their experiences at Castel Sant'Angelo, where they had suffered extensive bouts of torture. Even so, by the end of the fifteenth
century it was clear that Italian experts on antiquity were not necessarily subordinate to the Church. It was likewise clear that the
Olympian gods were no longer simply Christian allegories, historical figures, or demons. They now spoke of human love and strength.
And they could inspire lust and arrogance. Whether this transformation of the gods was indeed a return to classical antiquity and
whether it announced a distinctively European future remain debated
issues—but it seems to me that Malatesta's gods offer a specific
answer to such questions. The deities of the Tempio Malatestiano
were obviously not just Greek or Roman in inspiration, but Egyptian and Near Eastern, too, and they were not content to settle down
in Rimini. They had become symbols of human confidence and
power, and they would travel as far as their champions would go.

18

Old Gods in the New World

Exploration across time and space went together in the Renaissance: people simultaneously studied antiquity and moved forward
into new landscapes. Many historians have noted that the discovery
of the "New World" was directly inspired by the revival of ancient
culture. At the same time, transatlantic explorations cast new light
on the ancient world—not least because new forms of religion discovered by explorers seemed, to European observers, to resemble the
antique cults of the Olympian gods.

In the second century AD, Ptolemy had calculated the circumfer-
ence of the earth with remarkable accuracy. His monumental
Geography explained, moreover, how to draw a geometrical grid
with lines marking latitude and longitude and gave detailed information about some eight thousand different places on that grid. Arabic scholars preserved and revised Ptolemy's text, adding to it their
own theoretical developments and empirical discoveries. By the end
of the fourteenth century, Ptolemy's *Geography* was finally translated into Latin, but it did not have an immediate impact in the West.
On a practical level, the so-called portolan charts used by merchants
and navigators crisscrossing the Mediterranean were more helpful;
and on a theoretical level, Ptolemy's worldview did not fit medieval

assumptions. Christian geography was symbolic and schematic: maps put Jerusalem at the center and organized the earth around it. They represented God's plan rather than any human, measurable perspectives. Slowly, however, Ptolemy's *Geography* began to command attention, and a new edition published in 1482 would fire the imagination of many educated Europeans—including Christopher Columbus.

Even before then, however, geographic explorations had gathered momentum in close conversation with ancient literature. In 1341, an expedition led by the Genoese Nicoloso da Recco and the Florentine Angiolino de' Corbizzi set out to explore the Canary Islands. To their surprise, the European seamen found the islands to be inhabited by an unknown people, who had their own strange and distinctive culture. The discovery resonated with other Renaissance developments. This was the age when poets like Petrarch were offering a new vision for humanity. As we have seen, the most humane character in Petrarch's epic was Mago, a pagan African. Mago was modeled entirely on ancient Latin texts, but now Italian sea captains were confronted with actual pagans living off the coast of Africa. Indeed, historian David Abulafia has argued that the Renaissance was marked by two simultaneous discoveries of humankind, one achieved through historical research, the other through geographic exploration—even if the second one turned out to be incomplete, because not all observers accepted that the newly encountered people were in fact human.[1] His argument is convincing, particularly since the same Renaissance men who studied the ancient world were also deeply interested in transatlantic explorations.

Petrarch's friend Boccaccio, for example, author of *On the Genealogy of the Gentile Gods,* also wrote a brief account of the 1341 expedition to the Canary Islands, a text that is now all but forgotten. He based his account on the narratives of the seamen themselves, thus lending his learned voice to their discovery. *On Canaria and the Other Islands Recently Discovered in the Ocean Beyond*

Spain adopted the plain, factual style of exploration reports while revealing Boccaccio's intense curiosity about the people living on the islands.[2] His interest was not limited to the possibility of commerce. Thirsty for details of Canarian culture, he expressed regret that the available accounts offered only scant information: "They saw many other things, which this Nicoloso did not choose to report," he grumbled. His *De Canaria* reported on manufacture and agriculture but also lingered on the characteristics and habits of the local people:

> Their language was, they report, quite polished, and they spoke quickly, like Italians. . . . They understood no other language, for they tried addressing them in several different ones. They are no taller than us, well formed, spirited, strong, and very intelligent, as is immediately obvious. They talked to them gesticulating, and gesticulating they answered, as deaf people do. They treat each other with respect, and seem to pay especial honor to one man. . . . They sing very tunefully and dance rather like the French. They are pleasant and quick, and more domestic than many Spaniards.

Boccaccio described the stone houses where the islanders lived and their frightened reaction when the Europeans forced their way into them. He then added that the explorers had discovered a religious building:

> They found a place for prayer, or a temple, which had no painting or decoration except for a statue carved out of stone, the image of a man who held a ball in his hand: he was naked, except for some pants made of palm, covering his genitals, as is the local use. They took the statue and brought it in their ships to Lisbon on their return.

Boccaccio's uncertainty about the exact nature of the building on Gran Canaria is evident from his use of both a Christian and a pagan term to describe it: perhaps it was a place of prayer, an *oratorium,* or perhaps it was a *templum.* This uncertainty about how to categorize the religion of transatlantic natives lasted for many centuries. They seemed to be pagans, worshipping multiple gods like the Greeks and Romans—which raised the troubling question of why God had left them in ignorance for so long. Another theory held that the natives somehow knew about the true God even without scripture. A wooden sculpture of a female figure with a child was adduced in support of this notion: the Dominican friar Alonso de Espinosa argued that the people of Tenerife had led such a pure and simple life before the arrival of Europeans that the Virgin Mary had taken them under her direct protection, leaving a statue of herself by their beach. Espinosa saw this amazing relic himself when he traveled to the island in 1590, and he described it in detail. The figure was apparently half life-size, "very beautiful," and decorated with incomprehensible writing. Espinosa denied that it could have been a piece of flotsam—for example, a figurehead from a shipwrecked European vessel, with Gothic letters on it; the appearance of this relic on the beach, he insisted, long predated the age of transatlantic travel.

As for Boccaccio's stone statue of a naked man holding a ball, nothing is known of what happened to it once it reached Lisbon—if it ever existed, that is. Some readers of his account, though, assumed that it must have been classical in appearance. In the late sixteenth century, Leonardo Torriani drew a *Fquenes*—a temple of the Majoreros, the people living on the Canarian island of Fuerteventura. His picture cannot easily be matched with specific archaeological remains on the ground, but it seems that the spiral shape of the temple is more or less credible. The statue at the center, however, is not: possibly inspired by Boccaccio's report, it resembles an Apollo rather than any local deity. Having already made their way as far east as India and China, the Olympian gods were continuing to expand their range.

It is hardly surprising that European observers recognized in the

Leonardo Torriani's drawing of a *Fquenes,* or temple, on the Atlantic island of Fuerteventura. The classical statue on a plinth seems to be a European fantasy, perhaps inspired by Boccaccio's *De Canaria.*

New World aspects of the Old. Discovery, after all, always involves connecting the unexpected with what is already known. Just as Alexander thought that he saw traces of Dionysos in India, and Julius Caesar insisted that the Gauls worshipped Mercury, so the conquistador Pedro Cieza de León suggested that the Inca women whose duty it was to serve the sun-god resembled vestal virgins.[3] In the process of being documented, the myths and rituals of the Americas often shed the very characteristics that made them look new. The first European conquistadores who witnessed the Inca cult of the Sun, for example, accurately noted that the deity was represented as a young boy sculpted in gold. When the friar Bartolomé de las Casas—who had not seen the cultic statue—wrote about it, however, he assumed that the Incas' Sun had a round face with rays emanating from it, exactly as the Greek sun-god Helios had been depicted in antiquity and as Renaissance horoscopes represented him. At the beginning of the seventeenth century, the Inca scholar Garcilaso de la Vega likewise assumed that this was how the original cultic Sun must have looked. Soon, Peruvian statuettes of the deity were combining original Inca iconography with the European-style circle of rays.[4]

There were deep theological arguments that underpinned this process of assimilation. From classical texts, European scholars had learned that according to the Greeks and Romans, the same pagan deities ruled everywhere under different shapes and guises. When the Fathers of the Church tried to integrate pagan knowledge with Christian theology, they adopted and reinterpreted this ancient assumption, carefully incorporating classical accounts into a chronology that began with the Garden of Eden, continued with the Flood, and then listed events in biblical and pagan history in parallel chronological tables. Different nations had drifted apart after Noah and the Flood, but they could all be traced back to Adam, to a true and close relationship with God.

On the basis of this chronological scheme, Christian scholars had long read classical literature and philosophy as *praeparatio evangelica,* a preparation for the arrival of Christ. Now, in the sixteenth century, this approach seemed especially relevant. Missionaries working in the New World thought that they could hear in local legends echoes of the same narratives that they already knew from classical texts. And all these stories, they believed, preserved an initial knowledge of God, however muffled and obscure it had become over time. It is easy to see how this approach to mythology would be helpful for transatlantic evangelical missions: Amerindian mythology could be presented as a first step toward the true faith.

Attempts to line up indigenous and classical myths carried on for centuries. As late as 1724, the Jesuit Joseph-François Lafitau, who worked as a missionary in Canada, published two illustrated volumes comparing the customs of American Indians with those of the ancient Greeks and Romans. He thought that the myth of origins of the Iroquois, for example, told essentially the same story as the *Homeric Hymn to Apollo.*[5] According to the Iroquois, before the creation of the earth, a woman living in the sky was seduced by a wolf-man and was therefore expelled from heaven. As she dropped from the sky, her fall was arrested by a sea turtle, and an island came into existence beneath her. There, on that island, she gave birth to twin brothers. Lafitau identified this Iroquois island as Delos and argued that the woman in question was in fact Leto, even if not all mythical details matched. To confirm that the Iroquois had roughly the same ancestral stories as everybody else, Lafitau also carefully collected references to sea turtles in Greek, Roman, Egyptian, Indian, and Chinese mythology and art. All this effort was meant to prove the truth of the Bible, according to which all humanity descended from Adam and Noah before God "let all nations go their own way."[6] The task, as the conservative Lafitau saw it, was to reassemble a unified vision of the past. Ultimately, both the Iroquois myth and the story of Leto were just twisted memories of Eve expelled from terrestrial paradise.

To be sure, some observers who noted the vast range of human myths and cults argued against trying to make them cohere. For all that he mixed up Inca and classical visions of the sun-god, Garcilaso de la Vega, for example, insisted that Andean stories about the gods were best understood on their own terms, without trying to identify them with European "allegories."[7] (As the son of a Spanish conquistador and an Inca noblewoman, Garcilaso was especially well-placed to appreciate just how fraught the process of translation and cultural convergence could be.) But despite such reasonable comments, the process of assimilation left a lasting mark. To this day, many historians take at face value early Spanish reports that the Aztecs worshipped a pantheon of twelve deities, without realizing that these are in fact the Olympians in disguise.[8]

The missionaries' zeal for merging all pagan mythologies did not universally obliterate the distinctions between Old World and New World deities, however. Back in Europe, at a remove from the immediate need to save native souls, scholars were far more interested in the diversity of human mythology and its creative potential. This impulse is perhaps most obvious in the development of mythological manuals. Boccaccio's fourteenth-century *On the Genealogy of the Gentile Gods* remained the basic guide on the Olympians for a long time, but it was eventually replaced by other handbooks. As

readers became increasingly curious about the various manifestations of the gods, competition and one-upmanship shaped the work
of mythological writers. They wanted to be more accurate than
their predecessors, but also more wide-ranging.

Georg Pictor was the first author to renew the project of cata-
loging pagan gods. His *Mythological Theology* of 1532 took the
form of a dialogue between teacher and pupil and was decidedly
more visual in orientation than Boccaccio's book. When the teacher
failed to offer a description of a god, the pupil would immediately
demand, *"Dic imaginem!"* ("Tell me the appearance!") Pictor also
endeavored to provide new and exotic information about the gods
whenever possible, in order to feed his pupil's insatiable curiosity.
Time and again, the pupil in his story inquired, "Apart from those,
do you have other less common images?" And so the teacher broad-
ened his geographic scope, ranging across classical sources to
describe strange Near Eastern and African manifestations of the
gods. He talked about an Assyrian Apollo with a basketlike head-
dress, for example, and introduced his pupil to a peculiar bearded
Venus from Cyprus. Such reports, bizarre as they sounded, were in
fact based on meticulous research. The bearded Venus, for instance,
was attested in the Latin author Macrobius. Pictor learned from
him that in Cyprus there once was a beautiful female-looking statue
that also sported a beard and a penis, and that men sacrificed to it
dressed up as women while women worshipped it dressed as men,
in order to pay homage to a deity of love that was simultaneously
male and female. Pictor also used classical authors to offer disquisi-
tions on the Egyptian gods, trying to imagine how they might have
looked based on the scant evidence available.

Three other manuals followed Pictor's: *History of the Gods* by
Lilio Gregorio Giraldi, *Mythology* by Natale Conti, and *Images of
the Gods* by Vincenzo Cartari, all published within a decade of one
another in the mid–sixteenth century. With each handbook, scholarship became more exact, and Boccaccio stood corrected on many
issues. His most famous error was the mysterious Demogorgon,

who he thought was a pagan deity but was probably just a misunderstanding of Plato's concept of the "demiurge." (As Jean Seznec put it, this was "a grammatical mistake turned god.")[9] Boccaccio's Demogorgon, a kind of mythological prince of darkness, enjoyed some success in the Renaissance, appearing in carnival floats and other celebratory displays and later showing up in the works of Spenser, Marlowe, Dryden, and even Milton and Shelley.[10] In his mythological handbook of 1548, however, Giraldi became quite exercised about his authenticity, and a few years later Cartari exploded: "I have never yet found or seen mention of this Demogorgon in any ancient writer at all!"[11]

As well as checking their claims against ancient sources, mythological writers now increasingly took into consideration archaeological evidence, not least because they were trying to be helpful to artists. Giraldi explicitly omitted myths and explanations when they had no interest for those wishing to draw the gods, while Cartari deliberately focused on providing authentic representations of the Olympian deities. "Authentic," however, did not mean "authentically Greek or Roman." Since Renaissance mythographers wanted to satisfy a broad curiosity about the pagan gods, reports of strange cults, myths, and images in newly discovered lands began to have an impact on their handbooks. Cartari, for example, discussed the gods of Greece, Rome, Egypt, Syria, Phoenicia, Persia, Scythia, and Arabia—and then briefly mentioned the gods of the "new islands" discovered across the Atlantic.

In 1615, Lorenzo Pignoria further expanded Cartari's work by adding a supplement that dealt extensively with the gods of Mexico and Japan. After collecting what was known based on the few descriptions and artifacts that had reached Europe, he produced careful and accurate drawings. The gods of Olympus were now joined by a stunning Tonacatecuhtli, the Aztec lord of life and nourishing, and several other gods "of the eastern and western Indies," as Pignoria put it. Deities from the "new" and the "ancient" worlds thus came to feature together in the same collection of mythology.

As for the relationship between them, Pignoria subscribed to the dominant view that they were representations of the same pagan gods, under various shapes and guises. Indeed, he argued that these gods were originally Egyptian rather than Graeco-Roman. He remembered that according to Herodotus, Egyptian priests were the keepers of more ancient and authoritative traditions of divine knowledge than the Greeks, and that Homer and Hesiod had allegedly learned from them. So he assumed that in some way or other, these Egyptian priests had managed to convey their knowledge as far as Mexico and Japan.

In line with the argument about *praeparatio evangelica,* Pignoria believed that the Egyptians spoke cryptically and allegorically about the gods, hiding Christian truths in their mythology. A fascination with their incomprehensible hieroglyphic script helped to foster the Renaissance impression that the Egyptians were the keepers of esoteric knowledge. But Pignoria was not overly interested in theological argument or allegorical interpretation. Above all, he wanted to offer accurate, novel, and wide-ranging depictions of the gods, as his very title made clear: *On the True and New Images of the Ancient Gods.* The whole trajectory of the mythological manuals spoke of both a desire for new knowledge and a delight in the diverse manifestations of assorted deities. The Olympian gods thus exemplified two strands of the humanities that, in my view, are always best kept tightly bound together: the pursuit of increasingly accurate scholarship and a devotion to the human imagination—in all its multiform variety.

A Marble Head

The gods of Olympus did not vanish after the Renaissance. They lived on for many centuries and seem set for immortality as I write this. The popular notion that they died at the end of antiquity and were then born again, announcing the arrival of modernity, is a rather blatant fiction. History does not work like this and indeed cannot be neatly packaged into periods at all. The ancient gods survived right through the ages. They never died, but rather evolved, reinventing themselves as the circumstances demanded. Still, it is no accident that their different manifestations fit into the conventional divisions scholars use to parcel up history. Those periods were defined, at least in part, by their relationship to classical civilization. It was by reaching out to antiquity, and lamenting the Christian centuries that separated him from it as a time of darkness, that Petrarch helped along the invention of the Middle Ages.

The gods of Olympus experienced their most important transformation precisely at the end of that "in between" period. Rather than a rebirth, the Renaissance in the first instance certified a loss: the gods were no longer credited with supernatural powers, whether demonic or divine. They were increasingly seen as figments of the imagination, and that—despite the variety of their subsequent appearances—is what they have remained. Although a few Renaissance scholars and artists were accused of worshipping the ancient gods, and some pagan outbursts have occurred since, the Olympians ceased to attract widespread religious interest. Allegory won out. The gods lived on, but only as figures through which people could express different, human truths. Once fear of the Olympian gods had vanished, what remained was admiration for the people who had created them in poetry and art.

The link between Olympian deities and the celebration of human talent was not a new one. In antiquity, athletic competitions, poetry contests, theater festivals, statues, and paintings were intended to both please the gods and showcase the most impressive human accomplishments. It was no coincidence that Plato and Aristotle developed their theories of literature by engaging with the Olympian gods. Nor was it by chance that vase painters chose to reflect on progress in art—on innovations in the human ability to represent the human body—by depicting gods next to images of gods. And as time went on, the Olympians became the standard by which the most impressive mortals were measured.

The achievements of Alexander the Great, who claimed to have traveled farther than Dionysos, seemed divine; so did the doctrines of Epicurus, the philosopher of pleasure whose followers hailed him as a benefactor even greater than the god of wine. It is because the Olympians presided over the culture of Greece, and because the Romans admired that culture, that the gods eventually made themselves at home in Rome. And again, it was because Christian readers recognized the value of classical culture that they preserved the memory of objectionable pagan deities. (We can read Homer and Virgil today, after all, only because monks and bishops copied and studied their epics.) In the long run, it was this honoring of human talent, now unmoored from the practices of religion, that enabled the long journey of the Olympian gods from antiquity to modernity.

After the Renaissance, the Olympians continued to inspire

impressive human endeavors. Indeed, if we want to understand what people have valued and wanted at different times over the past few centuries, we could do worse than consider how they represented the gods of Olympus. In the accelerated account of modern manifestations of the gods that follows, then, I continue to refer to the conventional periods of European history—knowing all the time that they are fictions, but also that they are related to the more specific fictions that are the Olympian gods.

In the baroque, the gods took part in all kinds of excesses. They frolicked in literature and on canvas, but above all, they burst onto the stage. The basic technologies of the theater that we still use today—the ropes, curtains, pulleys, and other backstage machinery—were mostly designed in that era and often to facilitate the movements of the gods. Like the ancient deus ex machina, the baroque deities descended from the heavens and leapt onto the stage, rescuing heroes, resolving conflicts, and generally intervening in the most complicated, marvelous, and unlikely plots. Opera was born as a remake of the ancient theater: classical texts made it clear that Greek drama involved lyric songs and choral odes mixed with recitatives, and it was the musical theater of ancient Greece that baroque composers sought to re-create. Monteverdi's *Orfeo* was largely an excuse for Apollo to start singing again. In literature, painting, and sculpture, meanwhile, the gestures of the gods became more theatrical, reflecting their extraordinary stage presence. The desire to be marvelous and unlikely, to dazzle and seduce, typified the period and suited the gods very well. Venus and, above all, a proliferation of Cupids became emblems of the baroque. But the fundamental problem with all this had already been pinpointed by Ovid: "Love and dignity do not go well together."[1]

The backlash was swift and brutal. During the Enlightenment, as the scientific foundations of knowledge took hold of the imagination, the gods of Olympus went once more into hiding. Or rather, they went Greek. It was as a result of the Enlightenment that ancient Greece was rediscovered as a culture distinct from that of Rome.

A baroque Cupid by a painter in the school of Guido Reni, possibly Elisabetta Sirani (1638–1665).

In an act of resistance against the excesses of the baroque and the rococo, artists and intellectuals turned to the Greeks as the champions of aesthetic measure, rational restraint, scientific inquiry, and social justice, while the Romans were broadly dismissed as gruesome gladiators and deranged emperors. The art historian Johann Joachim Winckelmann was an important figure in this development: he elevated Greek art to an ideal (on scant evidence, it must be said, given that hardly any had survived) and treated Roman copies as derivative and hence inferior. Greek temples became models for the new civic buildings. Town halls, hospitals, museums, and even prisons were fashioned like ancient sanctuaries, complete with columns, pediments, and marble figures of the Olympian gods. In England, Wedgwood put the gods on a diet and softened their features; in that guise, they took pride of place in the drawing room, embellishing teapots, saucers, and cups. Greek divinities were thus admitted into civilized society, but only as pale images of virtue, moderation, beauty, and justice.

Josiah Wedgwood (1730–1795), potter, industrialist, and man of science, created polite representations of the Olympian gods, suitable for use in the drawing room.

Nothing in these anemic figures spoke of their aggressive vitality. Yet around the turn of the nineteenth century, it suddenly burst forth, again signaling a change of mood—or, as historians might put it, period. In the Romantic age, the gods of Olympus seemed to abandon civility. Escaping their marble effigies, they inspired extreme passion and, at times, even madness. Apollo, for example, struck down the poet Hölderlin as he was traveling on foot from Bordeaux back to his native Germany on a November day in 1802. Exactly what happened is unclear, despite the panicked letter the poet wrote a friend, but it was no polite encounter. It seems that Hölderlin experienced in his own life the tragic fall of Hyperion, a victim of Apollo whose fate he had described so movingly in "Hyperion's Song of Fate." Fortunately, Ernst Zimmer, a carpenter whose favorite poem this happened to be, heard of Hölderlin's mental breakdown and offered to help. For forty-odd years, Zimmer and his family kept

Hölderlin in their own home, fed him, cared for him, and hoped he might recover. He never did, showing that human kindness was no match for the romantic beauty and cruelty of the gods.

Other divine attacks of the time were more lighthearted and quintessentially French. Baudelaire, for example, described a young man standing up and proposing a toast to the gods at a fashionable Parisian party. "They are about to return," he declared in all earnestness.[2] Baudelaire and his friends made fun of this young pagan, but he was adamant. "Juno looked favorably on me," he said. "I was sad and miserable; I implored her, and she gave me a profound and benevolent look, she cheered me up and gave me courage." Baudelaire commented with a wink: "Juno threw him one of her *regards de vache,* the cow-eyed Hera. Possibly the poor fellow is mad." His friends joined in: "He saw all those girls with pagan eyes at the circus last night. Ernestine was playing Juno—she tipped him an allusive look, a really sluttish stare." "Call her Ernestine if you like," rejoined the young man, "but her effect on my morale was just the same."

Heine, who moved from Germany to France, captured the spirit of the age. In *The Gods in Exile* he claimed that the gods were about to return after a long and terrible life spent hiding "among the owls and toads in the dark hovels of their past splendour."[3] Their arrival would be astonishing: "Venus will come and meet us as a demon, a she-devil of a woman who, beneath all her Olympian arrogance, reveals herself as a courtesan perfumed with ambrosia, a divinity *aux camélias,* a divine entertainer." So much for Winckelmann's noble, quiet, enlightened marble gods. Romanticism harked back to the Middle Ages and to medieval visions of the Olympians: the toads, the hovels, and the demons were all references to that earlier period of darkness.

Romantic poets often used the language of religion to express their newfound devotion to the gods, but in fact what they revered was human creativity. Giacomo Leopardi celebrated the gods as survivors of a time when reason had not yet "spread its dreadful power, making everything small, petty, and lifeless."[4] Yet he also intuitively understood that the gods would forever remain outsiders, that they could never fit into the modern world. Some of his most ferocious prose condemned the affectation, the crude delusions, of poets who "pretend to be ancient Italians and conceal as far as possible the fact that they are modern Italians."[5] The problem with that attitude, as Leopardi rightly saw, was that the moderns lacked the necessary conviction: "Though we have inherited their literature, we did not inherit Greek and Roman religion along with it." For him and many other Romantic artists, writers, and poets, the gods stood for a sense of alienation from the present, mingled with feelings of social exclusion, loneliness, and a keen awareness of beauty.

Friedrich Nietzsche was the heir of much of this—of the passion, the loneliness, the crystalline visions, the divine visitations, the aesthetic justification of everything, the attractions of the demimonde, and finally the madness. All those were expressed in one of his last letters to Professor Jacob Burckhardt, eminent scholar of classical antiquity and the Renaissance at the University of Basel: "Actually, I would much rather be a professor in Basel than God: but I didn't dare push my private selfishness so far as to neglect, just for myself, the creation of the world."[6] Signed: Dionysos. As to what this world was that Nietzsche/Dionysos was in charge of creating, opinion was (and is) divided.

Thinkers, poets, and artists of nineteenth-century Europe commonly claimed to have a special, exclusive relationship with the gods of Olympus. They did so for a variety of reasons: convention, vanity, awe, but also simply to seem inspired and unique. It was only in the twentieth century that connecting with the gods became a collective aspiration. The 1936 Berlin Olympics were probably the occasion on which the Greek gods and the modern masses came into closest contact. Athletes imitated the postures of ancient statues, and, for the first time, thousands of runners carried the fire that

This cartoon, published in *The Philadelphia Record* on December 7, 1935, contrasts the Berlin Olympics with the values represented by the ancient Mercury, seen here as an ambassador of international goodwill.

Prometheus had stolen from Zeus all the way from Olympia to Berlin. That brilliant piece of propaganda—the first relay of the Olympic torch—was meant to symbolize the special connection between ancient Greece and modern Germany, though this was a link that many contested. A cartoon in *The Philadelphia Record* entitled "The Modern Mercury," for example, contrasted the noble Greek god of athletics with his thuggish German counterpart. In response to the 1936 Olympics, antifascists worldwide planned an alternative People's Olympiad in Barcelona. Unfortunately, we shall never know what Olympian gods that event would have presented, because the Spanish Civil War broke out before it could take place.

From Apollo singing the tunes of Monteverdi to Juno winking at an impressionable young Parisian, from Wedgwood's polite drawing-room deities to Dionysos's mad correspondence with a professor in Basel, the gods of Olympus have shown up across Europe in countless forms since the Renaissance. A common trait in all those appearances, though, has been their distance from ancient reli-

Romare Bearden's *Roots Odyssey* (1976) reinterprets ancient black-figure pottery, and classical culture more generally, in light of the traumatic experience of the Middle Passage.

gious practice. It was largely by venturing beyond Europe that the Olympians reconnected with the rituals they once enjoyed. In 1973, for instance, the Nigerian playwright Wole Soyinka cast Dionysos as the Yoruba god Ogun in an acclaimed version of Euripides's *Bacchae*. That same year, the Italian writer and film director Pier Paolo Pasolini took the plays of Aeschylus to Tanzania and Uganda in his film *Notes for an African Oresteia*. These Afro-Greek visions of tragedy (whether conceived in Africa or Europe) insisted that the world of the Olympian gods was by no means exclusively European and appealed to ancient ritual in order to make this point. Ritual sacrifices—with the slaughtered animals, buzzing flies, blood, heat, and dust—were simultaneously African and Greek. Comparisons across cultures also inspired a new academic interest in ancient religion, as historians developed new anthropological approaches to its study.

In Buenos Aires, meanwhile, Jorge Luis Borges was sleeping. He dreamed that he was having a conversation with a professor at the university before one of his lectures. Suddenly, in the dream, there was a great commotion outside the lecture hall. Borges thought that there were street musicians outside or perhaps student demonstrations. But then a mob burst into the lecture hall, screaming about a momentous arrival: "The gods! The gods!" Four or five creatures suddenly came out of the crowd and occupied the podium. "Everyone clapped, weeping," Borges recalls. "It was the gods, returning after a banishment of many centuries." Events unfolded quickly:

> Perhaps excited by our applause, one of them—I no longer know which—burst out in a triumphant, incredibly bitter clucking that was half gargle and half whistle. From that point on, things changed. It all began with the suspicion (perhaps exaggerated) that the gods were unable to talk. Centuries of a feral life of flight had atrophied that part of them that was human; the moon of Islam and the cross of Rome had been implacable with these fugitives. Beetling brows, yellowed teeth, the sparse beard of a mulatto or a Chinaman, and beastlike dewlaps were testaments to the degeneration of the Olympian line. . . . Suddenly, we felt that they were playing their last trump, that they were cunning, ignorant, and cruel, like aged predators, and that if we allowed ourselves to be swayed by fear or pity, they would wind up destroying us. We drew our heavy revolvers (suddenly, in the dream, there were revolvers) and joyfully killed the gods.[7]

So here they are, these multifaceted, migrating Olympian gods. In Borges's vision, as in many other modern manifestations, there is the sense that the gods can come and go, that they may die and reappear, and that when they do show up, we might not like them after all. There is an anxiety about their identity and racial purity in Borges's story: the gods turn out to be nothing like the pristine visions of ancient Greece promoted by centuries of idealizing scholarship. Indeed, there is a suggestion that professors will kill the gods if they finally meet them, though (at least judging from the effort of writing this book) it seems likelier that the gods will finish off the professors. Still, the whole assassination plot—no matter who might be killing whom—seems rather beside the point. The gods will always live, as long as people care about them. They do not need worshippers, necessarily, but they do need people. The question arises, then, as to why the gods of Olympus still attract such widespread interest.

There is, of course, the possibility that the gods are handed down from generation to generation for no reason whatsoever. In the Renaissance, that thought struck people quite suddenly and seemed rather convincing. Perhaps the gods were neither deities nor demons, wrote Bernard de Fontenelle in the seventeenth century, but "mere chimaeras, day-dreams and absurdities."[8] Fontenelle read about the alleged similarities between classical myths and Amerindian stories, concluding that all accounts of the gods, wherever they originated, were inescapably primitive—the product of stupendous ignorance rather than culture.

But there are other ways of thinking about the gods. Ancient philosophers, no matter how skeptical they were, treated them with respect precisely because, as Cicero put it, "no people, no race of men, lacks some untutored conception of the gods."[9] Viewed from this perspective, the gods of Olympus help us see ourselves as part of a broad and diverse humanity. Their history and our own have always been intertwined. Today, people are sometimes inclined to think that ancient cultures were somehow "pure," unmixed, and that they became intermingled only in our present-day multicultural world. This is not so: always, from the beginning, the gods of Olympus were shaped by long-distance encounters among different people, and the results of those encounters were momentous. They had weight.

In a modern Greek poem entitled "Mythistorema," George Seferis claims that he did not dream the gods—on the contrary, he woke up one day with a marble head in his hands. The head was heavy, it exhausted his elbows, and he did not know where to put it down. Sometimes, to receive something substantial and inexplicable is the best thing that can happen to us. As we struggle to make sense of the Olympian gods—debating their origins, nature, and utility—we speak of the things that are most important to us and that we do not quite understand. In this there still is, perhaps, a trace of divinity.

APPENDIX:
THE TWELVE GODS

The Greeks agreed that twelve supreme gods lived together on Olympus, though they did not always agree about which twelve gods those were. The Parthenon frieze includes the following gods, which are listed here in the order in which they are arranged on the frieze, from Zeus, moving to the left, and then from Athena, moving to the right (see p. 8 for a line drawing):

ZEUS is the supreme ruler of the universe, son of Kronos and Rhea, grandson of Gaia and Ouranos (Earth and Heaven). He is the only Olympian god whose name has a clearly traceable etymology. A comparison between some forms of the name Zeus (for example, the genitive Dios) with the Indic sky-god Dyáus Pitār, the Roman Diespiter/Jupiter, and Germanic forms of the supreme god (from which, for example, our word "Tuesday" derives) points to the existence of an earlier, Indo-European ruler of the sky.

HERA, daughter of Kronos and Rhea, is the sister and wife of Zeus. Her marriage with Zeus violates the taboo of incest and simultaneously points to a unique equality of birth between husband and wife, who enjoy exactly the same exalted ancestry. The marriage is unstable, and Hera is jealous of Zeus's other sexual partners. She is identified with the Roman Juno and the Carthaginian Tanit (this latter identification is important in Roman epic).

ARES is the only son of Zeus and Hera and represents war at its most violent and senseless. Zeus describes him as "the most hated of the gods" at *Iliad* 5.890. He is a minor deity in the Greek pantheon, and the Greeks believe that he receives greater honors in Thrace, a barbarous northern land. He is identified with Mars, a god who is, by contrast, very important in Roman religion.

DEMETER, sister of Zeus and Hera, is the goddess of agriculture. She is the mother of Persephone, who was raped and abducted by Hades, lord of the underworld. (Hades is also brother to Zeus, Hera, and Demeter herself.) Demeter and Persephone are often worshipped together as the Two Goddesses; and they preside over the Eleusinian mysteries, rituals that promise to ease the transition to the underworld. They are identified with the Roman Ceres and Proserpina, respectively.

DIONYSOS is the son of Zeus and the mortal woman Semele (daughter of Harmonia and Kadmos, the founder of the city of Thebes). He is the god of wine and ecstasy, including collective madness and orgiastic sex. The vine and the ivy are sacred to him; many Greek tragedies and comedies were composed for performance at the Great Dionysia, an Athenian festival in his honor. In Rome, he is known under his (Greek) cult title Bacchus.

HERMES is the son of Zeus and the minor goddess Maia. As soon as he was born, he stole cattle belonging to his half-brother Apollo and habitually engages in all manner of other trickery and mischief. He is the god of boundaries and boundary crossing, protector of thieves and interpreters, and escort of souls traveling to Hades. Hermes is sometimes identified with the Egyptian Thoth and the Babylonian Nabu and always with the Roman Mercury.

ATHENA was born, fully armed, out of the head of Zeus and often fulfills his plans. She is the goddess of war, military tactics, and discipline; she also oversees peaceful activities, especially the work of women at the spindle and the loom. She is a virgin goddess, though the Athenians treated her almost as a mythical mother. In Rome, she is identified with Minerva.

HEPHAISTOS is the son of Hera and has no father. In myth, this explains his physical imperfection: he is lame either because Hera did not manage to generate a perfect son without male seed or because Zeus maimed him out of jealousy and anger. He is the god of forges and crafts and is identified with the Roman Vulcan. He is married to Aphrodite, who is unfaithful to him.

POSEIDON explains, in *Iliad* 15.185–93, that he and the other two sons of Kronos and Rhea drew lots to apportion the world. Zeus was allocated the sky, Hades the underworld, and Poseidon the sea, while the earth and Olympus continued to be held in common. Poseidon is thus equal to Zeus in principle, though subordinated in practice. He is, partly for this reason, rather explosive: one of his epithets is "earth-shaker." He is identified with the Roman Neptune.

APOLLO is the son of Zeus and the goddess Leto and the twin brother of Artemis. He presides over the oracle at Delphi and is the patron god of prophecy, music, measure, and beauty. Apollo is often seen as the ritual opposite of Dionysos; he is closely associated with the Muses and is the father of Asclepius, patron god of doctors. He is known in Rome by his Greek name and is associated with the sun.

ARTEMIS, daughter of Zeus and the goddess Leto and twin sister of Apollo, is a virgin goddess. Patron of both hunters and their prey, in Homer she is called "mistress of the animals," and she is often portrayed in the company of animals in early art. She is also associated with childbirth and female puberty, overseeing the life changes from which she herself is exempt. In Rome, she is identified with Diana. She is widely associated with the moon.

APHRODITE is the goddess of love and sex, especially sex with women. According to Hesiod, she was born out of the severed genitals of Ouranos, which, tossed into the sea, washed up near Cyprus, whence she emerged. This account makes her a generation older than Zeus. Homer, by contrast, claims that Aphrodite is the daughter of Zeus and Dione, a minor goddess. She is identified with the Roman Venus; for identifications with ancient Near Eastern goddesses, see p. 48.

Dionysos and Demeter are not always included in ancient lists of the twelve Olympian gods. Possible candidates to replace them include **Heracles** (Roman Hercules), son of Zeus and the mortal woman Alcmene, who earns his immortality after completing twelve heroic labors; **Leto** (Roman Latona), mother of Apollo and Artemis; and **Hestia** (identified with the Roman Vesta), who presides over the hearth and, as a stay-at-home goddess, does not feature much in ancient art and literature.

ILLUSTRATIONS

NOTES AND FURTHER READING

PREFACE: SIMONIDES WAS WISE

1. The story of Simonides is told in Cicero, *On the Nature of the Gods* 1.22.60. On ancient and modern attempts to define what a god is, see the brief and brilliant article by A. Henrichs, "What Is a Greek God?," in J. N. Bremmer and A. Erskine, eds., *The Gods of Ancient Greece: Identities and Transformations* (Edinburgh, 2010), 19–42. A. B. Lloyd, ed., offers a good collection of essays on the subject: *What Is a God? Studies in the Nature of Greek Divinity* (London, 1997).

INTRODUCTION: A FAMILY PORTRAIT

The Greeks encountered the Olympian gods, as a group of twelve, primarily in poetry and art. Ancient cults tended to focus on one, two, or three deities at most, although there were some cults of the twelve together, for which see I. Rutherford, "Canonizing the Pantheon: The Dodekatheon in Greek Religion and Its Origins," in Bremmer and Erskine, eds., *The Gods of Ancient Greece*, 43–54. C. R. Long, *The Twelve Gods of Greece and Rome* (Leiden, 1987), collects and discusses a vast range of ancient textual and visual representations of the twelve Olympian gods. Some scholars, particularly those associated with the Paris school, argue that the gods of Olympus can be studied only as a group, because their individual characteristics

254   NOTES AND FURTHER READING

emerge in their interactions with one another: see, for example, G. Sissa
and M. Detienne, *The Daily Life of the Greek Gods,* trans. J. Lloyd (Stan-
ford, 2000). This view is now increasingly questioned, and Routledge is
currently publishing slim, informative volumes on individual gods and
heroes of the ancient world. The following studies have already appeared:
K. Dowden, *Zeus* (2006), R. Seaford, *Dionysos* (2006), S. Darcy, *Athena*
(2008), F. Graf, *Apollo* (2008), M. S. Cyrino, *Aphrodite* (2010), and E. Staf-
ford, *Herakles* (2011). Although individual portraits constitute, in my view,
a possible approach, beginning with the gods as a family of twelve makes
sense. E. Simon, *Die Götter der Griechen,* 2nd ed. (Munich, 1998), offers
beautifully illustrated essays on each of the twelve gods of Olympus, while
emphasizing how they interact with one another, especially in the poetry of
Homer. The twelve gods on the Parthenon are judiciously interpreted by
J. Neils, *The Parthenon Frieze* (Cambridge, 2001). M. Beard, *The Parthenon* (London, 2002), is a riveting general introduction to the temple and its
later reception.

Within any given local community, it was possible to worship each of
the Olympian gods, so by studying the relationships among different cults
in one specific city, we begin to see how the gods worked together for the
people living there. R. Parker, *Athenian Religion: A History* (Oxford,
1997), gives the best possible insight into the relationships among different
gods and cults in Athens. V. Pirenne-Deforge, ed., *Les Panthéons des cités:
des origines à la Périégèse de Pausanias* (Liège, 1998), collects essays on
several different cities and thus begins to offer a more general overview.
Greek religion is generally treated as an aspect of ancient civic life, partly
under the influence of two seminal essays by C. Sourvinou-Inwood, "What
Is Polis Religion?" (1988) and "Further Aspects of Polis Religion" (1990),
conveniently reprinted in R. Buxton, ed., *Oxford Readings in Greek Religion* (Oxford, 2000), 13–55. For a good overall introduction to civic religion, see L. Bruit Zaidman and P. Schmitt Pantel, *Religion in the Ancient
Greek City,* trans. P. Cartledge (Cambridge, 1992). New approaches, which
explore how the gods worked beyond the social and political structures of
the ancient city, are now beginning to gain momentum: see, for example,
J. Kindt, *Rethinking Greek Religion* (Cambridge, 2012). My book contributes to this rethinking in two ways: it focuses on travelers who took
their views about the gods to many different cities; and it discusses works
of literature, philosophy, and art that appealed (and were always intended
to appeal) to a wide range of different communities.

1. The most famous feast of reconciliation on Mount Olympus concludes the first book of the *Iliad*.
2. I follow the most widely accepted interpretation of the scene depicted on the Parthenon frieze. For a careful defense of this interpretation, and a discussion of the main alternatives, see Neils, *Parthenon Frieze*.
3. Homer, *Iliad* 5.890.
4. For Demeter and the sorrows of ancient mothers, see H. P. Foley, ed., *The Homeric Hymn to Demeter: Translation, Commentary, and Interpretive Essays* (Princeton, NJ, 1993).

PART I: BIRTH: ARCHAIC GREECE

R. Osborne, *Greece in the Making: 1200–479 BC,* 2nd ed. (London, 2009), offers an excellent overview of the archaic period. It discusses breaks and continuities in relation to Mycenaean Greece, the rise of the polis, the spread of epic poetry, the foundation of Panhellenic sanctuaries, and the development of cult statues and temples—all the while keeping in sight how we modern observers construct a historical period. M. Gaifman, *Aniconism in Greek Antiquity* (Oxford, 2012), offers a salutary reminder that even after temples and cult statues became central to religious practice, the Greeks continued to represent and worship the gods in other ways, too: sacred stones, wooden planks, pillars, and other mysterious objects continued to be treated as images of the gods. M. Scott, *Delphi and Olympia: The Spatial Politics of Panhellenism in the Archaic and the Classical Periods* (Cambridge, 2010), investigates how the two most important sanctuaries of the archaic period shaped and defined Greek religion and culture. S. Price offers a short analysis of how the Delphic oracle operated: "Delphi and Divination," in P. E. Easterling and J. V. Muir, eds., *Greek Religion and Society* (Cambridge, 1985), 128–54. J. Fontenrose, *The Delphic Oracle: Its Responses and Operations with a Catalogue of Responses* (Berkeley, 1978), collects the evidence. On the gods in early Greek epic poetry, see J. Strauss Clay, *The Politics of Olympus: Form and Meaning in the Major Homeric Hymns* (Princeton, NJ, 1989), and B. Graziosi and J. Haubold, *Homer: The Resonance of Epic* (London, 2005), chapter 3. R. Lane Fox, *Travelling Heroes: Greeks and Their Myths in the Epic Age of Homer* (London, 2009), investigates the impact of travel on epic visions of the gods. On early criticism of the gods in Homer and Hesiod, see D. C. Feeney, *The Gods of Epic: Poets and Critics of the Classical Tradition* (Oxford,

1991), chapter 1. I found the following article on the beginnings of philosophical reflections on the gods particularly stimulating: G. R. Boys-Stones, "Ancient Philosophy of Religion: An Introduction," in G. Oppy and N. Trakakis, eds., *History of Western Philosophy of Religion,* vol. 1 (Durham, 2009), 1–22.

There are many available English translations of Homer. Those by R. Lattimore and A. Verity are the most faithful and respect the line numeration of the original Greek, thereby allowing readers to follow references to specific passages. The best English translation of Hesiod is M. L. West, *Hesiod: Theogony and Works and Days* (Oxford, 1988). For the *Homeric Hymns,* see D. J. Rayor, *The Homeric Hymns: A Translation with Introduction and Notes* (Berkeley, 2004). The fragments of Xenophanes, Theagenes, and other early critics of the epic tradition are collected in H. Diels and W. Kranz, eds., *Die Fragmente der Vorsokratiker,* 3 vols., 6th ed. (Berlin, 1951–1952), and are translated in G. S. Kirk, J. E. Raven, and M. Schofield, *The Presocratic Philosophers,* 2nd ed. (Cambridge, 1983). The abbreviation "DK" in the following notes refers to the edition by Diels and Kranz.

1: AT HOME IN GREECE

1. Homer, *Odyssey* 6.43–45.
2. See J. Chadwick, *The Decipherment of Linear B* (Cambridge, 1958), and L. M. Bendall, *The Decipherment of Linear B and the Ventris-Chadwick Correspondence* (Cambridge, 2003).
3. With great perceptiveness, Walter Otto described Dionysos as *der kommende Gott,* the god perpetually arriving, even before the decipherment of Linear B, in *Dionysos: Mythos und Kultus* (Frankfurt, 1933), 71–80.
4. The phrase "most Greek of the gods" is Walter Otto's, in *Die Götter Griechenlands,* 4th ed. (Bonn, 1929), 78. For connections between Apollo and Resheph, see M. L. West, *The East Face of Helicon: West Asiatic Elements in Greek Poetry and Myth* (Oxford, 1997), 55.
5. Herodotus, *Histories* 8.144.2.
6. According to Herodotus's *Histories* 1.14.2, the first "barbarians" who consulted the Delphic oracle and left their gifts there were the Phrygian king Midas and the Lydian king Gyges.

2: EPIC VISIONS

1. Herodotus, *Histories* 2.53.2–3.
2. Hesiod, *Theogony* 18–20.
3. Ibid. 26.
4. Ibid. 115.
5. Ibid. 176–78.
6. Later Greek thinkers teased out the implications of Hesiod's myth of origins. Plato, for example, etymologized the name of Athena as "the mind of god" (*Cratylus* 407b).
7. Hesiod, *Works and Days* 640.
8. Homer, *Odyssey* 8.360–66.
9. Ibid. 8.62–64.
10. Ibid. 8.487–91.
11. See Homer, *Iliad* 20.22–25.
12. *Homeric Hymn to Aphrodite* 6.
13. That description was first coined by K. Reinhardt, *Das Parisurteil* (Frankfurt, 1938), 25: "erhabener Unernst."
14. The text and translation are published by L. R. LiDonnici, *The Epidaurian Miracle Inscriptions* (Atlanta, 1995), 104–5. F. Naiden offers an excellent discussion of it in "*Hiketai* and *Theōroi* at Epidauros," in J. Elsner and I. Rutherford, eds., *Pilgrimage in Graeco-Roman and Early Christian Antiquity: Seeing the Gods* (Oxford, 2005), 73–96.
15. Homer, *Iliad* 15.80–83.

3: CRITICAL VIEWS

1. Homer, *Iliad* 13.18–19.
2. Sappho, fr. 1.9–12 Voigt.
3. I have quoted the following hexameter fragments of Xenophanes, and they constitute a significant proportion of all that remains of his work: frs. 21 B 16, 15, 11, 23, 26, and 18 DK.
4. Heraclitus, fr. 22 B 5 DK.
5. Ibid. B 32 DK.
6. See Homer, *Iliad* 14.225–30 and 15.80–83, quoted above, p. 42.
7. See further Beard, *The Parthenon*, 147.

8. According to Pausanias, writing in the second century AD, "In early times, all the Greeks worshipped unshaped stones instead of statues" (*Description of Greece* 7.22.4).

9. Herodotus, *Histories* 1.131.1–3.

10. Theagenes 8 fr. 2 DK. For an excellent discussion, see D. Feeney, *The Gods in Epic: Poets and Critics of the Classical Tradition* (Oxford, 1991), 9.

11. This is a summary offered by Philodemus in the second century AD, in the second book of his work *On Poems* 2 (*P. Herc.* 1676 fr. 2); see also Metrodorus of Lampsacus, fr. 61 A 4 DK.

12. Homer, *Iliad* 21.6–7.

13. Heraclitus, *Homeric Problems* 1.1.

14. Xenophanes, fr. 21 B 1.22 DK.

PART II: DIALOGUE: CLASSICAL ATHENS

P. J. Rhodes, *A History of the Classical Greek World, 478–323 BC,* 2nd ed. (Oxford, 2005), is a superb guide to classical Greek history. For the term *classical,* see Edith Hall's eye-opening reflections in "Putting the Class into Classical Reception," in L. Hardwick and C. Stray, eds., *Blackwell Companion to Classical Receptions* (Oxford, 2008), 386–97. M. H. Hansen, as director of the Copenhagen Polis Centre, has done more than any other scholar in investigating the advent of democracy not only in Athens, but in other Greek cities, as the *Acts of the Copenhagen Polis Centre I–VII* (Copenhagen, 1993–2005) and the *Papers of the Copenhagen Polis Centre I–VIII* (Copenhagen, 1994–2007) testify. J. D. Mikalson, *Athenian Popular Religion* (Chapel Hill, NC, 1983), offers guidance on the religious life of classical Athens but overstates, in my view, the separation between popular culture and new intellectual approaches to the gods. Classical art, for example, was both popular and often innovative in its treatment of the gods, as was Athenian drama. Robin Osborne, *Archaic and Classical Greek Art* (Oxford, 1998), offers general guidance on visual representations of the gods: *The History Written on the Classical Body* (Cambridge, 2011), chapter 7, discusses in particular how divine bodies were represented in the classical period. For vases displaying classical-looking gods next to archaic statues of themselves, see M. de Cesare, *Le statue in immagine: Studi sulle raffigurazioni di statue nella pittura vascolare greca* (Rome, 1997), especially 91–106.

W. K. C. Guthrie, *The Sophists* (Cambridge, 1971), offers a readable introduction to some of the main intellectual currents of Greece in the fifth century BC; Jacqueline de Romilly, *The Great Sophists in Periclean Athens,* trans. J. Lloyd (Oxford, 1992), assesses their impact on Athenian culture. The fragments of the sophists are collected by Diels and Kranz, eds., *Die Fragmente der Vorsokratiker,* and are translated in Kirk, Raven, and Schofield, *The Presocratic Philosophers.* On atheists, see J. Bremmer, "Atheism in Antiquity," in M. Martin, ed., *The Cambridge Companion to Atheism* (Cambridge, 2007), 11–26. R. Waterfield, *Why Socrates Died: Dispelling the Myths* (London, 2009), provides full guidance on the extant evidence for Socrates's trial, though I disagree with his interpretation of it. On Socrates's *daimōn* and its extraordinary afterlife—that is, the eventual proliferation of demons—see Walter Burkert, *Greek Religion,* trans. J. Raffan (Oxford, 1985), chapter 7, which also discusses philosophical religion more generally. S. Halliwell assesses Plato's theory of imitation and its later reception in *The Aesthetics of Mimesis: Ancient Texts and Modern Problems* (Princeton, NJ, 2002); he is also the author of an excellent translation and commentary of Aristotle's *Poetics* (London, 1987). On how Plato and Aristotle developed their theories of literature by criticizing poetic visions of the gods, see Feeney, *The Gods of Epic,* chapter 1.

4: AN EDUCATION FOR GREECE

1. F. Nietzsche's first book, *The Birth of Tragedy from the Spirit of Music,* first published in Leipzig in 1872, posits the opposition of the Dionysiac and the Apollinian. Though highly creative in its approach to ancient culture, it draws from an opposition between Dionysos and Apollo that can clearly be discerned in Greek myth, cult, and art.
2. Protagoras, fr. 80 B 1 DK: "man," or more correctly "human being," since Protagoras used the gender-neutral term *anthrōpos* rather than *anēr* ("man" as opposed to "woman").
3. Euripides, *Hecuba* 799–801.
4. Protagoras, fr. 80 B 4 DK.
5. Diogenes Laertius, *Lives of Eminent Philosophers* 9.24, writes about Melissus: "As for the gods, he denied that there was any occasion to give a definition of them, for there was no certain knowledge of them." (Melissus fr. 30 A 1 DK.)
6. Cicero, *On the Nature of the Gods* 1.22.60; see above, p. 2.

7. Prodicus, fr. 84 B 5 DK.

8. Democritus, fr. 68 A 75, cf. B 30 DK.

9. See Anaxagoras, fr. 59 A 42 DK. As well as claiming that the sun was larger than the Peloponnese, Anaxagoras argued that celestial bodies were "red-hot stones snatched up by the rotation of the aether." For Anaxagoras's interest in a meteorite that fell in Aegospotami in 467 BC, see Diogenes Laertius, *Lives of Eminent Philosophers* 2.10 (= fr. 59 A 1 DK). The event must have contributed toward his belief that the heavenly bodies were made of stone.

10. The fragments of Diagoras are collected in M. Winiarczyk, ed., *Diagorae Melii et Theodori Cyrenaei reliquiae* (Leipzig, 1981).

11. See Strabo, *Geography* 8.3.30.

12. Thucydides, *History of the Peloponnesian War* 2.37–41.

13. Ibid. 5.84–116.

5: EXILE AND DEATH

1. Gorgias, *Encomium of Helen* 6.

2. Ibid. 8.

3. Ibid. 21.

4. *On What Is Fine and What Is Shameful* 2.28: the text is published in T. M. Robinson, ed., *Contrasting Arguments: An Edition of the Dissoi Logoi* (New York, 1979).

5. Homer, *Iliad* 3.383–420.

6. Euripides, *Trojan Women* 989.

7. Euripides, *Heracles* 1345–46.

8. See Aristophanes, *Thesmophoriazousae* 450–52.

9. For Mubaššir, see F. Rosenthal, *Greek Philosophy in the Arab World* (London, 1990), 33 (= *Orientalia* 6, 1937, 33).

10. Diogenes Laertius, *Lives of Eminent Philosophers* 2.40; Plato, *Apology* 24b–c; Xenophon, *Memorabilia* 1.1.1.

11. Thucydides, *History of the Peloponnesian War* 2.53.3.

12. Lysias, *Against Eratosthenes* 12.5.

6: FICTIONS AND FANTASIES

1. Plato, *Republic* 378a.

2. Ibid. 390c.

3. Ibid. 388e–89a.
4. Ibid. 381e. The mothers described in this passage take their inspiration from Homer, *Odyssey* 17.485–6:

Gods in the likeness of wandering strangers take on
all sorts of appearances, and go roaming from city to city.

5. D. Roochnik, "The Political Drama of Plato's *Republic*," in S. Salkever, ed., *The Cambridge Companion to Ancient Greek Political Thought* (Cambridge, 2009), 165.
6. Homer, *Iliad* 1.47–8.
7. Homer, *Odyssey* 1.320.
8. Plato, *Phaedrus* 229b–d.
9. Homer, *Iliad* 6.181.
10. Plato, *Phaedrus* 229e–30a.
11. Ibid. 247a–b.
12. Aristotle, *Poetics* 1449b 24–28.
13. Ibid. 1451a 36–38. M. Hubbard offers a good summary of the differences between Plato and Aristotle on the issue of poetry: "Plato had claimed that an instance of mimesis has less reality than an individual particular, which in turn has less reality than the *idea*. Aristotle replies that statements of the poet, so far from being inferior to statements of particulars, are more comprehensive and more philosophical"; in D. A. Russell and M. Winterbottom, eds., *Ancient Literary Criticism: The Principal Texts in New Translations* (Oxford, 1972), 88.
14. Aristotle, *Poetics* 1460b 22–26.
15. Aristotle admits that poems may contain things that are, strictly speaking, impossible: "That is a fault," he says, but it is excusable if the poem thereby achieves *katharsis* of the emotions and produces something more thrilling (*ekplēktikōteron*) than it could otherwise produce: *Poetics* 1460b 22–26.

PART III: TRAVEL: HELLENISTIC EGYPT

There are many histories and biographies of Alexander the Great. One of the most authoritative is A. B. Bosworth, *Conquest and Empire: The Reign of Alexander the Great* (Cambridge, 1988), not least because Bosworth has also written commentaries on the most important ancient account of Alexander's conquests: Arrian's *History of Alexander,* to which he dedicates two volumes (Oxford, 1980–1995). A. de Sélincourt translates Arrian in *The Campaigns of Alexander,* rev. ed., with an introduction by J. R. Hamilton (London, 1971). Other important sources are collected and translated in I. Worthington, ed., *Alexander the Great: A Reader,* 2nd ed. (London, 2011). R. Lane Fox, *Alexander the Great* (London, 1973), is as thrilling a read as a historical novel and informs Oliver Stone's Hollywood film *Alexander* (2004). P. Cartledge, *Alexander the Great: The Hunt for a New Past* (London, 2004), gives an equally accessible account to the general reader. P. Briant offers an important corrective to Graeco-centric views of Alexander in his seminal, and brief, *Alexander the Great and His Empire: A Short Introduction,* trans. A. Kuhrt (Princeton, NJ, 2010; original French, 1974): Briant looks at Alexander also through Persian eyes, assessing him as Darius's successor.

On Alexander's divinity, see E. A. Fredricksmeyer, "Alexander's Religion and Divinity," in J. Roisman, ed., *Brill's Companion to Alexander the Great* (Leiden, 2003), 253–78, and the excellent study by A. Chaniotis, "The Divinity of Hellenistic Rulers," in A. W. Erskine, ed., *A Companion to the Hellenistic World* (Oxford, 2005), 431–45. R. L. Gordon discusses anthropomorphic statues and, indirectly, contributes to explaining how they could help establish the divinity of rulers, in "The Real and the Imaginary: Production and Religion in the Graeco-Roman World," *Art History* 2 (1979): 5–34. Specifically on the Siwah oracle, see S. Caneva, "Depuis Hérodote à Alexandre: L'appropriation gréco-macédonienne d'Ammon de Siwa, entre pratique oraculaire et légitimation du pouvoir," in C. Bonnet, A. Declercq, and I. Slobodzianek, eds., *Les représentations des dieux des autres* (Palermo, 2011), 193–220. The Greek *Alexander Romance* is translated by R. Stoneman (London, 1991), who also offers a good introduction to the wider legends it inspired. In her groundbreaking monograph, *Seeing Double: Intercultural Poetics in Ptolemaic Alexandria* (Berkeley, 2003), S. Stephens discusses both the *Alexander Romance* and Euhemerus's *Sacred Register* in chapter 1, "Conceptualizing Egypt."

On the gods of Olympus as planets, see T. Barton, *Ancient Astrology* (London, 1994), and R. Beck, *A Brief History of Ancient Astrology* (Oxford, 2007). On Alexandria, P. M. Fraser, *Ptolemaic Alexandria* (Oxford, 1972), remains the standard work of reference; on scholarship in the Museum, the first port of call remains R. Pfeiffer, *A History of Classical Scholarship, from the Beginnings to the End of the Hellenistic Age* (Oxford,

1968). A. Sens's "Hellenistic Poetry," in G. R. Boys-Stones, B. Graziosi, and P. Vasunia, eds., *The Oxford Handbook of Hellenic Studies* (Oxford, 2009), 597–607, offers a succinct and masterly introduction to the Alexandrian poets. M. Fantuzzi and R. Hunter, *Tradition and Innovation in Hellenistic Poetry* (Cambridge, 2004), is an excellent general study; and G. Radke, *Die Kindheit des Mythos: Die Erfindung der Literaturgeschichte in der Antike* (Munich, 2007), considers, in particular, why the Greeks of Hellenistic Egypt focused on the childhood of their gods. The fragments of Callimachus mentioned in the following notes are collected and numbered in R. Pfeiffer, *Callimachus*, 2 vols. (Oxford, 1949–1953). Several more fragments have been discovered since then; some are collected in H. Lloyd-Jones and P. Parsons, *Supplementum Hellenisticum* (Berlin, 1983). I recommend the following English translations of Hellenistic poetry: P. Green, *Apollonius: The Argonautika* (Berkeley, 1997); F. Nisetich, *The Poems of Callimachus* (Oxford, 2001); and A. Verity, *Theocritus: Idylls* (Oxford, 2002).

7: FARTHER THAN DIONYSOS

1. Almost every aspect of Alexander's Asian campaign is hotly debated, but as A. B. Bosworth points out, "There is no doubt about the historicity of the altars": *A Historical Commentary on Arrian's History of Alexander,* vol. 2 (Oxford, 1995), 356. The altars are mentioned in all the ancient Alexander traditions and, as an act of celebration and closure, make perfect sense.

2. On the altars of the twelve gods as symbols of Hellenism, see "Canonizing the Pantheon: The Dodekatheon in Greek Religion and Its Origins," in Bremmer and Erskine, eds., *The Gods of Ancient Greece,* 53.

3. See Arrian, *Anabasis of Alexander* 2.14.5: "My father was murdered by conspirators whom you Persians organized."

4. Ibid. 1.16.7.

5. Ibid. 3.1.5.

6. See Aeschines, *Against Ctesiphon* 3.160; cf. Harpocration's *Lexicon* s.v. Margites.

7. See A. Kuhrt, *The Persian Empire: A Corpus of Sources from the Achaemenid Period* (London, 2007), 447.

8. On these burial heaps, see Bosworth, *A Historical Commentary on Arrian's History of Alexander,* vol. 2, 31.

9. Lane Fox, *Alexander the Great,* 313.

10. Arrian, *Anabasis of Alexander* 5.2.1.
11. Ibid. 4.28.1–30.9.

8: DEAD GODS AND DIVINE PLANETS

1. Arrian, *Anabasis of Alexander* 7.23.2.
2. For Zeus at Olympia, see Strabo, *Geography* 8.3.30. For Artemis, see Pliny, *Natural History* 36.13: the statue looked severe when worshippers entered their temple and glad when they left after paying homage to her.
3. Arrian, *Anabasis of Alexander* 7.1.4.
4. All quotations of Euhemerus are taken from the summary in Diodorus Siculus, *The Library of History* 5.42–46.
5. Diodorus Siculus, *The Library of History* 1.70.1–4 (= *FGrHist* 264 F 25).
6. For the relief in Amenhotep III's temple at Luxor, see B. J. Kemp, *Ancient Egypt: Anatomy of a Civilisation* (London, 1989), 198–99.
7. The quotations are taken from the Greek *Alexander Romance* 1.3 (Nectanebo and the wax ships), 1.7 (the encounter between Olympias and the pharaoh), and 1.11 (the birth of Alexander).

9: AT HOME IN ALEXANDRIA

1. See the Dalai Lama's foreword to M. Wenzel, *Echoes of Alexander the Great: Silk Route Portraits from Gandhara* (London, 2000).
2. On the wind-gods traveling along the Silk Route, see K. Tanabe, "The Kushan Representation of Anemos/Oado and Its Relevance to the Central Asian and Far Eastern Wind Gods," *Silk Road Art and Archaeology* 1 (1990): 51–80; for a more general study, see R. C. Foltz, *Religions of the Silk Road: Overland Trade and Cultural Exchange from Antiquity to the Fifteenth Century* (New York, 1999).
3. Theocritus, *Idyll* 17.16–19.
4. Ibid. 17.126–34.
5. Stephens, *Seeing Double*, discusses the Ptolemaia, 245–46.
6. See Callimachus, *Epigram* 28 Pfeiffer, and *Hymn to Apollo* 107–12.
7. They are mentioned at the beginning of Callimachus's *Aitia*.
8. Callimachus, *Aitia*, fr. 178 Pfeiffer.

9. Theocritus, *Idyll* 11.
10. Meleager of Gadara in the *Palatine Anthology* 7.417.5–8 = 3988–91 in
A. S. F. Gow and D. L. Page, eds., *The Greek Anthology: Hellenistic
Epigrams*, 2 vols. (Cambridge, 1965).

PART IV: TRANSLATION: THE ROMAN EMPIRE

The second series of *The Cambridge Ancient History,* vols. 7.2–10 (Cambridge, 1990–1996), offers authoritative accounts of the history of Rome, from the origins to the end of the Augustan principate. For a basic (and affordable) overview, see M. T. Boatwright, D. J. Gargola, and R. J. A. Talbert, *The Romans: From Village to Empire* (Oxford, 2004). On republican history, see M. H. Crawford, *The Roman Republic,* 2nd ed. (Cambridge, MA, 1993). R. Syme, *The Roman Revolution* (Oxford, 1939), is the most influential study of the end of the republic and the Augustan principate: inspired by the rise of fascist regimes in Europe, it offers a brilliant, and disenchanted, portrait of Augustus. M. Beard, J. North, and S. Price, *Religions of Rome,* 2 vols. (Cambridge, 1998), is essential for any study of Roman religion. Feeney, *The Gods of Epic,* is the best study of the gods in Roman literature.

S. Hinds, *Allusion and Intertext: The Dynamics of Appropriation in Roman Poetry* (Cambridge, 1998), offers a brilliant account of how Livius Andronicus, Naevius, and Ennius chose to translate the Muses. Livius Andronicus is still best served by S. Mariotti, *Livio Andronico e la traduzione artistica* (Urbino, 1950). The fragments of Ennius are collected in O. Skutsch, *The Annals of Q. Ennius* (Oxford, 1985), to which the following notes refer. E. Gowers offers a detailed account of Ennius's three hearts, "The *Cor* of Ennius," in W. Fitzgerald and E. Gowers, eds., *Ennius Perennis: The Annals and Beyond* (Cambridge, 2007), 17–37. On Ennius, Fulvius Nobilior, and the temple of Hercules of the Muses, see M. Martina, "Aedes Herculis Musarum," *Dialoghi di Archeologia* 3 (1981): 49–68.

Cicero, *On the Nature of the Gods,* is translated by H. Rackham (Cambridge, MA, 1961). A. S. Pease offers a full introduction and commentary to this work: *M. Tulli Ciceronis: De Natura Deorum,* 2 vols. (Cambridge, MA, 1955–1958); A. R. Dyck introduces and comments on book 1 (Cambridge, 2003). A. Momigliano, "The Theological Efforts of the Roman Upper Classes in the First Century BC," *Classical Philology* 79 (1984):

199–211, is excellent on Roman religious discourse, as is M. Beard, "Cicero and Divination: The Formation of a Latin Discourse," *Journal of Roman Studies* 76 (1986): 33–46. On Augustus's cultural revolution and his eclectic "classicism" in art, see G. K. Galinsky, *Augustan Culture* (Princeton, NJ, 1996). On Roman cults of the emperor, see two seminal articles by S. Price: "Between Man and God: Sacrifice in the Roman Imperial Cult," *Journal of Roman Studies* 70 (1980): 28–43; and "Gods and Emperors: The Greek Language of the Roman Imperial Cult," *Journal of Hellenic Studies* 104 (1984): 79–95. There are many excellent translations of Virgil's *Aeneid* and Ovid's *Metamorphoses;* I recommend D. West's version of Virgil, 2nd ed. (London, 2002), and Raeburn's verse translation of Ovid's poem, which has the advantage of including an excellent introduction by D. Feeney (London, 2004).

10: THE MUSES IN ROME

1. For most Italians today, "Carneades" simply means "unknown Greek or Roman." This is because, in Alessandro Manzoni's nineteenth-century novel *The Betrothed,* Don Abbondio is famously muttering to himself, "Carneades . . . who he?" when the two innocent lovers, Renzo and Lucia, burst into his study demanding to be married. Manzoni's poor priest never manages to look up Carneades; he has enough trouble preventing those two from tying the knot. And thus Carneades remains a faceless name—even if Manzoni is, of course, having a little joke. As it happens, Carneades's skepticism is a perfect match for Don Abbondio's own lack of moral direction.
2. Ennius, *Annales* 240–41 Skutsch.
3. Cato the Censor, fr. 98, in E. Malcovati, ed., *Oratorum Romanorum Fragmenta,* 4th ed. (Turin, 1976).

11: ANCESTORS, ALLIES, AND ALTER EGOS

1. The methods used for calculating the population of Rome are discussed in W. Scheidel, ed., *Debating Roman Demography* (Leiden, 2001).
2. Caesar, *Gallic War* 6.17. For discussion, see Beard, North, and Price, *Religions of Rome,* vol. 2, 55.
3. Plutarch, *Life of Pompey* 27.3.
4. Cicero, *On the Nature of the Gods* 1.4.7.

5. Beard, "Cicero and Divination," 40.
6. Horace, *Epistles* 2.1.156.
7. Tacitus, *Histories* 1.3.

12: MUTANTS

1. Plutarch, *Life of Antony* 4.1–2.
2. Ibid. 24.3–4.
3. Ibid. 26.1–3.
4. R. Syme, *The Roman Revolution,* corrected ed. (Oxford, 1960), 448.
5. Virgil, *Aeneid* 8.698.
6. Ibid. 1.279.
7. Ibid. 1.279–82.
8. Ovid, *Metamorphoses* 6.7–8.
9. Ibid. 6.103–4.
10. Ovid, *Tristia ex Ponto* 2.207.

PART V: DISGUISE: CHRISTIANITY AND ISLAM

D. MacCulloch, *A History of Christianity* (London, 2009), is compulsively readable and learned. Beard, North, and Price, *Religions of Rome,* offers excellent guidance on the early history of Christianity, within the context of the many other religions and cults that flourished in the first centuries AD. The fall of the Roman Empire and the rise of Christianity is the subject of many books. E. Gibbon wrote his celebrated *History of the Decline and Fall of the Roman Empire* at the end of the eighteenth century, and the book is available in an authoritative critical edition by D. Womersley, 3 vols., 2nd ed. (London, 2005). A. von Harnack, *Die Mission und Ausbreitung des Christentums,* written at the turn of the twentieth century, 4th ed. (Leipzig, 1924), was influential; sociological and demographic arguments inform R. Stark, *The Rise of Christianity: A Sociologist Reconsiders History* (Princeton, NJ, 1996). J. N. Bremmer helpfully discusses these three books in his valedictory lectures, *The Rise of Christianity Through the Eyes of Gibbon, Harnack and Rodney Stark* (Groningen, 2010). R. Lane Fox, *Pagans and Christians in the Mediterranean World from the Second Century AD to the Conversion of Constantine* (London, 1986), is perceptive and beautifully written. P. Brown is perhaps the most influential scholar of late antiquity: see especially *The World of Late Antiquity: AD 150–750,*

2nd ed. (New York, 1989). On the last pagans, see A. Cameron, *The Last Pagans of Rome* (Oxford, 2011); on the period AD 400–600, see R. Markus, *The End of Ancient Christianity* (Cambridge, 1990). On Christian attitudes toward the statues of the pagan gods, I learned a lot from C. Mango, "Antique Statuary and the Byzantine Beholder," *Dumbarton Oaks Papers* 17 (1963): 55–75; and J. Elsner, *Imperial Rome and the Christian Triumph: The Art of the Roman Empire AD 100–450* (Oxford, 1998). On the Christian reception of Ovid and the problem of allegory more generally, see L. Barkan, *The Gods Made Flesh: Metamorphosis and the Pursuit of Paganism* (New Haven, 1986). To investigate Christian attitudes toward the pagan gods, the best guide is Augustine himself in *The City of God Against the Pagans;* R. W. Dyson offers a good translation, with introduction and notes (Cambridge, 1998).

On the Arab conquests and the history of Islam more generally, see I. M. Lapidus, *A History of Islamic Societies,* 2nd ed. (Cambridge, 2002). On the Muslim reception of ancient Greek culture, see F. Rosenthal, *The Classical Heritage in Islam,* trans. E. and J. Marmorstein (London, 1975); G. Strohmaier, *Von Demokrit bis Dante: Die Bewahrung antiken Erbes in der arabischen Kultur* (Hildesheim, 1996); and D. Gutas, *Greek Thought, Arabic Culture: The Graeco-Arabic Translation Movement in Baghdad and Early 'Abbāsid Society* (London, 1998). More specifically on the gods, see D. Urvoy, *Les penseurs libres dans l'Islam classique: L'interrogation sur la religion chez les penseurs arabes indépendants* (Paris, 2003), and A. Etman, "Homer in the Arab World," in J. Nelis, ed., *Receptions of Antiquity: Festschrift for F. Decreus* (Gent, 2011), 69–79. For the gods as stars, see P. Kunitzsch, *The Arabs and the Stars: Texts and Traditions on the Fixed Stars and Their Influence in Medieval Europe* (Northampton, 1989). J. Seznec, *The Survival of the Pagan Gods: The Mythological Tradition and Its Place in Renaissance Humanism and Art,* trans. B. F. Sessions (New York, 1953), pays close attention to the Arabic reception and transmission of the ancient gods.

13: HUMAN LIKE YOU

1. Gibbon, *History of the Decline and Fall of the Roman Empire,* vol. 1, 446.
2. Tacitus, *Annals* 15.44.
3. The Gospel According to Matthew 5:5.

4. R. Seaford, *Dionysos* (London, 2006), makes the case in chapter 9.
5. Bremmer, *The Rise of Christianity Through the Eyes of Gibbon, Harnack and Rodney Stark,* 69.
6. It seems to me beside the point to insist that "trials of Christians could spring from personal and local enmities," as Mary Beard, John North, and Simon Price do in *Religions of Rome,* vol. 1, 238. Personal enmities always play a role, during all persecutions, but what is specific about the charges against Christians concerns their failure to sacrifice.
7. Acts of the Apostles 14.
8. Lane Fox, *Pagans and Christians,* 99–101, argues against the Ovid connection effectively, even though it has continued to surface since.
9. E. Haenchen, *Die Apostelgeschichte* (Göttingen, 1961), 374.
10. Augustine, *The City of God Against the Pagans* 7.9.
11. Ovid, *Metamorphoses* 2.846–47.

14: DEMONS

1. Jerome, *Chronicon,* ed. J. K. Fotheringham (London, 1923), 314.
2. The poem, by the Egyptian Christodorus, forms book 2 of the *Palatine Anthology.*
3. Historians generally claim that Christians represented between 8 and 12 percent of the population by the year 300, but there is very little evidence on which to base calculations; see R. MacMullen, *The Second Church: Popular Christianity A.D. 200–400* (Atlanta, 2009), 102 n. 18. The fact that the most recent estimate of the population of the Roman Empire as a whole wavers between sixty million and one hundred million gives a measure of the problem: see W. Scheidel, ed., *Debating Roman Demography* (Leiden, 2001), 63–64.
4. Eusebius, *Life of Constantine* 3.54.
5. Corinthians 10:20.
6. Marcus Diaconus, *Life of Porphyry* 59–61.
7. St. Gregory the Great, *Second Dialogue* (*Life of St. Benedict*) 8.
8. Zosimos, *New History* 5.24.8.
9. An important project, funded by the Arts and Humanities Research Council (UK) and directed by Professor R. R. R. Smith and Dr. Bryan Ward-Perkins, investigates the archaeology of ancient statues in the period AD 284–650. See further, http://www.ocla.ox.ac.uk/statues/index.shtml.

10. Theophylact Simocatta, *History* 8.13.7–15.
11. Arnobius, *Against the Pagans* 4.25.
12. Ibid. 7.41; see also the appendix to the text.
13. Arnobius, *Against the Pagans* 3.15.
14. Ibid. 4.21.
15. Ibid. 5.34.
16. Ibid. 5.23.
17. Barkan, *The Gods Made Flesh*, 98.
18. Lactantius, *The Divine Institutes* 1.11.24.
19. Augustine, *The City of God Against the Pagans* 7.18.

15: SACKCLOTH AND SCIMITARS

1. This version of the dream is preserved in Ibn-Nubāta, *Sar ḥ al-'uyūn fi šar ḥ risālat Ibn Zaydūn*, ed. M. Abū-l-Faḍl Ibrāhīm (Cairo, 1964), 213; translated and discussed in D. Gutas, *Greek Thought, Arabic Culture: The Graeco-Arabic Translation Movement in Baghdad and Early 'Abbāsid Society (2nd–4th/8th–10th Centuries)* (London, 1998), 97–104.
2. F. Rosenthal translates this and other key sources on Arabic theories of translation in *The Classical Heritage in Islam*, 18.
3. G. Strohmaier, "Homer in Baghdad," *Byzantinoslavica* 41 (1980): 196–200.
4. The comment features in the margin of a manuscript now kept in the Laurentian Library, Florence, 226/173 fol. 73 recto, 13f. For discussion, see Strohmaier, "Homer in Baghdad."
5. See P. Nwyia and K. Samir, eds., "Une correspondance islamo-chrétienne entre Ibn al-Munaǧǧim, Ḥunayn ibn Isḥāq et Qusṭā ibn Lūqā," *Patrologia Orientalis* 40, no. 4 (1981): 664–69.
6. The relevant illustration is in a manuscript now kept in Vienna: Nationalbibliothek, MS 14.38, fol. 247 verso. For a reproduction of the image and discussion, see Seznec, *Survival of the Pagan Gods*, 180–83.
7. F. Saxl pioneered work in this field; see "Beiträge zu einer Geschichte der Planetendarstellungen im Orient und Okzident," *Islam* 3 (1912): 151–77.
8. Tertullian, *De Idolatria* 9.
9. Dante, *Inferno* 20.115–17.
10. For discussion, see Seznec, *Survival of the Pagan Gods*, 162–63.

11. B. Caseau, "Late Antique Paganism: Adaptation Under Duress," in L. Lavan and M. Mulryan, eds., *The Archaeology of Late Antique "Paganism"* (Leiden, 2011), 111–34, puts paid to any easy arguments about continuity.
12. The liberal arts followed this scheme: Moon/Diana (grammar), Mercury (logic), Venus (rhetoric), Sun/Apollo (Arithmetic), Mars (music), Jupiter (geometry), Saturn (astronomy/astrology).

PART VI: BORN AGAIN: THE RENAISSANCE

J. Brotton, *The Renaissance: A Very Short Introduction* (Oxford, 2006), helpfully sets out how the period has been conceptualized and defined; L. Jardine and J. Brotton, *Global Interests: Renaissance Art Between East and West* (London, 2000), looks beyond the boundaries of Europe, investigating in particular the connections between the Italian Renaissance and the Ottoman Empire. For Renaissance explorations of the transatlantic West, see D. Abulafia, *The Discovery of Mankind: Atlantic Encounters in the Age of Columbus* (New Haven, 2008), and K. Ordahl Kupperman, ed., *America in European Consciousness, 1493–1750* (Chapel Hill, NC, 1995), especially the essay by S. MacCormack, "Limits of Understanding: Perceptions of Greco-Roman and Amerindian Paganism in Early Modern Europe," 79–129. On Petrarch and all his different enterprises, see V. Kirkham and A. Maggi, eds., *Petrarch: A Critical Guide to the Complete Works* (Chicago, 2009). On his treatment of the Olympian gods in the *Africa,* see T. Gregory, *From Many Gods to One: Divine Action in Renaissance Epic* (Chicago, 2006), chapter 2; the poem has been translated into English by T. G. Bergin and A. S. Wilson (New Haven, 1977). A. Pertusi offers an extremely well-informed, and sensitive, interpretation of Petrarch's relationship to Homer, showing how it intersects with his real-life friendship with Boccaccio, and his much more turbulent relationship with Leontius Pilatus, teacher and translator of Greek: A. Pertusi, *Leonzio Pilato fra Petrarca e Boccaccio* (Venice, 1964).

Seznec's *Survival of the Pagan Gods* questions any stark division between the Middle Ages and the Renaissance. S. Settis, in his introduction to a new Italian edition of Seznec's work (Turin, 2008), vii–xxix, rightly points out that Seznec overstates continuity because he focuses on the subjects of Renaissance art rather than the new visual idioms used to represent them. M. Bull, *The Mirror of the Gods: Classical Mythology in Renaissance Art* (London, 2006), considers many different objects and media, thus revising traditional distinctions between decoration and high art; he then offers individual chapters on Hercules, Jupiter, Venus, Bacchus, Diana, and Apollo. L. Freedman, *The Revival of the Olympian Gods in Renaissance Art* (Cambridge, 2003), discusses freestanding statues and argues that they posed special theological challenges because they recalled the cult statues of antiquity. For an enjoyable account of the Tempio Malatestiano, see E. Hollis, *The Secret Lives of Buildings: From the Ruins of the Parthenon to the Vegas Strip in Thirteen Stories* (New York, 2009), 157–81. I. Pasini discusses the temple in an exhibition catalog edited by F. Arduini: *Sigismondo Pandolfo Malatesta e il suo tempo: Mostra storica* (Vicenza, 1970). A. F. D'Elia, *A Sudden Terror: The Plot to Murder the Pope in Renaissance Rome* (Cambridge, MA, 2009), offers a lively portrait of mid-fifteenth-century humanists (or "pagans" in the pope's description), their networks, and their aspirations.

16: PETRARCH PAINTS THE GODS

1. See Dante's *Divine Comedy, Paradiso* 1.13–33 and *Purgatorio* 6.118.
2. For example, Brotton, *The Renaissance: A Very Short Introduction,* 12–13.
3. Petrarch, *Africa* 7.506–728.
4. Ibid. 3.136–262.
5. Ibid. 6.839–918.
6. Petrarch in a letter to his friend Boccaccio, *Seniles* 2.1.108.
7. The relevant passages from the letters are collected in Pertusi, *Leonzio Pilato fra Petrarca e Boccaccio,* 40–41.
8. Petrarch's second letter to Cicero: *Familiares* 24.4.12.
9. T. E. Mommsen, "Petrarch's Conception of the 'Dark Ages,'" *Speculum* 17, no. 2 (1942): 226–42.
10. The quotation is from *Familiares* 8.3.12. On his second, more inclusive plans for a *De viris illustribus,* see R. G. Witt, "The Rebirth of the Romans as Models of Character," in V. Kirkham and A. Maggi, eds., *Petrarch: A Critical Guide to the Complete Works* (Chicago, 2009), 106–8. Petrarch planned to include Jewish, Asian, African, Greek, and Roman illustrious men in his collection.

17: A COSMOPOLITAN CARNIVAL OF DEITIES

1. Bull, *Mirror of the Gods,* 60.
2. Pope Pius II, *Commentaries* 2.32.
3. Hollis, *Secret Lives of Buildings,* 163.
4. Pope Pius II, *Commentaries* 2.32.
5. Macrobius, *Saturnalia* 1.23.10.
6. F. Nietzsche, *Vom Nutzen und Nachteil der Historie für das Leben* (*On the Uses and Abuses of History for Life*), in *Kritische Studienausgabe,* ed. G. Colli and M. Montinari, vol. 1 (Munich, 1999), 243–334.
7. Leon Battista Alberti, *De re aedificatoria* 6.1.
8. One concerned ecclesiastical commentator suggested that Correggio's painting was "meant to impress nuns who might be tempted to forsake their vows"; see *Ragionamento del Padre Ireneo Affò sopra una stanza dipinta del celeberrimo Antonio Allegri da Correggio nel monasterio di San Paolo in Parma* (Parma, 1794), 47–8.
9. The charges are discussed in D'Elia, *A Sudden Terror: The Plot to Kill the Pope in Renaissance Rome,* 87: "Some say that you are more pagan than Christian and that you follow the pagan practices more than ours; some say that you call Hercules your god, others Mercury, Jupiter, Apollo, Venus, or Diana; that you habitually swear by these gods and goddesses, especially when you are with men of similar superstitions."
10. Pomponio Leto, in an unedited manuscript: MS Marc. Lat. Classe XII, n. 210 (4689) fol. 34 recto.

18: OLD GODS IN THE NEW WORLD

1. Abulafia, *The Discovery of Mankind,* especially 312f.
2. Boccaccio's *De Canaria* is published in *Monumenta Henricina,* vol. 1 (Lisbon, 1960), 202–6.
3. See Justus Lipsius, *De Vesta et Vestalibus Syntagma* (Antwerp, 1603), chapter 15, citing Cieza's comparisons. For discussion, see S. MacCormack, *Religion in the Andes: Vision and Imagination in Colonial Peru* (Princeton, NJ, 1991), 106f.
4. For a reproduction, see Ordahl Kupperman, ed., *America in European Consciousness, 1493–1750,* 105, together with the excellent discussion by Sabine MacCormack, 98–101.

5. J.-F. Lafitau, *Moeurs des sauvages Amériquains comparées aux moeurs des premiers temps,* vol. 1 (Paris, 1724), 97–98.
6. Acts of the Apostles 14:16, discussed above, p. 166–69.
7. Garcilaso de la Vega, *Comentarios reales de los Incas,* vol. 1 (Lisbon, 1609), 30b (in the edition by C. Saenz de Santa Maria, Madrid, 1963).
8. This is a point A. Laird makes in his forthcoming study of classical influences in early reports about the New World, "Atzec and Roman Gods in Sixteenth-Century Mexico: Strategic Uses of Classical Learning in Sahagún's *Historia general,*" in J. Pohl, ed., *Altera Roma: Art and Empire from the Aztecs to New Spain* (Los Angeles, 2014).
9. Seznec, *Survival of the Pagan Gods,* 222.
10. Most famously, Demogorgon headed a procession of Olympian carriages celebrating the marriage of Francesco de' Medici with Johanna of Austria in 1565. M. Castelain collected references to Demogorgon in Spenser, Marlowe, Dryden, Milton, and Shelley in an article alarmingly entitled "Démogorgon ou le barbarisme déifié," *Bulletin de la Association Guillaume Budé* 36 (1932): 22–39.
11. Lilio Gregorio Giraldi, *De deis gentium historia* (Basel, 1548), dedicatory epistle, and V. Cartari, *Le imagini con la sposizione de i dei degli antichi* (Venice, 1556), 8–9.

EPILOGUE: A MARBLE HEAD

The first port of call for an investigation of the Olympian gods from the Renaissance to the present is J. D. Reid, ed., *The Oxford Guide to Classical Mythology in the Arts, 1300–1990s,* 2 vols. (Oxford, 1993). This essential work of reference provides guidance on works of literature, art, music, and film organized under the names of individual gods. It would take several lives and afterlives to follow up on even a small proportion of the references contained in this work. For a short and stimulating account that focuses on the Romantic period, see R. Calasso, *Literature and the Gods,* trans. T. Parks (London, 2001), 28.

1. Ovid, *Metamorphoses* 2.846–47.
2. C. Baudelaire, "L'École païenne," in *Oeuvres complètes,* ed. C. Pichois, vol. 2 (Paris, 1976), 44–45.
3. H. Heine, *Elementargeister,* in *Sämtliche Schriften,* ed. K. Briegleb, vol. 3 (Munich, 1978), 686.

4. G. Leopardi, *Zibaldone,* ed. R. Damiani, vol. 2 (Milan, 1997), 1856.

5. Ibid., 288f.

6. F. Nietzsche, letter to Burckhardt, 4.1.1889, in *Briefwechsel,* ed. G. Colli and M. Montinari, vol. 3.5 (Berlin, 1984), 574.

7. J. L. Borges, "Ragnarök," in *El Hacedor* (Buenos Aires, 1960), 63–65.

8. See B. de Fontenelle, *Oeuvres complètes,* ed. A. Niderst, vol. 3 (Paris, 1989), 187–202.

9. Cicero, *On the Nature of the Gods* 1.16.43.

ACKNOWLEDGMENTS

I would like to thank:

Catherine Clarke, my agent, who waited some ten years just to see a book proposal and was a constant source of encouragement, wisdom, and inspiration.

Sara Bershtel and Grigory Tovbis at Metropolitan Books, who insisted I do better, and showed me how, with great verve and humor.

Zoë Pagnamenta, my U.S. agent, for introducing me to them.

Peter Carson, John Davey, and Penny Daniel at Profile Books, for their keen editorial eye, patience, and trust.

Susanne Hillen, my U.K. copy editor, who worked so quickly and precisely in order to give me more time to write and still meet deadlines.

Sona Vogel, who prepared the U.S. manuscript and saved me from several mistakes and infelicities.

Lisa Kleinholz, for compiling an excellent index.

Robin Osborne, for suggesting I consider the wit and wisdom of Praxiteles's Apollo and for correcting many errors scattered through the book.

Robin Lane Fox, for making one long phone call, revealing some tricks of the writing trade, and suggesting enough ideas for a whole new and better book.

George Boys-Stones, for telling me that Cicero was actually quite a good philosopher and for reading a whole draft in record time as a "St. Nicholas's gift."

Philip Hardie, for talking about Petrarch's *Africa* during a wild car journey between São Paulo and Campinas and for reading and correcting the Roman and Renaissance sections.

Andrej and Ivana Petrovic, who read several chapters and offered detailed insights on ancient ritual and Hellenistic poetry.

Anna Leone, for her hospitality in Rome, for tracking down the amazing picture on p. 176, and for telling me what to read.

Massimo Brizzi, for his mapmaking skills and archaeological advice.

Julia Kindt, for Skyping from Australia early in the morning to tell me what's wrong with the way people study Greek religion.

Greg Nagy and everyone at the Center for Hellenic Studies (Harvard) for a beautiful six months spent writing and researching there, the Institute of Advanced Study (Durham University) for a fellowship, and all colleagues at the Department of Classics and Ancient History (Durham University) for letting me off teaching for a while.

Laura and Roberto Haubold, for keeping me happy and entertained, even while I struggled to write this book.

And Johannes Haubold, for everything.

INDEX

Page numbers in *italics* refer to illustrations.

planetary gods, 113–14, 189, 192–96, 215–17, *216*
Plataea, Battle of, 13, 53
Platina, Bartolomeo, 223
Plato, 38–39, 73, 77–87, 108, 236
  Aphrodite and, 38–39
  Aristotle and, 86–87
  Arnobius and, 180
  attack on gods and poetry, 77–87
  Bellerophon and, 84–86
  demiurge and, 233
  Hecataeus and, 109
  Platonism and, 81
  Socrates's trial and, 73, 78–79
Plutarch, 149–50
Poetics (Aristotle), 86, 187
poetry, 6, 15, 39–40, 46, 67. *See also* epic poetry; *and specific poets*
  Alexandria and, 89, 120–21
  Arab scholars and, 187–89
  archaic Greek, 20–24, 197
  Aristotle and, 86–87
  Homer on, 36
  Plato on imitation and, 79–87
  poetic license and, 181
  truth and, 77–78
Politian, 207
Polybius, 128–29
polytheism, 80
Pompey, 140–43, 146
Pontius Pilate, 163
Poros, ruler of India, 91
Porphyry, Bishop of Gaza, 175
Porphyry of Tyre, 217
Poseidon, 56. *See also* Neptune
  Athena and, 11
  Euhemerus and, 107
  Homer and, 20, 37, 43, 87
  Mycenaean rituals and, 20
  Parthenon frieze and, 6, *8*, 11, *12*, 249
  Pegasus and, 83, 85
  Prodicus and, 56
  Theagenes and, 49
  Zeus and, 249
Pound, Ezra, 215
praeparatio evangelica, 230, 234
Praxiteles
  Apollo Sauroktonos, *58*, *59*
  Cnidian Aphrodite, 174
priests, 70, 98, 130–31, 141, 143
Prodicus, 56, 61, 108
Prometheus, 242
Proserpina. *See* Persephone
Protagoras, 55–56, 61
Ptolemaia, festival of, 119
Ptolemy, Claudius, 189, 190, 192, 225–26

Ptolemy I, King of Egypt, 116–17, 120, 143, 151
Ptolemy II, King of Egypt, 117–20, 143
Punic Wars, 127–29, 202
Pylos, 19–21
Pythia, 27–28
Python, 22, *58*, *59*, 83

Quṣṭā ibn Lūqā, 188–89

Raphael
  Sacrifice at Lystra, 168, *169*
Recco, Nicoloso da, 226, 227
Renaissance, 14, 197, 200–26, 230–37, 245
Renaissance, The (Pater), 201
Reni, Guido, *238*
Republic, The (Plato), 79–80, 85
Resheph (Canaanite god), 20
Rhea, 31, 247, 249
rhetoric, 65–67, 81, 134
ritual practice, 5–7, *8*, 9, 13–14, 20–21, 24, 46–47, 57, 78, 87, 89, 98–99, 104–5, 120–23, 131, 133, 142, 166, 229, 249, 243
Roman Senate, 125, 133–34, 142, 145, 151
Romantic age, 239–41
Rome, 1, 109, 123, 125–58
  Christianity and, 162–66, 171–75, *176*
  and Empire, 138–40, 147–58, 215
  Enlightenment and, 237–38
  Olympian gods translated in, 131–37
  Renaissance and, 202–3
  republic, 125, 127–47, 149
Romulus and Remus, 135, 141, 153
Roxane, wife of Alexander, 105

Sacred Register (Euhemerus), 106–10, 114, 137, 144
Sacred Way, 25–28
sacrifices, 13, 20–21, 48, 89, 101, 130, 165–68, *169*, 174–75, 232, 243–44
St. John Lateran, basilica, 173, 175
St. Peter's church, 173, 175
Salamis, Battle of, 13, 53
Santa Maria del Fiore (Florence), 193–95, *194*
Sappho, 43
Saturn, 182–83, *183*, 204, 216
Saturn (planet), 112, 192, 194
satyrs, 5
Savonarola, 208
scholia, 49
Scipio, 202

1   ANC GREECE